THIRZA VALLOIS

AVEYRON,

A BRIDGE TO FRENCH ARCADIA

To Experience my France
Bon Voyage!
Thirza Vallois

ILIAD BOOKS

Published in 2007
Copyright © 2007, Thirza Vallois
ISBN 978-0-9525378-4-7

Iliad Books
5 Nevern Road
London SW5 9PG
www.thirzavallois.com

Designed and produced by Cyril Hude, Paris
pao@cyrilhude.fr

Imprimé par
Industrias Gráficas Ferré Olsina SA Viladomat
158-160 int. 08015 Barcelona. España

My deepest love goes to
— my enlightened and enlightening mother, who taught me how to look and how to travel, and who, to the very end, supported the writing of this book with her intelligent suggestions and wise comments. She would have been thrilled to see it published.
— my dear father, who was gone before I started writing this book, and who was on my mind throughout.
Both had travelled extensively in France and would have loved the Aveyron as much as I do.
— Nathaniel, who kindly took so much time off his very busy schedule to read my manuscript and, with his precious critic's 'eye', helped me improve it as I went along.

This book is especially dedicated, with deepest gratitude, to Georges and Odette, without whom none of this would have happened. Thank you for your amazing hospitality.

And in memory of Bob.

ACKNOWLEDGEMENTS

Heartfelt thanks to Mary Yost who was involved in this project for several years and did her best to help.

My deepest gratitude to the friendly and highly professional team at La Maison de l'Aveyron —Stéphanie Augeyre, Bernadette Catusse-Bazet, Anne Goutal and Christine Gaudru — who were always available to assist me in my research and queries and were consistently helpful during the long process of writing this book.

My gratitude also goes to Francis Castan, Catherine Ciberras-Delmas and Nadine Bonal from the Comité Départementale de Tourisme, and to Christian Sabathier, also from the CDT, who supplied me with an excellent map of the Aveyron.

Special thanks to the wonderful people of the Aveyron who gave me their time and hospitality, drove me around, hiked with me, invited me over, and shared with me their stories and erudition. Thanks to them my journey into the Aveyron has been a memorable lifetime experience. Please forgive me if I have forgotten to mention anyone.

Pierre Albanois, Catherine André, Delphine Atché, Isabelle Aronovitz, François Auriac, Elisabeth Baillon, Isabelle Baldit, Christine Barrès, Eric and Claudine Belin, Christian Bichwiller, Françoise Blanquet, Gérard Boissins, Olivier Bonnemaire, Jean-Yves and Flavie (Mamie) Bonnet, Raymond

Bouscayrol, Hubert Bouyssières, Agnès and Yves Calvetti, Max Capdebarhtes, Raymond Capoulade (Capou), Marilyne Chassang, Marie-Hélène Causse, Claude Chauvet, Solange Colin Perez, Régine Combal, Compagnie Eiffage du Viaduc de Millau, Marine Crouan, Henri Dardé, Simone Dardé, Georges Desirat, Christophe Evrard, Gérard Fabri, Laurence Fric, the Friends of La Bastide-l'Evêque, Jacques Godfrain, André Gouzes, Serge Itkine, Annhick and Lionel Izak, Thérèse Jacob, Jacques Jambon, Brigitte Julien, Pierre Lançon, Delphine Lapeyre, Myriam Laur, Jean Laurens, Claudine and Philippe Long, Jean-Pierre Marc, Jean-Luc Matha, Jacques Mazières, Paul Mestre, Jean-Henri and Katlène Meunier, Jacques and Claudine Miquel, Alain Montrozier, Martine Mouls, Jean and Maïté Mouly, Zoé Mourat, Claude and Michèle Mourino, Alain Ory, René Pagés, Sébastien Persec, Stéphanie Pezé, Jean et Danièle Puech, Jeanne Pujol, Yannick Raminez, Jean-Pierre Raynal, Hugues and Mathilde Robert, Jean-Pierre Romiguier, Mylène Roques, Raymond Rouquier, Henri Sauzeau, Jean-Philippe Savignoni, René and Jacqueline Serieys. Colette Terrasse, Philippe Teulier, Guy Tourette, Laurence Toutet, Philippe Varsi, Hervé Vernhes, Alain Vernhet, Nadine Vignolo, her superb team and the people of Valon and Prat, René Vigne, Marie-Louise Vigouroux, Jean-Pierre Viguier, Sylvie Vuilloz, Michel Wolkowitsky, Patrice Wursching, Sabrina Zède

To Lucy Smith who was an invaluable editor, and with whom it was a great pleasure to work, and to Patrice Geniez whose photos added beauty, atmosphere and poetry to my text. A special thank you to Jeff Berner who provided me with the picture of the back cover, and to all the other photographers who lent me a helping hand: Delphine Atché and the Tourist Office of Roquefort, Giovani Bertolissio, Christel Caruso, Régine Combal and the Tourist Office of Conques, Anaïs Combes, Philippe Larroque, Pierre Soisson, Please forgive me if I couldn't use all your pictures.

To Jackie for her invaluable help in making the selection of photos that went into the book, to Susan who, likewise, gave me a helping hand, and her time, to Barbara who lent me her attentive ear, and to Pauline and Raymond who took the time to read some of my manuscript, as did Susan. Thank you all.

CONTENTS

PROLOGUE

It all began with a riot of wisteria. I was out on Ile de la Cité, checking out a walking itinerary for my book *Romantic Paris*. It was an unusually warm April afternoon and the garden by Notre Dame was a Monet-like symphony of pastel blossoms and white light — the kind of sight that will force a smile onto the grumpiest of faces. I left the garden with its pairs of lovers and doll-like little girls behind me, and headed for the site of Héloïse and Abélard's love story, along rue Massillon, one of the old streets north of the cathedral that Baron Haussmann didn't have time to demolish. At the junction of rue Chanoinesse I looked to my left, and there was the wisteria! Draping in purple glory the island's oldest house (1524), further down the street. The house had been a restaurant for as long as I could remember, but at such a short distance from Notre Dame, I assumed it must be a tourist trap and never bothered to check. However, on that enchanted afternoon the clusters of wisteria were irresistibly enticing — Héloïse and Abélard would have to wait till later.

Before I knew it, I had pushed open the stiff old door and found myself peering into a dark, dimunitive woodsy interior and scanning its sundry contents — a wooden statue of a benevolent-looking churchman in a praying posture, a painting of a hunting scene, an old violin... a portrait of an elderly countryman in a traditional black hat in particular caught my attention. Gazing at me from the wall behind the counter, he seemed to have risen from another age, telling a tale of a faraway land that I couldn't quite place, although it was clearly French, a slice of a *France profonde* I had a hunch I had never been to.

The owner, Georges, did not look typically French. His checked shirt sleeves and floppy corduroy trousers gave him rather the air of an English gentleman farmer. A silky mane of silver locks framed his rosy face and large blue eyes whose mischievous twinkle melted every now and then into dreams. The menu he handed me was exclusively French, and included the promisingly named *saveurs d'Odette* — suggesting the hand of a woman behind the smells that came from the kitchen. The woman, indeed Odette, was from the Aveyron, Georges told me, a remote, rural area I had very vague notions about, except that it was situated somewhere towards the south.

Georges, who himself was from the Vendée, was inexhaustible on the topic of the Aveyron, waxing lyrical about it with even more conviction than a tourist brochure would. He and Odette owned an 18th century priory, Las Canals, by the village of Nuces, where within moments he invited me to stay, promising me a *Relais-et-Château* style holiday. Almost in the same breath, he was already fancying me, a total stranger, writing a book about the Aveyron and opening up to the world the last hidden gem of France. Of course, I found his suggestion a little premature. I had never set foot in the Aveyron, had never considered doing so, knew nothing about it and, besides, had no time to get involved in such a project. Moreover, he knew nothing about me or my credentials and whether I had what it took to carry off something like this. It did seem rather ludicrous.

Meanwhile, Odette emerged from the kitchen with a big smile and lots of golden curls. As she and I were talking, Georges slipped out and returned with a stack of books on the

Aveyron intended for my education. There followed, mostly out of politeness, a non-commital consent on my part to come down to Las Canals for the *vendanges* (grape harvest) in early October. I didn't take the invitation very seriously and, besides, October lay six months away, far enough into the future not to warrant much thought. So much water might flow under the bridge by then. Georges mentioned a large American party who would be flying out from the States for the occasion. But it was 2001, and, of course, he hadn't anticipated September 11, following which the Americans cancelled their trip. And so it was I, who had never intended to visit the Aveyron, that found myself going there instead, unaware of the extent to which it would get under my skin.

We left Paris early on Sunday October 7th, so as to beat the traffic, and arrived at our first port of call in the Aveyron in time to catch the weekly morning market at Marcillac, an astonishing red little town, carved out of the sandstone of its sunny valley, neatly streaked with bright green vineyards for over a thousand years. Several friends of Georges and Odette's were gathered by one of the stalls in the tree-filled square, enjoying a mix of wine and *charcuterie* amidst good-natured banters. After the interminable round of handshakes, we too were poured wine and handed a dish of freshly sliced *saucisson* as a preliminary to being absorbed by the group. While talking to Bernard, who was standing next to me, I realised that it was at his place that the *vendanges* took place, except that Georges had got the dates wrong and they were over the night before.

There was something else Georges got wrong: he had assumed everyone would welcome the idea of a book on the Aveyron and introduced me to Bernard as the author of the future book. Well, Bernard didn't like the idea at all and didn't mince his words about it. He would gladly have some visitors around, as long as they came in discreet trickles, but he did not want the area contaminated by the *A Year In Provence* syndrome. A quick mental revision of the local geography and its recent history reminded me that it was at Millau, in the very Aveyron, that the celebrated storming and dismantling of the new McDonald outlet took place in 1999 — we are talking of the heart of *la France profonde*, a sensitive place, jealously self-protective, to be handled with silken gloves.

I was beginning to feel uncomfortable. Bernard seemed a genuinely nice chap and I certainly did not wish to upset him. But how was I to disentangle myself from this awkward situation without upsetting Georges who was so keen on my writing the book? As the days moved on I felt increasingly indebted to him and to Odette who had lavished on me so much hospitality and chauffeured me through the best of the Aveyron. Every meal was a feast sprinkled with fresh ingredients picked directly from nature by Odette during our drives — she could spot a herb, mushroom, or ripe bunch of grapes from behind the closed window of a speeding car. Her concoctions were shared at the long bare table next to the kitchen where everyone squeezed up at the end of the day. On special occasions, for example when Madame la Préfète was invited over, dinner was served in the more formal dining room, glowing with silver candelabra, where we played out a scene from *la vie de château* to the sound of baroque music. Unlike Bernard, Madame la Préfète liked Georges's idea of a book on the area, but she was an administrator appointed from Paris on a temporary post, whereas Bernard belongs to the

Aveyron and talks with a regional lilt that went straight to my conscience and made me stall and waver for eighteen months: Should I divulge the secret and risk the Aveyron being spoilt, or should I just let it be?

But time was moving on, with or without my meddling. Ryanair had eyed up capital Rodez, and was negotiating a direct daily connection with London at a €50 fare, to start operating in May 2003. 50,000 Brits were expected to discover it in the first year. In the meantime, the construction of the Millau Viaduct was under way over the river Tarn further south. Once completed, it would inevitably contribute to opening up the region. If you can't beat them, join them, I had often been advised. Since *la France profonde* was going to be assaulted by modern times, I might as well sing its praises before it disappears.

INTRODUCTION

I was surprised to discover that people in the Aveyron resent the expression *la France profonde*. They interpret it as condescending, implying a backwater inhabited by country bumpkins. No matter how hard you insist you meant it as a compliment to a rural area that has preserved its authenticity, the Aveyronnais will look at you suspiciously, or at best dubiously, and understandably so, since not so long ago the Aveyron was precisely this, backward and underdeveloped. Today, still, the keen observer will detect remnants of those times here and there, even in its main towns (the largest of which, Rodez, has only 53,785 inhabitants, and that's including the suburbs).

The phrase sounds particularly offensive when uttered by the 'cousins' who have made it in Paris, *les Parisiens* — not a very popular lot down here who, I've been told, behave as if they own the place when they come down for their holidays. Some 320,000 of them live in the Paris area, sometimes going back several generations. There are many more who have by now been diluted into the general population and no longer identify with the homeland. This is the largest French community living in the capital, outnumbering the Bretons and the 263,000 who reside in the Aveyron, over half of whom are actually outsiders. That's without counting their compatriots who moved further afield and left us no statistics, and whose success stories reach as far as California and the Argentinean Pampas.

No matter where they have settled, the Aveyronnais diaspora has always been dynamic, enterprising, hard working and intelligent — the perfect combination of ingredients for success. Added to this is a shrewd business sense inherited from their peasant ancestors which, in Paris, helped them conquer the entire café industry. All the legendary cafés once frequented by Jean-Paul Sartre, Simon de Beauvoir and other Ernest Hemingways, belonged to Aveyronnais. Many still do. In California, some of them were equally successful in the laundry business, which later shifted into Chinese hands. I am yet to find out whether Thomas Keller's famous restaurant The French Laundry in Napa Valley was not initially a French laundry owned by an Aveyronnais.

Life was no bed of roses back home, a hilly, rugged land, spreading over 873,512 hectares (3386 sq. m) on the southern edge of the Massif Central. Winters were harsh, hillsides were steep, the soil was poor and the road network was inadequate, leaving its mosaic of miniature regions cut off from one another, and the area as a whole isolated from the outside world. Other than in Roman times, highways always shunned it in favour of the more convenient basin of the Rhône to the east and the Garonne Valley to the west. Even today, when technology can defy natural obstacles, the high-speed TGV has chosen to skirt it, simply because it would not have paid off to bring it over. Guidebooks followed suit, inexcusably, brushing over one of the country's most compelling areas with impunity. No wonder most foreigners have never heard of the Aveyron. Those who think they have are often embarrassed to find out they had confused it with the town of Avignon. When guidebooks do mention some of its sites, rather than situate them in the Aveyron, where they belong, they incorporate them into overlapping geographical or historical regions — the Quercy for instance, which takes in Western Aveyron, thus adding to the confusion.

To clarify matters, the Aveyron was one of the 83 *départements* (administrative districts) created during the French Revolution, when the nationalised territory was redistributed (today there are 95 *départements* in metropolitan France). By and large, it replaced the old province of Rouergue and was renamed after the most central of its three main rivers, the other two being the Lot and the Tarn, to the north and to the south respectively. All three rivers are tributaries of the Garonne, but the Aveyron alone takes its source in the *département*, by Sévérac-le-Château. Owing to its isolation, the Rouergue remained a distinct entity and developed a strong individual character and a unique identity, at once quintessentially French yet mysteriously different, going back to the ancient Celts for sure, perhaps to dawns unknown. This is *la France profonde* at its deepest, as tenaciously rooted in its identity as it was in its struggle to survive in an inhospitable environment. It was that tenacity that enabled the Aveyronnais of Paris to pile up small fortunes of francs behind their café counters, when given half a chance. But the homeland offered no such opportunities and lagged behind. It was archaic, remote, and deserted *en masse* by its natives.

But France was changing, putting aside the unpleasant parenthesis of the Occupation and shaking off the dust of the past. Optimism reigned supreme in the 1960s, striding towards prosperity to the delight of French households, and also towards the advent of the consumer age, which was not to everyone's liking. Following the legacy of the May 1968 '*événements*', many young people turned their backs on the alienating city and wandered through the French countryside in search of Arcadia. Some found it in the Aveyron where they settled under the newly coined label of *néo*-Aveyronnais, often in old, deserted farmhouses they bought and did up for a song. The natives eyed them with suspicion and overall did not welcome their arrival, but it's a good thing they came, because they injected young blood and breathed new vitality into an area that was in danger of dying out.

Imbued with the energy of 1968, the politically-minded among these *néo*-Aveyronnais headed south, towards the vast uplands of the Larzac, where they joined forces with some natives under the umbrella of the Confédération Paysanne. Led by the high media profile José Bové, they fought a ten-year, nationwide battle, from 1971 to 1981, against the extension of a military camp at a place called La Cavalerie. Since then the Larzac has remained a hotbed of political activism, taking on all the planet's ideological struggles, focusing at present on the ecological repercussions of globalisation. Hence their fight against *malbouffe* (junk food), which led to the dismantling of the McDonald in nearby Millau and to the destruction of genetically modified crops, of which more later. How extraordinary that this remote, empty corner of France was picked out in August 2003 to host a gigantic protest with international coverage against the World Trade Organisation meeting in Cancun, Mexico. Driving through the empty Larzac, the Confédération Paysanne's giant graffitis stand out against the vast horizons, yet the majority of Aveyronnais are hardly sympathetic to the movement. On the other hand, they often do share their dislike for Brussels whose agricultural legislation is threatening to destroy that very rural France the *néo*-Aveyronnais came seeking.

Your average Aveyronnais is no revolutionary. He is hard working and wished to enjoy some of the windfalls of the post-war national prosperity, which he converted into boring modern bungalows that scarred the landscape but had running water and bathrooms. This was only a gesture towards progress, however. Big-scale development could only be hoped for by breaking through the area's isolation. It took twenty years of Aveyronnais tenacity to persuade the authorities in Paris to bring over a north-south axis of the motorway, but it still needed to be joined to the strip lying south of the Tarn Valley. The Millau Viaduct now provides the hitherto missing link that will eventually bring together northern and southern Europe. It is a twist of history that faraway Aveyron may one day become a major pivot of international communications. No less paradoxical is the fact that the world's tallest and most spectacularly contemporary bridge should stand like an emblematic spearhead towards the future in an area where the most ancient past of France has been recorded.

While we visitors meander through the countryside in search of a quaint, perched village, the local inhabitants of the Aveyron get wired to the internet. Today's Aveyron has become the breeding ground of a new creative, forward-looking generation, a mix of natives and *néos*, who are no less miffed by the old picture-postcard image of the Aveyron than others are by the phrase *la France profonde*. But somehow they have managed to update the picture-postcard rather than do away with it — and this is the key to their unique achievement. My journey to the Aveyron allowed me to see and hear several of their success stories. Thanks to this new breed of inhabitants, the Aveyron is undergoing a stupendous transformation which is turning it into the up-and-coming *département* of contemporary France. This was confirmed by a survey conducted by the French magazine *l'Express* which examined quality of life in metropolitan France by *départements*. Amazingly, the one-time destitute, backward Aveyron came out the winner!

Until recently the direct day train ride between Paris Gare d'Austerlitz and Aveyron's capital Rodez took 7 hours, a lovely slow-pace journey from Figeac on, stopping on its way at every little town. Despite petitions, the train was cancelled in December 2006 because the line wasn't deemed profitable enough, so now it takes even longer to get here by train. Distances in the Aveyron are still measured in time rather than in mileage. Modernity has stepped in, but tactfully. The slow-paced traveller will rejoice.

Chapter 1

GREEN AND BLUE INFINITIES

I wanted to go to the beginning of time. There was something about the Aveyron that I sensed might give me that feel. I wanted silence, lofty altitudes and open spaces. Should anything come between the silence and me, let it be only the sound of the wind, or of murmuring water. I wanted to arrive from the top, embrace the view, then make my way down a slope like a river. It would have to be the Aubrac, *la Montagne* — over here the generic merges with the name, and that in itself is a journey into the beginning. I traced a finger down the map: I would have to come from the north, like the mountain itself which starts in the Auvergne. I could catch the local train from St-Flour, on the Auvergne side of the border, and on to Laguiole, the main town here.

    -"Nope, you will need a car", Georges was adamant.

    -"That's impossible! Surely there are trains?"

I had totally forgotten about that dreadful walk-out in Rodez on a recent visit, when I couldn't get back to Paris because the SNCF (French Rail) employees lay dramatically on the tracks to protest the scheduled closure of a local line. Is it the French government's fault if people prefer to use their private cars these days? Later I found out that the Paris train never went beyond St-Flour, not even in the old days when the Aveyronnais expats would come down from Paris for their summer holidays (a good number of them were from the Aubrac, since it was the area closest to Paris). St-Flour was the terminus where everyone would alight with their substantial luggage and carry on to Laguiole by stagecoach. This is all history, except that they still come down for their holidays, but they do so by car nowadays, and several times a year rather than once.

Eventually Odette's son conceded that some places might be reached by local buses, but it would be a drag and a hassle, as they would be unlikey to run more than once a day at best. Besides, once they reached their final destination, it would still be a long stretch to the middle of nowhere, which is necessarily where the beginning must lie and therefore where I was heading. Some acquaintances came to my rescue and offered me a ride down from Paris. It was a good thing they did, because it turned out that there were no local buses, not even once a day. The dual carriageway between St Flour and Laguiole could hardly evoke the days of the *diligence* (stagecoach), but the hilly landscape flanked pleasingly on either of its sides had remained virtually unchanged.

The centre of Laguiole is nothing much - a few characterless multi-storeyed buildings that could have been put up anywhere in France, and a village 'square' — le Foirail — once the livestock market, now a car park, the price to be paid for prosperity. Countless displays of Laguiole knives stared me in the face from adjoining shop windows as we shifted to lower gear, but luckily sculptor Georges Guyot's bronze Aubrac bull gave me new hopes that what I had come for might still be found in the vicinity: Looming above the car park, dark and massive, it looked like some stupendous force of nature, emerging out of a primeval age. Much of the impression is lost in the summer, when tourist parties line up in front of the beast for a 'must' photo. The bull is somewhat overshadowed these days by designer Philippe Starck's colossal knife blade, which flashes against the sky from the rooftop of La Forge, the local manufacturer, hailing proudly some 100 jobs, 200,000 knives per year, and an annual turnover of €4.5 million.

Originally the knives came from Catalonia, and were introduced here in the early 19th century by the seasonal migrant population of woodcutters when they returned home. The *navaja*, as it was called, had a fixed blade and the peasants wore it in their belts in country fairs to show off its elegant elongated shape. A certain Pierre-Jean Calmel noticed it, liked it, and inspired by the traditional *capuchadou*, refined it in 1840 into a multi-purpose tool by adding to it a folding awl. From then on the 'Laguiole' (pronounced La'yol, like the town) became the indispensable extension of every peasant's hand and was kept routinely in every male's pocket. Occasionally, when things got out of hand, it could be used to settle scores with a foe.

By dipping the blade into the streams and rivers of the volcanic Aubrac, Calmet improved its quality, while the horns of bulls provided the characteristic curved handles. Jean Mouly, from les Pesquiés, a one-time hamlet now devoured by Villefranche-de-Rouergue, and by a huge McDonald advert at its entry, recalls having been given a Laguiole knife by his grandfather on his seventh birthday, in 1940. It was to accompany him into manhood, as was customary. He also remembers how, in this deeply pious part of France, Grandfather would use his Laguiole knife to mark a cross on the freshly baked loaf before cutting it up and passing it round the table. Pulling out his own Laguiole, Jean pointed to the stamped bee on the handle's bolster, a guarantee of authenticity. There are different theories regarding the origin of the bee, some trace it back to Napoleon III or earlier still, to his uncle, meaning it to stand for industry and diligence, two highly rated virtues among the Aveyronnais. Gérard Boissins, one of the founders of the Forge de Laguiole, refutes this theory. He claims the bee was simply substituted to the original fly, to make it more appealing.

The knife created a sense of identity among the Parisian immigrants. They added to it the corkscrew in the late 19th century, when they started serving wine in their coal retail outlets, '*bougnats*' (from *charbongard* — coal vendor). A generation or two down the line, when the *bougnats* evolved into a flourishing café industry, the Laguiole knife remained in every *cafétier*'s pocket, as it still often does today.

In the early 20th century, when Laguiole's manufacturers could no longer satisfy the growing demand, they relocated to Thiers in the Puy-de-Dôme, which had been the French cutlery capital for over five hundred years. 75% of Laguiole knives are still made in Thiers, which creates some confusion in people's minds as to their authenticity. Demand decreased in the 1950s; sales plummeted to a record low, and it seemed that the commercial career of the knife was over. However, in 1987, designer Philippe Starck, hailing from Paris, stepped in with two other trendy contemporaries and gave the knife a new lease of life by updating it and reaching out to new markets. By the 1990s, world-renowned fashion houses such as Sonia Rykiel and Courrèges put their stamp on the one-time rustic tool, and converted it into a luxury item sold at hundreds of euros apiece. The beautiful people who use it at elegant dinner parties round the world would probably be taken aback if they found out that Jean Mouly's grandfather used his Laguiole to fix a scrap of string on his oxen's yoke. This was only sixty odd years ago.

A three-star Best Western hotel, le Relais de Laguiole, stands by the car park. It is conveniently placed, pleasantly decorated, and offers all the amenities the modern visitor would expect. It is run efficiently by a young couple, Annick and Lionel Izac, who even refurbished the hotel by themselves with the help of family and friends. Raymond Capoulade, a farmer from nearby Soulages, and one of the prominent characters on this side of the Aveyron *profond*, booked me a room there, assuming that coming from the city it would offer me the level of comfort I am used to. He was right — I was very comfortable, and everyone was very friendly, and the food was fresh, good and plentiful. There was even a sauna and a great swimming pool, and my room was perfectly restful. But it had little to do with my quest.

Capou, as he is known down here, drove me to the old section of Laguiole, which can easily be missed. Driving past Guyot's Bull into town, we took the road that forks to the left, winding uphill between two rows of dark houses, whose stripped stone was cut out of the local basalt and granite many years before. The blue sky and the flowery gardens helped brighten the scene, but I can imagine it being as bleak as the Yorkshire of Wuthering Heights' in winter, and just as exposed to the winds. The rue du Couvent, named after a convent that no longer exists, leads to the church of St-Mathieu, on the site of the old medieval castle that has left the neighbourhood with the name Le Fort. From there we enjoyed commanding views extending as far as the grey-blue summits of the Plomb du Cantal and Puy Marie to the North, in the Auvergne, the

Quercy to the west, and Rodez and the hills of the Lévézou to the south. A scallop (*coquille St-Jacques*) carved in the stone above the porch pointed to the medieval pilgrimage to Compostela, another item on my list of quests, but not for now.

For the time being I had come here to seek the pristine time that had preceded all pilgrimages and all civilisations, and I found it on the lofty empty plateau barely a few minutes away from Laguiole. But it took me a while. For a start, I had to arrange to arrive there before dawn so as to witness the moment when chaos gave way to the birth of Creation. Moreover, nature is capricious in these parts, as is the weather, and scheduling a sunrise when you are only a passing visitor can be complicated. In the meantime Sylvie from Villefranche-de-Rouergue offered me a taster over an ancient Celtic dolmen in Western Aveyron.

It was still dark when the alarm clock went off. We grabbed a quick coffee in the kitchen, without even sitting down, and made a dash for the car. But the sky was already smeared with grey, which filled me with misgivings that we might have started out too late. Faint pink pigments began to colour it before we even reached the outskirts of Villefranche, melting rapidly into a rosy glow as we raced eastwards along the D911 in the direction of Rieupeyroux, trying to keep abreast of our contender. No matter how hard Sylvie came down on the engine, the odds were not in our favour: what chance does a rickety old car stand against the faultless mechanism of a perfectly lubricated universe? The engine made so much noise, I thought it might come apart any moment. Sylvie pressed on the accelerator while keeping an eye on the sky, which seemed to be swelling into an ever redder lustre at an alarming speed.

Under normal circumstances I would have been overwhelmed by such majesty, but not now when the spectacle of a sunrise over a dolmen was at stake. Around us the pastoral Ségala, all gentle curves, had been dipped in an ocean of golden light. Even the cattle seemed to have been cast in gold, frozen into a motionless posture on the gilded meadows.

We continued in the direction of Carmaux, then turned right towards Lescure Jaoul. Le Cheval du Roi dolmen, named after a carving of a horse on its stone, was signposted soon after. Sylvie swerved to the right without slowing down, bumping and rattling along a narrow dirt track, between cornfields also cast in gold. The dolmen was tucked away at the end of the track, still out of sight. But peeping out between two hills on the horizon was a blood-red dot, gleaming at us through the windscreen. We jumped out of the car and sprinted to the dolmen on our right just as the dot waxed into a blazing crown.

Dolmens were collective burial sites consisting of an enclosed roofed rectangular structure made of dry walls. These were eroded by time into dust and disappeared. The rudimentary structure we see today — a horizontal slab supported by two vertical ones — served as the entrance to the mortuary chamber and faced the sun for ritualistic reasons. 1,000 dolmens have been recorded in the Aveyron, more than in any other *département*, enhancing the sense of ancientness imprinted on many travellers. Unfortunately, the effect was impaired that morning by ugly barbed wiring, installed close to the dolmen to fence off the cornfields — you can't expect the local farmer to wax mystical over an ancient shrine. Sylvie pointed to a couple of boundary-stones (*bornes*) at several corners of the fields. She said they were often the destination for a Sunday stroll — '*On va voir les bornes*' — an opportunity to check on a neighbour who might have shifted them an inch or two on the sly. Apparently they do the same in the border *département* of the Lot. Watching the sun begin its daily climb along the exact axis of a dolmen, you can't help thinking about the futility of such preoccupations.

When eventually I made it to genesis, a veil of silver mist billowed over the plateau, now flowing and ebbing like a silent ocean, now gliding in an eddy of perpetual metamorphosis, coiling around invisible mountains, then unrolling into a vapour of faint blush. Little by little the fuzzy landscape came into focus. Then came the moment of grace, when the sun pierced the horizon, and the sky and the earth burst into blue and green splendour. All around lay a grass-covered wilderness of granite, born out of an ancient battle between glaciers and lava. It seemed that after the great reshuffle, once the fury had abated, a piece of Connemara (or Iceland, Mongolia, or the Scottish Highlands) somehow tore itself from Western Ireland and found its way to the south of the Auvergne. Here it settled into a territory of 2,500 km² — now l'Aubrac, Ambra (meaning 'altitude') in Roman times — a world unto itself, indifferent to administrative partitions, extending deep into the Cantal and the Lozère. In spring time, it becomes a riot of 2,000 varieties of flowers, the country's record, among them some rare species that are found nowhere else other than in Greenland or remote parts of Scandinavia. I suppose their seeds were brought over by migrating birds. These are only medium-size mountains, averaging 1,300 metres above sea level and culminating at 1,442. Over here you don't feel dwarfed by eternally snow-capped summits but the thrilling call of a horizontal infinity. You don't encounter the vertical drama of the Mont Blanc but a forceful, windswept landscape under skies that never seem to end.

I stood beneath those skies, watching the earth complete its daily act of birth. The world was still. Across the empty plateau the sun returned my gaze, a disk of burning fire pursuing steadily its inexorable ascent — the first of all gods, the parent of all life. There wasn't a living soul in sight to carry out the ritual of its worship, other than myself, but I, like my contemporaries, had vowed allegiance to other gods. Even the fawn-colour Aubrac cows, which are so much part of the scenery in the summer months, were conspicuously absent. It was too early in the season; they would only make it up here during their annual migration from the valley, known as *transhumance*, on the third weekend of May, as close as possible to the 25th, once known as St Urbain's Day — a Christian pope and saint to mark a date in this Christian phase of the Aubrac. The druids, who officiated over the dolmens, were here much earlier, replaced in turn by the Romans who marked their conquest with a road. Thay have all gone. Including the fast-moving ferocious aurochs, recorded on the cave walls of Lascaux before they were domesticated into the Aubrac cattle, it is believed.

Then came the Christians, who signaled their presence with crosses, notably La Croix des Trois Evêques. I was intrigued by it as soon as I spotted it on the map. Who were those three nameless bishops and what on earth were they doing on a lonely heath in the middle of the wilds? I had a hunch they must have lived a very long time ago. I thought the site of a cross with such a mysterious name would make a grand location from which to watch the spectacle of the first sunrise of Creation. Later I found out that the cross marked the meeting point of the Aveyron, the Lozère and the Cantal *départements*, and of the provinces of Rouergue, Gévaudan (Lozère) and Clermont (Auvergne) in earlier times. Further reading instructed me that the bishops of the three provinces had held a council there in the year 590 A.D., as reported soon after by their contemporary Gregory the Bishop of Tours in his *History of the Franks*.

Gregory was from nearby Clermont-Ferrand and died in 594, which makes his testimony all the more credible. I was delighted to stumble upon an old English paperback copy of Gregory of Tours' precious document among my own books, having forgotten that I had once picked it up for 50 pence in Chelsea's secondhand bookshop. It had been in my possession all those years, waiting for the right moment to reveal itself to me. How neat to watch the three anonymous bishops from a faraway mountain materialise into factual history from the comfort of my armchair. I had to read till the Tenth Book to find out, to my amazement, that they had travelled all that way in order to arbitrate on a private matrimonial case, not unlike those brought before the court today:

> "*A council of bishops was convened on the borders of Clermont, Gévaudan and Rouergue to judge the case of Tetradia, the widow of Desiderius, in a law-suit brought against her by Count Eulalius for the restitution of the property which she had taken with her when she left him.*"

Gregory provides the full story and points an accusing finger at Eulalius who had made Tetradia's life a misery, and was believed to have murdered his own mother. I was surprised that such allowances were made for women by a churchman in those remote times. It was an interesting window onto the early Middle Ages, a time about which little is known.

In 1238 a 300kg granite cross was erected by the monks of Aubrac (of which more later) on the site of the three bishops' council. It weathered the centuries and stood undisturbed until 1990 when, following another gathering of officialdom, it disappeared mysteriously. This time the meeting was headed by the three Conseillers Généraux of the Midi-Pyrénées, the Languedoc-Roussillon and the Auvergne — three of France's modern-day regions — which also meet here, keeping the historical thread running on a solitary mountain through 1400 years. Incidentally, the representative of the Auvergne on that occasion was the one-time French president, Valéry Giscard d'Estaing. The cross has never been recovered and no one has figured out how anyone could have run off unnoticed with such a cumbersome booty, let alone of such considerable weight. Unless it was a trick played by the Devil, who is known to have been very active over here and would have naturally been tempted to remove crosses, especially since these were erected to offer protection against him. Apparently, he also interfered with the bread, which is why people marked a cross on the dough before it went into the oven. A new cross stands by the roadside of the D15 north of the village of Aubrac. Surrounded by conifers and hardly noticeable from a car, it offers no vistas and would certainly not have worked for the staging of my sunrise.

On 15 August 1997, the bishops of Rodez, St-Flour and Mende (capitals respectively of the Aveyron, Cantal and Lozère) had convened once more on the Aubrac, at the nearby

Moussous mountains, north of the D987, driving east from Aubrac. They had come to dedicate a new statue to Notre Dame d'Aubrac, the work of Hervé Vernhes whom I was to meet several years later in his home village of Peyrusse-le-Roc. His was not an ethereal Virgin, floating on a heavenly cloud, but a monolithic piece of granite, anchored to a 14-tonne rock that served as its pedestal, and stark like the surrounding landscape which it dominated. Like the emblem of the cross which bridges heaven and earth, she stood like a link between the earth out of which she had been carved, and the beyond where her detached yet benign gaze rested. By her side was Jesus the shepherd boy, evoking the area's pastoral traditions (sheep grazed on the Aubrac until recent times).

A 3,000-strong crowd had gathered around the statue on that Assumption Day of 1997, under an azure sky. The celebration was marked by a polyphony of 80 voices. When later Hervé Vernhes showed me a cutting with a photo from the local press, I was surprised to recognise the nuns of the Order of Jerusalem, whose crystalline acapella prayers I am very familiar with, having heard them many times at the church of St-Protalis-St-Gervais in the Marais, their Parisian base. Theirs is an original congregation insofar as their members hold regular jobs out in the world, then regroup in the nest for meditation and prayer. Their connection to the Aubrac surprised me at first, but on second thought it seemed the most appropriate environment for their earthy spirituality. The sculptures of Hervé Vernhes convey much the same, the glorification of Almighty God-given matter through sharp incisions in the bare rock. They have an unfinished aspect which subordinates them to the raw rock out of which they have been carved, as the living are subordinate to the earth. '*oh, ce ne sont que des cailloux!*' ("Oh, they are just pebbles!"), Hervé retorted almost bashfully when I expressed my admiration. That may be so, but I am thrilled to own one, the bust of a dreamy grape-picking lass, chiselled out of the red sandstone of the village of Conques.

Aubrac the place, as distinct from the plateau, is too small to be called a village, or even a hamlet, going by its number of permanent residents — three in total until very recently, all of whom were women. The legendary Germaine, who was Aubrac's oldest resident with pre-Revolution ancestry, is no more. Her daughter Adrienne gave up her mother's hotel business but has kept the homely restaurant. Those who knew Germaine claim things are not quite the same. I was not in a position to draw comparisons and enjoyed thoroughly both the daughter's company and her cooking. One comes to Adrienne, as one came to Germaine, for an *aligot* — a mix of potatoes and cheese believed to have originated here. It is the Aveyron's most famous speciality, but it spills over to border areas as well. Ours was preceded by a flavourful cheese soup, and followed by an enormous slice of Adrienne's celebrated *tarte aux fruits de la fôret*. Everything was served amidst a jovial bustle that kept me happy for the rest of the day.

At the other end of the spectrum, Catherine Painvin's luxury *chambres d'hôtes* have replaced Germaine's modest hotel. Catherine is a well known figure on the Paris show-biz scene, and the owner of Tartine et Chocolat, purveyor of all things nice to the BCBG (*bon chic bon genre*) children of the sophisticated neighbourhood of St-Germain. How on earth did someone from that kind of world make her way to the Aubrac? No less astonishing is the fact that she has Mongolian friends whom she brings over in the summer to help her fix the place. But then, the Aubrac does look like a miniature tundra. Be prepared to dish out €200 for Bed and Breakfast. In return you may lounge under a parasol in the lovely garden and enjoy the massage room. There is even a boutique where you can buy a miscellaneous bric-a-brac of ethnic and artsy gowns (some of which are her own designs) and artifacts, at ever-skyrocketing prices. The interior decoration is a whimsical recreation of the heath outside, and of Mongolia, Tibet, or whatever Catherine may fancy. And it works. Even the picket-and-wire snow fencing she grabbed from the roadside works. There are five differently designed rooms, with five different bathrooms. My favourite was filled with conifers and had twin bathtubs ensconced side by side inside two mounds of granite boulders, inspired by the dry walls that grace the curves of the Aubrac.

The third woman, 34-year-old Marie-Claude David, has taken over the management of the 2-star hotel-restaurant La Dômerie, a five-generation business on the maternal Auguy side of the family. Marie-Claude's great-great-great-grandmother took part in the Commune (which opposed the bourgeois authorities in Versailles during the 1871 civil war) and was nicknamed *le tablier rouge* (Red Apron) because she was in charge of feeding the Communard fighters. Marie-Claude's great-great-great-grandfather was from the Lozère side of the Aubrac and traded in wine from the Languedoc. Occasionally he travelled up to Paris to sell his wine, where the couple met. In 1880 they decided to settle in the Aubrac and opened the hotel. Having come down from Paris, they named it l'Hôtel Parisien. Marie-Claude's mother was the last member of the family to have been born on the premises, as was customary in the countryside, and is still in charge of the kitchen, keeping regional traditions alive — including, of course, that of freshly made *aligot*. The establishment cannot compete with the luxury of Catherine Painvin's but it is delightfully genuine, homely and welcoming, and does provide all the basic modern amenities.

Recently, some noticeable changes have taken place in the tiny village of Aubrac. For one, the number of its residents has more than doubled, jumping from three to seven! Furthermore, one of the newcomers is a man, Cyril Lerisse, bringing to an end the century old female homogeneity.

Things were quite different in the year 1120, when the plateau was covered by a thick forest, through which the *Via Podiensis* pilgrim route wound its way to Compostela in northwest Spain, coming from Puy en Vélay in the Auvergne. Only unflinching faith could have driven the wayfarer into such Biblical desolation '*In loco horroris et vastae solitudinis*' ("of horror and vast solitudes"), to quote Deuteronomy, of howling winds and packs of wolves, blinding snowstorms and lurking bands of brigands. This was the scenario faced by Adalard in the above mentioned year, when, coming from the court of the Count of Flanders on his way to Compostela, he was assailed by bandits in the wilderness of the Aubrac.

As in all moralistic struggles good prevailed over evil and Adalard came out of the trials unharmed and fortified, vowing to build here a shelter for fellow pilgrims, upon his return. Basalt stone was yielded by the volcanic soil and wood by the forest, and before long the black, horizontal silhouette of the monastery of the Dômerie, so called after its head, the Dom, stood out against the sky like a beacon of hope to the exhausted pilgrim. Here he was offtered hospitality for up to three nights, just enough time to refuel his energy, receive medical care in the adjacent hospital, and spiritual solace in the chapel. Further assistance was provided by the chimes of a bell, *la cloche des perdus*, which would guide him to safety through bad weather, as a lighthouse helps the seafarer to the shore. Even today it is easy to get lost here during a snowstorm, or when the fog descends; it can happen in no time, with no forewarning, even in the middle of summer. Sébastien Persec, a young farmer from the nearby hills above Laguiole told me how his grandfather had got lost in his own farmyard in the midst of a white blizzard and had to grope his way into the house. Had he been on less familiar grounds, he would have certainly perished.

The surrounding forest was gradually cut down by the friars and turned into pastures, cattle and sheep were introduced (the latter having since disappeared) and dairy farming developed, benefiting from the aroma of the Aubrac flora and herbs, which added a wonderful flavour to the milk and the cheese. The *tomme* and the blue-veined *fourme* of Laguiole have their origin in the Dômerie of Aubrac. It is believed that two of the Aveyron's most common specialities — the above-mentioned *aligot* and the *fouace* — also originated here. According to one theory *aligot* comes from the Latin *aliquid*, meaning 'something'. It is to the Aveyron (and the neighbouring areas) what couscous is to North Africa and curry to India and no social gathering can be conceived without it. Initially, it was made from bread and cheese, but in the 19th century mashed potatoes were substituted for bread, and garlic was added more recently for extra flavour: according to another theory '*ali*' derives from *ail*, the French for garlic.

Today, you can buy it packaged and frozen at the local supermarket, as you can couscous, curry, chili con carne, and the rest of it, but some natives will sniff at such outrageous sacrilege. Obviously, nothing can match the freshly made *aligot*, especially when partaken of in its Aubrac homeland. The pleasure is all the greater when you have developed an appetite because it's miserably cold and wet outside. It goes so well with the open fire over which it cooks in a huge black cauldron until it reaches perfect consistency. A magical performance begins, with a wooden spatula dipped into the preparation to reemerge trailing an endless yellow piece of drapery and everyone oohs and aahs and claps their hands like delighted children.

The *fouace* is a hearth cake and keeps longer than bread. It is said to have been offered the pilgrims by the friars upon their departure, which some claim accounts for its ring shape: The pilgrim would hang it from a string round his neck and have that much less to carry. Today the *fouace* is as basic a staple as bread (someone defined it as "bread with added sugar and eggs"), kept in every Aveyronnais household as a matter of course.

Little remains of the old Dômerie, gone the way of many abbeys during the French Revolution, except for the church of Notre Dame des Pauvres, built around 1198, some sixty years after the death of Adalard. Its treasures, however, were dispersed or lost, and its Renaissance rood screen is said to have made its way to America. The 15th-century bell tower has survived too, but the *cloche des perdus* was melted down in 1772. The Tour des Anglais (1353) next to the church is the only other survivor, now a stopping-place (*gîte-d'étape*) for pilgrims and hikers. Despite its misleading name, the tower was not built and never occupied by the English, nor was it erected to fend them off. Rather, the name alludes to the

hordes of ruffians who scoured the western reaches of France
during the unstable times of the Hundred Years' War, and were
referred to as *les Anglais* as a matter of course! At present the
tower is beautifully floodlit by night, and is further enhanced
by star-lit skies so pure they seem to display the entire cosmos
before your eyes. In August, a festival of shooting stars adds to
the enchantment.

I visited the church for the first time on Friday 3 October
2003, during a special mass that marked the annual *Fête des
buronniers*. It was a sunny, morning outside, and the
contrasting stripped basalt walls looked just right in this
rustic environment. I was standing at the doorway when I
noticed a series of wall paintings across the nave, practically
the only decoration around. Although the church was dim,
and even from that distance, I recognised at once the touch
of Hervé Vernhes' hand whom I had met by then on several
occasions. In character with his modesty, he hadn't
mentioned these paintings, and this unexpected encounter
with his work thrilled me like the connection between the
Order of Jerusalem and La Croix des Trois Evêques. It
seemed as though some invisible thread had strung together
all those kindred souls. I crossed the nave to get a close view
of the paintings, a six-piece pictorial narration of the history
of the Dômerie, beginning with the arrival of its Flemish
founder Abalard. In keeping with traditional medieval
church art, such paintings were meant for the edification of
the beholder. Hervé Vernhes had no moralistic purpose, but
his work is steeped in his heritage and environment, a
modest '*caillou*' as he refers to it, which he adds quietly to
the overall edifice.

The church was beginning to fill up. It could barely hold the 230 plus *buronniers* and their families who had gathered for their annual fete. The term *buronnier* is derived from *buron* (or *mazuc* in Occitan, the one-time flourishing language of southern France). It is a low-lying stone hut characteristic of the Aubrac and of the neighbouring mountains of the Auvergne. During the summer months, while the cattle were left to graze the open pastures, the *buronniers* spent their days making cheese, which enabled them to extend the lifespan of milk from a day and a half to a year and a half, and thereby ensure the economic survival of the territory. All the successive chores that were woven into their intricate and busy schedule, from sunrise to nightfall, were ingeniously coordinated and had the Laguiole cheese as their final goal. The lower level of the *buron* was buried underground for the ripening of the cheese. Their steep, pointed roofs therefore seem to emerge out of the grass, creating a picturesque effect further enhanced by the silvery crystals of their characteristic schist tiles known as *lauzes*.

Life was harsh and rigorous organisation was necessary in order to manage the community's livelihood. An all-male microcosmic society, usually of six, gravitated around each *buron* with the same rigid hierarchy you would find on a sea vessel. At the top of the ladder, the *cantalès* ruled supreme, often ironhanded; at the bottom, the *roul*, sometimes a mere child of 8, had to carry out the most strenuous chores. Occasionally, when the master overstepped the tolerable, his subordinates took the law into their own hands, referred to as '*la Justice de Laguiole*'. This was administered not with the celebrated knife, but with a knotty rod whittled out of a service-tree (*drillier*), a hardy shrub that weathers the winds of

Chapter 1

the plateau and which you might sight here and there framing prettily an abandoned *buron*. When, one day, a notoriously ruthless *buronnier* was left dead after a session of flogging, no one called for an investigation. It was an internal matter, responded to with eloquent silence. Occasionally an enterprising *roul* would brace himself and take his destiny into his own hands, such as 16 year old Marcellin Cazès who, following a clash with his boss, left for Paris where he later opened what was to become the illustrious and glamourous Brasserie Lipp, while he and and his son became iconic figures of St-Germain-des-Prés.

As I write this chapter, the last *buronnier*, Jean Fournier, has just closed down the last *buron* of the Aubrac, ending 200 years of history which began with the dismantling of the Dômerie during the French Revolution. As elsewhere in France, the abbey's land was parcelled up and sold to local farmers. Each parcel was known as *la montagne* and its owner as *montagnard* (*Mountanhiès* in Occitan). They were the summer extension of the farms which lay down in the valley, providing pastures of wonderful wild grass, where the cattle would graze between late May and mid-October. There were as many as 300 of them at the time, collectively known as *les estives*. This additional territory enabled them to increase the size of the herds, whilst the rich soil led to an improvement in the quality of the cheese.

So now all the *buronniers* are retired, but once a year they walk down memory lane to commemorate their past life. They start off at the church of Aubrac for an emotional mass, which I was privileged to attend on that October day. The theme picked for the sermon was the Hand of man, the ultimate gift given him by God. Although it was His Spirit that commanded

20

Creation into being, according to the Holy Scriptures, it was His Hand that shaped Creation. In these rural parts manual tasks are highly valued, and, as I had noticed earlier, spirituality is never disconnected from the earth. Paradoxically, this deeply Catholic land is imbued with the spirit of the Old Testament. Yet despite Père Ricard's eloquence, why should anyone wish to pursue a life of hardship in this day and age, when one can drive up to the plateau and back home in less than an hour each way? Why shiver through the night in a drafty stone hut on top of a desolate mountain when a comfortable bed and a hot bath or shower are available down the valley?

When we were all seated at long tables in the Salle des Fêtes of St-Chély-d'Aubrac, and Capou called Jean Fournier to the mike, I sensed I was witnessing the closing of the last chapter of *la plus profonde de toutes les Frances profondes*. This was confirmed by the fact that the *aligot* we were about to be served had been prepared by la Coopérative de la Jeune Montagne, the new generation of Laguiole cheesemakers who have secured the survival of the tradition with an ultra-modern plant-cum-museum, where a popular exhibition on the local history of cheesemaking is on display. Today the cheese is no longer pressed by unhygienic knees, as was customary, a method which I doubt would have passed the test of the Food Safety Agency in Brussels, and enjoys the AOC (Appellation d'Origine Contrôlée) label, a guarantee that the entire chain of production — from the grazing of the cattle to the maturing of the cheese — takes place on the Aubrac.

There is little difference between the Laguiole cheese and that of the neighbouring and somewhat better known Cantal, but native connoisseurs discern a subtle superiority in the

Laguiole (I suspect the inhabitants of the Cantal would argue to the contrary). Naturally, now that the *buronniers* have entered the pages of history, their communal way of life is viewed through the distorted mirror of nostalgia, to which the entertainment provided by Capou contributed that afternoon. Yet neither his wooden *sabots* (clogs), black hat and red kerchief, nor his accordion, could halt the march of time. When I asked Jean Fournier why he had closed down and whether he felt a twinge about walking the path of no return, he simply shrugged his shoulders philosophically. I suppose he meant it was time to let go, although others have told me he drops into his *buron* daily.

Letting go entails an acceptance that all must end, except the memory of things, which continues so long as there is someone out there to perpetuate it and someone else to stand by as its witness: without spectators there will be no show. That's where the tourist industry steps in. Although too easily pointed at as the villain who is ruining the past and casting a blemish on the local colour, it's often the other way round. The past is gone by its very definition, leaving the present and future with no other choice than desolation, or survival through adjustment.

The entrepreneurial André Valadier, chairman of the Coopérative de la Jeune Montagne, has opted for adjustment: La Maison d'Aubrac has both the area's heritage and its present dynamism on display. Its attractive boutique carries some of the mountains' specialities, such as *thé d'Aubrac*, an infusion made from the calament's pink flowers, and *gentiane*, a refreshingly bitter *apéritif* made from its roots. The contemporary design of the building, the lavish use of glass, the sophisticated gift wrappings, all stand for modern Aveyron, which is moving proudly with the times. What a contrast to the mass earlier, when a lonesome *cabrette* (Aveyronnais bagpipe) poured out Schubert's Ave Maria like a lament surging out of the ancient totem of humanity. Over here, the past is obstinately resistant and won't let go.

Most of the *burons* are in a state of ill repair, eroded by the wind and the rain, and by unscrupulous locals who prey on their precious *lauzes*: once the roof goes, the rest disintegrates in no time. There is talk of restoration, to be undertaken by the Heritage Department, but for the moment several have been turned into summer restaurants. At the Buron de la Sistre, outside Aubrac, Monsieur et Madame Ramon provide a copious menu of *charcuterie*, Laguiole cheese, Aubrac meat and, obviously, *aligot* for €21, but no credit cards are accepted. This is the standard menu which we were also served at the Buron de Born with Georges, Odette and a long trail of friends, on the occasion of the *transhumance*. It is situated on the even more beautiful Lozère side of the Aubrac, (take the D52 beyond Nasbinals) facing the lake of Born after which it is named. People on the Aubrac will tell you that their plateau is a world of its own, indifferent to the arbitrary division into *départements* imposed by administrators from Paris. Besides, the *patron* happens to be an Aveyronnais.

Some sixty of us were hosted by Georges and Odette at Las Canals for the *transhumance*. We set out early the next morning, headed for St-Geniez-d'Olt. Sitting prettily on the river Lot (or Olt as the section of the river is named east of Entraygues), St-Geniez was one of the Rouergue's largest towns prior to the French Revolution, thriving on its textiles which were exported as far as America. Several elegant townhouses and religious establishments still bear witness to the *bourg's* (borough) past affluence. Today, St-Geniez nestles among fruit orchards and has gained quite a reputation for its strawberry farming, despite competition from Spain.

We started off with an Aveyronnais breakfast, a must as a one-off experience although I feel no urge to repeat it. After the usual charcuterie and sausages, I was doing fine on the *tête de veau* (as well as the skin of the head, the animal's tongue and brains also go into the concoction). According to Odette *tête de veau* is not part of a traditional breakfast, although some Aveyronnais claim the contrary. *Tripoux* (mutton or veal's stomach stuffed with parsley and garlic), on the other hand, are the backbone of an Aveyronnais breakfast. It is a speciality of the Ségala, in western Averyon, but it is served all over the *département*, although in the south they call it *trénel*. Ours was followed by a sizeable wedge of Laguiole cheese, and a chunky wedge of *prunat* (prune tart) to finish off, by which time I was ready to throw up the sponge.

Everything got washed down by coarse red wine of little merit, bringing to mind visions from my student years in the Latin Quarter, when I often breakfasted in a local café on a *petit crème* and *tartine beurrée* and watched the workmen in their blue overalls start their day with un *ballon de rouge* (a glass of red wine). This was swilled down at the counter, while engaging in long-winded discussions with the *patron* who every so often would refill his customer's glass. This would be done on an empty stomach, every single morning of a working week: How much wine must have gone into those bodies over the years! No wonder cirrhosis of the liver was the number one killer in France at the time, taking thousands of lives a year. As I am always game for trying something typically local, I am glad I had a go at an Aveyronnais breakfast, but the bunch of juicy red cherries I bought at the local shop when we left the restaurant gave me much greater pleasure and cost half of what I would have paid for them in Paris.

The square of St-Geniez is pleasantly shady and was decked with flags on that morning. A makeshift stage had been set up at one end, complete with sound equipment for the traditional string of speeches and music. As on all official occasions held far from the main urban centres, a variety of background noises and whistles spewed out of the mikes, scattering to the winds most of the content of the successive addresses. What my ears caught was candidly self-congratulatory, intermingled with encouraging statistics which would have been useful for my research, but it was much less taxing to just enjoy the speakers' regional lilt and the overall colourful scene — a living portrait gallery branded with centuries of wedlock to the ancestral soil; an assembly of red kerchiefs, black hats and tunics, an occasional beret; wooden clogs, cowherds' crooks, and especially those elderly weather-beaten faces lined with lifetimes of farming, the living 'cousins' of the portrait behind the counter at George and Odette's restaurant who may have been at the origin of my journey. It was hard to believe this was 21st-century France.

Everyone squeezed behind the metal barriers that fenced off the centre of the square, leaning over them whenever possible to get a better view of the herds as they ambled in one by one to make a spectacle of themselves before beginning the steeper climb up the mountains. Unlike me who had driven here from Las Canals, the farmers, cowherds and cows had been up and about since before dawn and had walked dozens of miles from the different farms to St-Geniez. Not so long ago even one-month-old calves made the journey on foot, marching close to 80 km in two days, much of it up a steep slope. Today the calves are driven up the mountains in trucks and their mothers get all distressed when they are torn away from their calves. Unfortunately, there is no telling them that they will be reunited on top of the mountain at the end of the day, a delightful scene as mothers and offspring single each other out without hesitation, even from a distance.

The anticipation began to build up in the square as soon as the melody of cow bells could be heard signalling the approaching steps of a herd. Everyone's eyes turned in the direction of the bells, where the vanguard of the herd would appear any moment, a beautiful fawn-coloured breed with big, black patches round their languorous eyes that look like kohl make-up. On the festive occasion of the *transhumance* they are also prettily decorated with paper flowers and *tricouleurs*. There were very few European Union flags, which I thought might be intended as a political statement against Brussels, but it turned out that they were simply hard to come by in remote Aveyron. I also wondered whether the red flags hoisted by one exceptionally well-groomed herd suggested any socialist leanings, but closer examination pointed to the logo of the Midi-Pyrénées region, which embraces the Aveyron and its seven neighbouring *départements*. Whilst herds came and went, the accordion teamed up with the bagpipe, firing off the village folks into a lively *bourrée*. I was standing close enough to the dancers to be able to read an expression of quasi-solemnity on their faces as they were getting ready to climb onto the stage and repeat the ancestral pattern of steps. Coming from sophisticated Paris, I was touched by their restrained blush here and there, the subtle throbbing of a cheek muscle... I guarantee this was no gimmick for tourists.

The climb up the mountain was tiring, the weather was iffy and got worse as we approached the plateau. I couldn't wait to spread my hands over the open fire which I knew was waiting for us inside the *buron* with a glass of red wine. But when we reached the top of the slope, and hit upon carpets of white narcissus, I stood transfixed, bewitched by their fragrance. Only mad dogs and myself were out there in the biting rain, inhaling as much as I could of the inebriating scent and soaking up the whipping wind. I could have stayed there forever. I wanted to pick all the flowers and hold them, or better still, bury myself among them, but since this was obviously an overambitious project, I contented myself with the purchase of some narcissus-scented soap on a subsequent visit to La Maison d'Aubrac. Sadly, the magic would be short lasting — in a few weeks' time they would be harvested mechanically to supply the scent industry of Grasse in Provence. I can well understand why the late Annick Goutal, having spent summertime on the Aubrac as a child, was inspired to turn its native flowers into her world-renowned scents, now part of the Taittinger empire. She had started out as a pianist.

Michel Bras, too, has spent his childhood on the Aubrac, but he lived in Laguiole all year round. Carrying his love of the heath to the kitchen, he is now the owner and chef of the eponymous 3-Michelin star Relais et Châteaux establishment, without a doubt the culinary flagship of the Aveyron. People make a special journey to the Puech du Suquet ('Bald Peak', in local *patois*) where he is situated from as far away as Japan, and among the foreign apprentices in his kitchen when we visited was a beaming Brazilian.

It was sunset when we arrived, having wound our way along the D15 between green and blue infinities of land and sky. Who ever claimed that abstract art is a distortion of nature? Eric Raffy* carried the abstraction into his architecture, playing on a palette of purple, blue and silver greys which the native basalt, granite, schist and slate had yielded to him willingly. Inspired by the traditional *burons*, the buildings lie low, but the generous use of glass marks them as our contemporaries, opening them up to the plateau and to its mystical light. To optimise the effect, the lounge and restaurant face west, thus setting the shrine aglow for the first two acts of the gastronomic celebration, when attended in spring and summer (at the end of October the establishment closes for the winter months).

Drinks are served in the lounge, and the above-mentioned gentian *apéritif* is a must, since the yellow-flowered plant is emblematic of the Aubrac. It blooms in June, but it takes ten years or more before it gives its first blossoms for all to see, two metres above the ground. The various liqueurs and *eaux-de-vie* are made from the roots, and these are even longer than the stalks, reaching three metres underground. Digging them out is a strenuous job, requiring the use of a pitchfork and a pickax. Sipping the result, however, requires no effort whatsoever, especially when accompanied by Bras's astonishing *oeuf à la coque*, a subtle tribute to his mother's cooking going back to his childhood. Many of France's chefs had inspiring mothers behind their success stories, notably bubbly and colourful Patrice Wursching from the wonderful Magnolias hotel in Plaisance, down south, whom I visited subsequently,

* Raffy has also redesigned the Ferme de Moulhac *chambres d'hôtes* at Moulhac, by Laguiole

and who insisted I should pay a tribute to his mother in this book. The promise is kept.

We sat there soaking up the scenery and the warmth of the sunset, dipping our spoons lazily in the smooth texture of the yolks, a pleasure that climaxed with a sensual thrill in each mouthful. How could a straightforward soft boiled egg turn into a gastronomic experience? Ingredients, ingredients, for sure, but combined with the mysterious *coup de main* of a great chef. Facing us, the red disk of the sun poured through the window pane. Eric Raffy must have had this in mind when he planned the position of the buildings in relation to the sun, not unlike the ancient Celts when they erected their stone monuments. I suspect Michel Bras also followed their example when he picked out his spot, judging by the energising breeze that greeted us out of the car. A footpath overhung with the aroma of wild herbs led us through the yellow broom to the top of the hill, where the breathtaking moors came into full view, slanting down towards the black forests below.

Although Michel Bras was recognised officially in 2005 as Europe's foremost chef, self-aggrandisement is foreign to the Aveyron. It is the Aubrac that you have come to celebrate, to which everything is subordinate, the architecture, the interior decoration, the cooking and the chef. The luminous skies are replicated in the red burbot caught in one of the native rivers, and the dark shadow of a cloud in the black olive preparation that accompanies it. The young sprouts of spring are gathered into a bright green mound of *gargouillou*, the delicate backbone of the establishment, which arrives at the table topped with a blue field flower to evoke a butterfly. The mousse of white cheese mirrors the mountain snows, the *coulant au chocolat* its ancient lava. Each dish is meant to connect the guests with the elements that lie beyond the glass walls, while local touches are provided by the Laguiole knives, the silk version of the Auvergnat tunic sported by the waiters, and the delicate, feather-weight side dish of aligot, the lightest I had ever tasted.

Our lunch in the *buron*, on the other hand, had no silk frills, no symbolic references, and no gastronomic claims. It was a straightforward hearty meal, comprising all the classics — *charcuterie*, Aubrac beef — claimed to be the best in the world — French beans, green salad, Laguiole *tomme* cheese, fruit tart... in other words, the usual Aveyronnais fare, served in generous quantities. Since our party was made up essentially of Georges and Odette's friends, it was a cosy affair, played out at long, bare wooden tables, as usual. When the long spatula emerged out of the pot with its streaming sheet of *aligot*, it received the same boisterous ovation I had encountered at the *fête des buronniers*, and at all the other Aveyronnais gatherings I have attended since. Some dishes just do this to you, like the *fondue savoyarde* and the *raclette*, for instance, both of which, incidentally, are cheese-based mountain specialities too. They create a sense of belonging by the sheer fact that they bring everyone close together, and also because the awkward handling of the melted cheese adds to the sense of *convivialité*. In the old days the *buronniers* ate the *aligot* straight out of the central pot, the way one still eats a *fondue savoyarde*. No matter how uptight, stuffy or self-important one might be back home, everyone loosens up on these occasions, because these homely dishes are great social levellers. And the colder and wetter the weather outside, the greater the effect.

It was time to look for the river that would take me down from the mountain to the valley of civilization, the Lot. I thought I might start with some afternoon exercise before setting off, just a short hike along the Devèze that would take me through the forest to a lovely hidden waterfall recommended by Capou. Capou was confident I would not get lost, "Just listen to the river and follow it..." He sent Céline with me as my guide, but she too was a stranger to these parts and before we knew it we had mistaken the rustle of the wind for the murmuring of the water, and lost both the river and our way.

It was autumn, and the opulent beech trees had strewn trails of rusty leaves on the ground; more came gliding down gently like clouds of glowing butterflies; an occasional blood-red toadstool shone with Disneyland white dots; a pheasant alighted at our feet and hopped in and out of our path with its glittering copper tiara; and all along the muted sound of the breeze and the overhanging balmy smell of conifers accompanied our steps. But we never found the waterfall. Feeling rather inadequate, I recalled my conversation with Sébastien who has the Aubrac in his blood and who can hear every bit and beat of its pulse with his internal ear. His pitch black hair and thick moustache, his fiery charcoal black eyes and his deep voice, seem to weld him to its volcanic soil. He had covered 2,000 km of unmapped territory in five years, never treading the same ground twice, always trying out something new. He's been through the thickest of forest and fog, even through an unexpected blizzard. Naturally when you are at one with your environment your senses become sharpened; but what about those medieval pilgrims who were first-timers? How many had perished without leaving a trace?

Capou was surprised we hadn't made it to the waterfall. We joined him in the evening on his farm in Soulages, which rolls in green tranquillity on the western foothills of the Aubrac. "But all you had to do was listen to the water..." Easier said than done when your ear has only been trained to pick up city noises. Capou has 35 dairy cows and grows 8 hectares of cereals to feed them. In the event of drought, their diet is supplemented by branches of ash, which grow in plenty all over the foothills. Initially he was supposed to accompany me to the waterfall, but the tilling and sowing had to be completed by the end of the week: Nature's clock is inflexible; no concessions are ever allowed for, not even on the Sabbath. Despite progress, the loose rock must still be removed by hand, a tough job for a 60-year-old farmer, and there is only Capou, his son and one helper to take care of the farm.

While I was lingering on the driveway, indulging in the evocative smells of my childhood, Capou was already in the cowshed preparing the machines for the evening milking session. This may be France, but over here nobody ever goes on strike. It's a seven-day-a-week, round-the-clock job, always up at dawn, always tending to the animals before nightfall. Not an easy life. A weary farmer's option is to try and sell the farm and leave, except that it may be difficult to find a buyer. Those who do want to hang on to their ancestors' farm, like Capou and Sébastien, have to branch off into other part-time activities, because a medium-size herd won't provide a living. Capou set up a campsite on his farm several years back, complemented by day visits for children. It was quite a pioneering initiative in those days, when the

French peasantry was even more leery of the outside world than it is at present.

For quite some time too, Capou has been unearthing memorabilia from the area's past, which has gradually built up into a stupendous collection, an extraordinary jumble of ploughs, yokes and carts, early wooden washing machines that would be set in motion with a crank, an early wireless, neat old cars... samples of all the tools and vehicles that accompanied previous generations have been piled up by Capou in his barn-cum-museum, something of an Ali Baba cave. For a one-man venture, this is quite a shrine to the heritage of rural France. Officialdom recognised his commitment and in July 2005 he became the first French farmer to have been knighted *chevalier des arts et des lettres*.

Chapter 2

THE *VIA PODIENSIS* —
THE ROAD TO COMPOSTELA

By a stroke of good fortune my journey from Genesis to the valley of civilisation coincided with a section of the pilgrim route to Santiago of Compostela. Since the two roads overlapped, I thought I might kill two birds with one stone and visit some of the pilgrim stopping-places along the way. The only self-imposed prerequisite was to start out from a source of a river, which I would then follow down to the Lot, because that's what I had planned initially, to please my fancy. I picked the month of March so as to take in the regeneration of nature, and kept my fingers crossed that my timing would coincide with the flowering of the daffodils. Once on site, I recruited a small party of locals to accompany me, among them Christian Bichwiller, a mountain guide who also runs a *gîte* for pilgrims. Before we set out, Isabelle Baldit from the tourist office confirmed that the daffodils were out. So far so good.

By another stroke of good fortune, St-Chely-d'Aubrac, the next stopping-place on the Compostela pilgrim route coming from Aubrac, happens to have a river which doesn't even have a name — what more could I wish for on this journey to primal beginnings. Maps and guidebooks call it La Boralde de St-Chély, although strictly speaking *boralde* is a generic designation for any watercourse that takes its source on the Aubrac. By a miraculous coincidence La Boralde de St-Chély emerges from the ground in the vicinity of La Croix des Trois Evêques, a few minutes' walk down the slope from Hervé

Vernhes's statue of the Virgin on the Monts Mossous. It felt as though my itinerary might have been mysteriously designed from above. A myriad of tiny crocus buds unrolled a frail mother-of-pearl carpet over the hillside, streaked here and there by dashes of daffodils that cowered from the slashing rain and wind in miniature size, tailor-made specifically to enchant me, it seemed. Yet beneath the exquisite offering of early spring lay an invisible snare of swamps and bogs that made it impossible to reach the spring of the river. I should have deduced that if the vitality of germination is magnified on the microcosmic Aubrac, it was due to the equally magnified impetus of the elements.

There was water everywhere, and not just one but a profusion of springs all over the place, none of them accessible. Besides, there was no river to be seen and followed, because no sooner had it surfaced than it was engulfed underground. As for us, we had no choice but make do with an unexceptional walk down the tarmac-covered D987 to the medieval bridge of St-Chély, where the river reappeared — a boisterous torrent, alive with the mountains' freshly melted snows. The only other time we saw it was at the end of its journey, when it flowed into the Lot between St-Colm-d'Olt and Espalion. There its frenzy subsided into glistening emerald ripples, and everything drifted westwards towards the Garonne.

We did much the same, but we first detoured in the opposite direction for a brief visit of St-Colm-d'Olt, an exquisite fortified borough of honey-coloured sandstone, recognisable from a distance by the unusual flame-like shape of its church tower referred to as *clocher flammé*. This was one of the crossing places of the pilgrim route over the Lot, although the present bridge dates only from 1535, as do several of the townhouses that line the narrow alleys, pointing to bourgeois prosperity in the fertile valley at the time. By then the heyday of the pilgrimage to Compostela had been over for hundreds of years.

It was the 11th and 12th centuries that marked the golden age of pilgrimages in Christian Europe, when heaven and hell had seeped into every-day life. In order to escape the wrath of eternal fires and gain salvation, the Christian faithful was willing to cross the entire continent headed for a holy shrine. Yet despite his unshakeable faith, before embarking on such a perilous expedition, he required tangible tokens of divine presence. The holy relics of martyrs seemed to provide such tokens since they could intercede on his behalf, work miracles in his favour, and ultimately grant him a ticket to paradise.

The most prestigious of all saintly relics were those of St James, because his body was believed to have reached intact Galicia in north western Spain, a feat the more remarkable considering that a) he had been decapitated and b) his decapitation took place in 44AD, that's 800 years before the translation of his remains from Palestine to Spain. No one ever questioned the authenticity of the relics when they were laid to rest in Santiago de Compostela, nor the fact that the Saint's head was believed simultaneously to be lying in the basilica of St Sernin in Toulouse — inconsistencies of this sort were readily disregarded. Although the Compostela pilgrimage ranked only third in importance, after Jerusalem and Rome, it became the most popular one, sending millions of wayfarers out into the wilds, at the risk of their lives. Occasionally, hangers-on and other profiteers filtered into their ranks, driven by darker motivations, but overall the journey to Compostela was a pilgrim's progress, with a view to spiritual betterment.

Coming from the north, the east and the south, everyone had to travel to Spain through France, along one of four pilgrim routes (that's without counting the proliferation of minor alternative ones), which merged into one route — *El Camino Francès* — once they crossed into northern Spain. Hence the expression, *y aller par quatre chemins*, i.e., to beat about the bush. This was news to me who, like all Parisians, believed that Paris was the centre of the world, and therefore presumed that the pilgrim route that started at the church of St-Jacques-de-la-Boucherie, north of Place du Châtelet, was the only one that existed. For many years I had fantasised about following it south, starting in Paris along the rue St-Jacques, the ancient Roman *cardo* (main thoroughfare) renamed after St James in the Middle Ages. I now found out that the Paris pilgrim route had nothing to do with the *Via Podiensis*. It never even got close to the Aveyron, but veered west towards the ocean after Tours. The *Via Podiensis* is the shortest of the four roads, roughly 800km, but it surpasses the others in beauty, winding its way through ravishing rugged scenery. It is indicated on contemporary maps as the GR5 (GR standing for *grande randonnée*).

The first pilgrim I sighted on that wet March day was a donkey, still up in the village of Aubrac. It was standing all by itself tethered to a pole by the Tour des Anglais, sporting a *coquille St-Jacques* (scallop) on its black, shining forehead by way of a brooch, the way many pilgrims stick them on their hats. It being France and just past noon, it didn't take a genius to figure out that its pilgriming master was probably feasting on an *aligot* at Germaine's. Unless he was one of the party gathered at the table next to ours at La Maison d'Aubrac, who were snacking like us on delicious open sandwiches made to Michel Bras' recipes. No doubt the pilgrim of the Third Millennium still roughs it to some extent, but today he needs his basic comfort. He may be content with Spartan lodgings, but he expects a decent meal, a hot shower and a dry, clean bed. He may be willing to cover a long mileage and negotiate arduous climbs, but he is more likely to pick a summer month for his journey — so far I have not stumbled on any pilgrims in the dead of winter. Few walk the entire route to Santiago, and I am yet to meet one who walked the route both ways.

Simone did walk the entire stretch of the *Via Podiensis* from Puy-en-Velay to Compostela. She did it in 52 consecutive days, which is pretty impressive for someone who had just been released from hospital after a long illness. But this is also why she made the vow to walk the route and what sustained her through the challenge. Different people, different motivations. I met several pilgrims who were committed Christians like Simone, and others who belonged to no specific church; even agnostics in search of an undefined spiritual experience. For several the pilgrimage provided a hiking holiday with an edge, for others a way of discovering a new area with an interesting slant. Others still used the pilgrimage to resolve personal issues, a therapy of sorts. To each their own incentive, which can include meeting new people, recovering from a divorce, or getting away from a stressful atmosphere at home, as was the case the following June when I met a pilgrim of that category.

It was during a rehearsal of the Monteverdi Choir conducted by Sir John Eliot Gardiner in the little church of St

Pierre at Bessuéjouls, a pink-stone gem tucked away among the foliage on the little travelled D566 coming from Espalion. Its upper chapel contains wonderful Romanesque vestiges from an earlier pilgrim church, which most visitors overlook. It was a warm cloudless day and the sunlight shining through the stain-glass windows added splendour to this occasion. Imagine the surprise that greeted the pilgrims who happened to walk into the church during that inspired moment, like the two fellows in their fifties who were clearly engrossed in the music and with whom I had a brief conversation at the end of the rehearsal. It turned out they were from the Paris area, and very keen on vocal music. I was thrilled that their pilgrimage should be enhanced by such quality singing, like a surprise gift to the deserving music lover. But as we pursued our conversation, it turned out that one of the men's 18-year-old daughter was taking her '*bac*' (*baccalauréat*, end-of-school exams) that week, a borderline neurotic time in many French households, which the father had no desire whatsoever to be put through. He therefore chose to leave his wife to cope with the situation on her own, whilst enjoying a two-week carefree hike in the lush green Valley of the Lot and thereabouts, in the relaxed company of one of his buddies. My friend Christine, who was standing next to me, gave me a look which implied, "What a jerk!" It takes all sorts to make a pilgrimage.

Espalion is the Aveyron's fourth largest town and an old economic hub due to its geographical position where mountain and valley meet. It is also the home town of several illustrious families, among them the Poulenc. One of the Poulenc was the founder of the company Poulenc Frères, the ancestor of Rhône Poulenc. He was also the father of the famous composer

▲ Nuces. by Las Canals ©Patrice Geniez

Hilly, rugged Aveyron ©Patrice Geniez ▼

"I wanted to go to the beginning of time"
©Patrice Geniez

▲ Village of Aubrac ©Patrice Geniez

Then came the Christians ©Patrice Geniez ▼

▲ Spring Transhumance ©Patrice Geniez

Back to the valley ©Patrice Geniez ▼

▲ *aligot* — "and everyone oohs and aahs and claps their hands like delighted children." ©Thirza Vallois

buronnier ©Patrice Geniez ▼

Francis Poulenc, who was born and bred in Paris and had little to do with the Aveyron. Classical music and a variety of other cultural activities are promoted here nonetheless by the Association du Vieux Palais, whose base is the beautifully restored Renaissance palace overlooking the Lot. If you are a musician, artist, writer or film director... working on a cultural or intellectual project, you can even stay in one of the six self-contained studio flats of the palace, at a low price and for any number of nights, weeks, or months.

The old section of town is enhanced by the medieval Vieux Pont which affords lovely river views, taking in the right bank with its row of old wooden tanneries and cheerful flowerboxes. Friday morning is the best, when the weekly market is held on the other side of the bridge, spilling out from the Place du Marché into neighbouring streets. Folk music and sunshine added to the local colour as we strolled among the stalls, and since these were organized by category, like in olden times, I let myself be guided along by the successive smells of fruit and vegetable, then cheese, then fish, meat, *charcuterie* and finally freshly baked bread... Needless to say we developed a serious appetite.

On the left bank side of the bridge, too, stands le Choc d'Aubrac, the best place in town, I have been told, for jam and all sorts of spreads that go so well with a crusty *tartine* of country bread. It also boasts wonderful ceramic wall panels depicting traditional trades. The shop is located on the corner of rue Droite in a straight line with the bridge, as was often the case in the Middle Ages, since this was the high street which usually ran through the length of the town, pointing back to an earlier Roman road. La Maison Fanguin Calsat at 2 avenue de la Gare is another unmissable address, a three-generation family business reputed for the best *fouace* in town, although I personally drooled over their sunny *tarte à l'abricot*. In 1911, when 32-year-old grandmother Noémie was left a widow, with no income and three young mouths to feed, a neighbour suggested she should bake and sell loaves of *fouace* for a living, and then proceeded to give Noémie the wrong recipe. Others might have been disheartened but Noémie went on experimenting on her own until she got it right. This is the recipe still used today by her granddaughter Marie-Thérèse, who has recently passed it on to her own daughter, also named Noémie. She is a school teacher in Toulouse for the time being, but you never know — after all, Marie-Thérèse previously lived down south in Montpellier and had no intention of taking over the family business. She changed her mind after her mother Maria had passed away and her elder sister Madeleine decided to retire.

Outside Espalion we climbed up to the ruins of the Château de Calmont d'Olt for a splendid bird's-eye view of the town, then visited the exquisite pink sandstone Romanesque church of Perse, blissfully empty at the time. The church stands on the supposed site of the martyrdom of St Hilarion, who is reported to have been decapitated by the Saracens in 730AD. The choir and the apse have survived the 11th-century monastery that stood here and came under the tutelage of Conques, the main stopping-place on the Compostella pilgrim route in the Aveyron and my destination.

As the valley widened, the river unrolled into a ribbon of emerald, then narrowed into a thread, squeezing its way through gorges of sheer red cliffs. Roadsides and meadows were sprinkled with pastel-coloured flowers underneath orchards hanging with white blossoms and with the promise of a juicy harvest in months to come. Here and there yellow blossoms had begun to cling timidly to the stringy broom, but it was mainly the wisteria that was making a show of itself as it luxuriated in the sun, dripping exuberantly from stone walls and trellises. Too bad that the little outdoor café with the pergola hadn't opened up for the summer yet. I would have given anything to stop there for lunch. Many establishments don't open up before May or June, because there aren't enough tourists to warrant it. Even in the height of summer I didn't find the valley overrun with tourists, despite the fact that the stretch between St-Colm-d'Olt and Estaing was listed by UNESCO, in 1998, as *patrimoine mondial de l'humanité* (world heritage site) for its beauty and architectural heritage.

Lovely Estaing clusters at the foot of its fabulous château on the sun-steeped right bank of the Lot. Its Gothic pilgrim bridge completes the pretty picture, for which the village has justifiably been awarded the '*un des plus beaux villages de France*' designation. Ten villages in the Aveyron enjoy this status, beating all other *départements*. Estaing bears the name of the great Rouergat family, whose most illustrious member, François d'Estaing was Bishop of Rodez from 1504 to 1529. It was during his term of office that he built the *château*, and subsequently the village and the bridge. Recently, the *château* was bought by Valéry Giscard d'Estaing, apparently with a view to a cultural project. However, no links have been established between the two families.

The south-facing hillside around Estaing, combined with the calcareous nature of the soil, made it particularly suitable for wine growing. The monks of Conques planted vineyards here back in the 9th or 10th century, but this may have already been wine country in Roman times. At their heyday the vineyards of Estaing extended over 350 hectares, leaping up the terraces of the sun-drenched slopes. Above the vineyards, to the north, lay orchards of chestnut which supplemented the local economy, providing food for the pigs and flour that went into several local specialities. But everything collapsed during the phylloxera epidemic of 1882 -1885, which destroyed the vines, followed by a wave of emigration to Paris, America and Argentina. The loss of lives during World War I was an even worse calamity, and as tough competition from Cahors and Bordeaux had already been threatening Estaing after the arrival of the railway in the 1850s, there was little incentive to replant the vineyards. Yet, in the 1960s several local enthusiasts banded together to resuscitate Estaing's age-old viniculture and set up a cooperative, often the only viable structure for an agricultural venture these days. Although they have expanded recently from 16 to 17 hectares, this remains a very small scale venture, the smallest cooperative in France, but their winery, on the other hand, carries perhaps the longest name — La Maison de la Vigne, du Vin et des Paysages (landscapes) d'Estaing — which emphasises the link between the wine and its *terroir*. It is situated at Coubisou, on the D920 in the direction of Espalion.

The cooperative is run by Jean-Pierre Marc who moved to the Aveyron from the Paris area in the late 1978. It was the call of nature, he explained. His father was Aveyronnais, but his mother was a 'thoroughbred' (to quote Jean-Pierre) *Bretonne*, which may account for his stubborness during the early years, when harrowing battles had to be fought in order to keep the business afloat, let alone make it sound.

This was after his military service, which by sheer coincidence he spent on the Larzac, but in the ranks of the 'bad guys' who were instructed to implement the unpopular military project at La Cavalerie. Not unlike my old friend Hubert whose contingent had to clean up the mess after the students in the Latin Quarter during the May 1968 riots known as '*les événements*'. While José Bové's friends unleashed the Larzac sheep in Paris to alert public opinion about the destruction of nature, Jean-Pierre was ordered to pour tarmac on the plateau to receive the army's vehicles. But then, on 10 May 1981, François Mitterrand was elected President and within less than 10 days the Larzac project was called off for the sake of national peace.

By the end of the month Jean-Pierre's battalion was dismantled and Jean-Pierre was discharged, went home and eventually bought himself an old vineyard. In 1983 he started replanting the lower part of the slope, waiting for three years before tackling the less convenient upper slope. However, that's the stretch that gets more sun and yields the better wine. His vineyard climbs up the steep hillside opposite the old cooperative's winery. I noticed several old stone sheds among the vines which Jean-Pierre has preserved out of respect for the local heritage and which add a welcome touch of history.

In order to improve the quality of the wine the coop has been experimenting in a laboratory. They have even hired the expert advice of a woman enologist — quite a revolution in a male-dominated profession. Karine Scudié works all over the Aveyron, and also down south in the Hérault, a living proof that times are changing even in the remote parts of France. The cooperative members are proud of their results but are unable to satisfy the growing demand, which increases further during the tourist season. Most of the wine is sold at their winery, and also in their makeshift village shop in July and August. Their wines are served in many of Northern Aveyron's restaurants and in the occasional one in Paris. The most obvious place to enjoy them is in one of the village restaurants, either on the flowery terrace of Aux Armes d'Estaing which faces the old bridge, or at the more gastronomic Auberge de St-Fleury, whose proprietor and chef, Gilles Moreau, was trained by Michel Bras. Gilles has installed a swimming pool in the backyard, next to the neighbours' henhouse. Apparently, he is upset because they won't clear this rustic blemish, but we citydwellers are quite charmed by this anachronistic co-habitation.

We were now ready for the main business of the visit — the tasting of the cooperative's various vintages. The ceremony was presided over by winemaker Jean Duiloz, who poured us first a 2001 vintage of Cuvée de l'Amiral, a refreshingly uplifting white with a lingering aroma of citrus. The Admiral in question was the last member of the Estaing family who was guillotined in 1794. A few years earlier he had been La Fayette's right-hand man, fighting for the freedom of the United States, but then made the fatal mistake of returning to France. Jean-Pierre told me they were thinking of changing the name of the vintage to Cuvée de la Liberté, which, I thought, would make a strikingly balanced response to America's 2003 vintage of freedom fries, although I prefer the more personal tribute to the Admiral and hope they will keep it. Next came a bottle of Cuvée des Brumes, a very satisfying rosé named after the morning mists of the Lot Valley, a compelling sight on no account to be missed when you are coming down from the mountains. Red wine came last, Cuvée Tradition which I found in some of the local restaurants, followed finally by a 2001 vintage of Cuvée St-Jacques, which won the cooperative a silver medal in the 2002 Paris Agriculture Show and a '*master d'or*' since. Meant to tickle the palate of the weary, thirsty pilgrim, it was a congenial way to nudge me back to the Compostela track...

And so to Conques.

All four cardinal points lead to Conques, but I wanted to view it first from above, so as not to miss the magic and the conch-like topography that has given it its name. Driving along the right bank of the Lot we headed towards Grand-Vabre past Entraygues (of which more later) and detoured up a very steep winding road to the gemlike hamlet of La Vinzelle, perched above Grand-Vabre with its *lauze*-covered pitched roofs, church tower and bell cote, and some 20 residents, affording spectacular river and valley views. This was big-time wine country (Vinzelle probably derives from 'wine' and 'cellar') before the phylloxera bug devastated the area and forced many to leave. A good number of the inhabitants of Grand Vabre made their way to California, possibly unbeknownst to their American offspring.

Back in the valley we crossed the Lot and followed its tributary the Dourdou upstream, heading south along the bottom of its wild wooded gorges. Like everything else, the river was very high, careering past us in the opposite direction in an exhilarating racket. At the entrance to Conques we followed the signpost to the Centre Européen and skirted the village uphill along another beautiful winding road when, all of a sudden, beyond a bend, there was Conques, revealed. Curled up snugly in its conch, the village lauze-covered pitched roofs closed ranks in amphitheatre like silvery sheets of coats of mail, clinging to the steep slope opposite the northern side of the abbey church of Ste-Foy. Beneath the roofs, the sandstone houses were graced with a mellow glow by the afternoon sun.

Rising from below, the proud honey-coloured medieval abbey church thrust its three colossal towers to the heavens, inevitably stealing the show (later I found out that the three towers were a 19th-century addition). Rolling above the village was a silent wilderness of thickly wooded hills. If you have made it to this bend of the road on foot, or even better, if you have done so all the way from Puy-en-Velay, the reward will be all the greater. Imagine the surprise of the weary pilgrim of yore when he reached Conques, having done no prior reading to prepare for his journey. In all likelihood he would have arrived here via Sénergues, east of Conques, a lovely route through green countryside, dotted with medieval heritage, which I took on a later occasion.

Eventually I tried all four possibilities and was equally awestruck by the viewpoints of Bancarel and the chapel of St-Roque, and just as astonished by the southern approach from Noailhac, which the above-mentioned pilgrim would have probably missed because he would have left Conques behind him at that stage of the journey, as he headed towards Spain. Unless he was endowed with an inquisitive spirit and had the good sense to turn round for a final glimpse of the magic, which would have sustained him through the rest of his journey.

No matter how inspiring, the spell and beauty of the site would not have sufficed to catapult Conques to a prominent position on the Compostela route without the possession of holy relics.

An early Christian shrine is believed to have been erected here back in the Merovingian era and to have been destroyed by the Saracens in the 8th century. In the early 9th century, the hermit Dadon (also referred to as Datus, Déodat, or Dieudonné – who "gave himself to God"), found here suitable conditions to retire from the world — solitude, shelter from the north wind, and a fountainhead (now la Fontaine du Plô, at the foot of the cloisters). He was joined by Medraldus in 819, which was fine so long as there were just the two of them. But when others followed suit and set up a monastic community under the Benedictine rule, Daton chose to push further down the Dourdou, and settled on the site of what is now the village of Grand Vabre. The Chapel of Danon, outside the village, may be the site of his hermitage.

That same year, Louis the Pious, the son of Charlemagne and King of Aquitaine, visited the abbey of Conques and placed it under his protection. This included substantial gifts of stretches of hillslopes, which the monks planted with vineyards. Pépin II of Aquitaine extended those royal favours to gold, silver, jewels and other precious *objets d'art*, the nucleus of what is today the most renowned medieval treasure on French soil, boasting a fabulous collection of enamels, cameos, instaglios and precious stones, and open to visitors on site. Pépin's reliquary joined the collection later, a richly decorated golden box studded with multi-coloured precious stones. Yet despite Pépin's lavish generosity, history preferred to retain the name of the more famous Charlemagne as the benefactor of the abbey, who is honoured in the village with the name of a street and with a privileged position at the vanguard of the procession of the elect, carved in the tympanum on the western façade of the church.

Pépin's favours were very helpful but could not make up for the absence of holy relics, and since no honest way could be figured out to get hold of any, Abbot Bégon resorted to robbery. It so happened that hundreds of years earlier, in the third century, 12-year-old Fidès (Faith, or Foy in French) from the remote, western city of Agen, chose to be martyred by the Romans rather than renounce her Christian faith. Her martyrdom was glorified through a multitude of miracles performed by her relics, mainly restoring their sight to the blind and breaking loose the shackles of captives. Needless to say the abbey of Agen cashed in on the worship of the holy maiden by way of substantial donations, which did not escape the attention of Bégon, who eyed with envy "the hen that lay the golden eggs". With a view to abducting the relics, a conniving monk, Arosnide (also referred to as Ariviscus), was sent out to Agen under the false pretence of joining its monastic community. Little by little he gained the trust of his fellow monks and manoeuvred his way to the post of guardian of the sanctuary where the relics were kept. In 866, after ten long patient years, he found an opportunity to break into the tomb and run off with the booty. When the monks of Agen discovered his felony, they set out in his pursuit but lost him in the fog, which allowed Arosnide to dodge his pursuers, and Conques to interpret the fog as a divine intervention in their favour.

Bégon, unabashed, refused to return the goods — too much was at stake to be burdened with moral considerations. Indeed, over and above enhancing the prestige of a shrine, the possession of holy relics generated substantial wealth through the flow of gifts of gold, silver and gems, which in turn attested to the holiness of the shrine, thereby increasing its reputation and attracting the flow of further gifts. In other words, holiness and opulence fed on each other and combined to further the good fortunes of church-sponsored ventures. As did the multiplication of miracles. Those performed by Ste Foy were renowned all over western Europe, indeed as far west as Horsham in England. Thus the star of Conques ascended as a result of outrageous plundering, but since history chose to narrate the event through the biased perspective of Conques, the sin was played down and recorded tactfully as "furtive translation". An alternative version of the episode suggests that the relics were transferred to the remote site of Conques to shelter them from the Normans, the terror of the Rouergue in the 9th century, as the Muslims had been a century earlier.

The prestige of Conques reached further heights in the 10th century, when the relics of Ste Foy were placed inside a golden statue-reliquary studded with precious stones, the highlight of its treasure ever since. It is a strange-looking statue with a face that could just as well belong to a man, exuding an ancient, somewhat fetishistic pagan feel, enhanced further by dark eyes that bulge out of their golden sockets with a sense of unfathomable mystery. She is seated on a gilded throne, especially made for that purpose, just as the colossal abbey church was built for the purpose of housing the reliquary. The better known Ste-Chapelle in Paris was also built for the sole purpose of housing the relics of the Crown of Thorns and the True Holy Cross. Moreover, the man of the Middle Ages was admirably daring in his faith and thought nothing of engaging in glamorous architectural ventures that exceeded several lifetimes, three hundred years in the case of Conques.

Glamour implied gigantic dimensions, and the new church had three vast naves that could hold thousands of pilgrims.

The reliquary of Ste Foy was displayed next to the altar for all to see and be edified by; but it also served an economic purpose, helping Conques to turn the pilgrimage into a prosperous business, which benefited, for instance, the hotel industry, which was shared between the innkeeper and those villagers who could spare a room, not unlike today's *chambres d'hôtes*. And just as postcards, T-shirts, mugs and the like make for profitable spin-offs in today's tourist industry, Conques drew a substantial income from the trade of tapers. Shoemakers too were in great demand, and gathered by the Porte de la Vinzelle (suggesting that la Vinzelle was a more prominent place than it is today, owing probably to its wine), while money exchangers clustered on rue Mounède (*monnaie*, money), many pilgrims having travelled from foreign lands. Thus so long as the star of St James shone, Conques remained a stopping-place on the Compostela road, maintaining an infrastructure that could accommodate thousands of pilgrims at any given time, and a treasure that surpassed all others in magnificence and wealth.

Before entering the church, the pilgrim received a lesson in morality, carved in the tympanum for the attention of the majority who could neither read nor write. Originally this Last Judgement was a polychrome bas-relief. The contrasting blue and red paints that once covered the carvings of heaven and hell have long peeled off, but the lesson in morality can still be read on the honey-colour stone, wonderfully aglow in the late afternoon. Sitting in state, in the centre, is Christ the Judge, his right hand pointing upward to heaven, where the procession of the elect is headed by Mary, followed by Peter (recognisable by his keys), then Abbot Bégon who is leading

Charlemagne towards virtue. The geometric order and harmony of the composition mirror the peace and serenity awaiting the righteous.

No such peace for the damned! Christ's left hand (with its sinister associations) points down towards a chaos of demons swarming about in a limbo of flames, meant to scare off the sinner. Present-day sinners like myself are more inclined to be astounded and entertained by the exuberant imagination of the anonymous artist and by his hilarious take of the human condition, admirably expressed in a profusion of playfully camouflaged tiny scenes. I'll leave it to you to decipher the details of what is arguably France's Romanesque masterpiece of its genre, which merits a special journey to Conques if only for its sake.

To mention just a few of the scenes, there is the weighing of the souls by St Michael and a demon, who challenge each other across a pair of scales. Although the demon cheats by pressing his forefinger on the tray in front of him, the scales are tipped in favour of the archangel, indicating that good works will prevail. The seven deadly sins are also wonderfully expressive in their allegorical representation, notably Avarice who is being hanged with a purse round her neck and a nasty toad crouching at her feet. Calumny has her tongue torn off by a demon, whilst Adultery is displayed as a pair, who are tied to each other by a noose. Typically, the female alone has been partially stripped, displaying two exquisitely pulpous breasts that are more likely to encourage sin than prevent it. The beholder is overwhelmed by the boundless perverse imagination of the human mind and its creative aptitude for devising prolific methods of torture, over and above the evident glee derived from inflicting it. Obviously the tympanum of Conques mirrored the kind of punishment some culprits endured at the hand of fellow humans well before crossing the threshold of hell, which, I am confident, would have proved an inspiring source of reference for the likes of the Monty Python. It was equally edifying to recognise the direct lineage between the content of the tympanum and the jokes we relish nowadays about heaven and hell. Then as now heaven is portrayed as placid, uneventful and dull, while hell is vibrant with vitality and excitement. I would have loved to find out whether the anonymous artist was working in earnest or tongue in cheek.

By the 13th century, the pilgrimage to Santiago was beginning to lose its momentum, and the fortunes of Conques went the same way. Nevertheless, it maintained its population of 3,000 inhabitants into the 14th century, a considerable number for those days. The Benedictine supremacy, however, had already been dented in the 12th century by the Cistercians, as well as by the Knights Templar who were solidly established in the Rouergue. The Wars of Religion in the 16th century and the plague in the 17th century accelerated the decline. The French Revolution dealt it a final blow. Close to a thousand years of history came to an end with the abolition of the religious orders and the departure of the last abbot, François René d'Adhémar de Panat, the one-time chaplain of the daughters of Louis XV, who retired to Rodez where he died in 1797. Fortunately, the abbey's treasure was salvaged by the villagers in 1792, who started a street riot when the state's agents came over to seize it. Most of the pieces were hidden away, some were negotiated, a small part had to be surrendered.

The abbey itself was in a pitiful state when Prosper Merimée arrived here in 1837. Although better known as the author of *Carmen*, Mérimée came here in the capacity of inspector for the French Heritage Trust (Les Monuments Historiques), as part of a nationwide tour to survey the country's monuments, all of which were severely damaged during the French Revolution. Mérimée's job was to determine which monuments could be rescued; fortunately, the abbey church of Conques passed his test. But he came too late for the cloister which the villagers had been plundering for the past few decades, using its stones as building material. Some vestiges were salvaged however, notably 30 sculpted capitals. A few of them have carvings that depict everyday life, providing a charming insight into 12th-century society.

Gone too were the medieval stained-glass windows, replaced in 1987 by 104 stunning pieces commissioned from Pierre Soulages, the Aveyron's sole contemporary painter to have achieved international renown. This is a just reward for the man whose artistic calling was triggered by his early encounter with the church during a school trip coming from Rodez. The 12-year-old was so taken by the architecture that he decided right away to become, paradoxically, not an architect but a painter. It was on subsequent visits to Conques that he started reflecting on art, and it was in Conques that he reached the unorthodox conclusion that there are only two colours: red, which is yielded by the iron oxide of the earth and is to be found in plenty around Conques, and black which, contrary to a common misconception, gets transmuted by light. (Interestingly, an Aveyronnais painter friend of mine claims that black doesn't exist...). Significantly, says Soulages, these are the first two colours used by man, as recorded in prehistoric caves.

As was the case for several other local artists I have met, it was the empty expanses of the Aveyron that moved him the most — the Aubrac of course, but also the various limestone plateaux (*causses*) and the uplands of the Lévezou. The abstract design he chose for the windows echoes the stark, luminous landscape, while the grainy texture of the glass evokes its stony surface. By playing on texture rather than colour, Soulages made the glass blend with both the bare stone and the overall austere character of the church. His palette, reduced to sobre greys and ivories, is inspired by the surrounding environment too, bringing to mind the skies of the Aubrac. As the day light filters through the opalescent glass, it fills the volume of the church with an iridescent glow; at night, when the church is lit up, the windows shimmer like flames of gold. When a choir joins in — as did the Monteverdi, one spellbinding Sunday afternoon in June 2004 — stone, light and voices become one, alive with music and prayer, uniting the disparate congregation of pilgrims and tourists in a communion of souls.

Chapter 3

TRAILS OF ELVES AND FAIRIES

Like many lawyers at the time of the French Revolution, Joseph Lambel became involved in local politics. In 1790, when the division of France into *départements* was under way, he managed to incorporate to the far north-western edge of the Aveyron a narrow strip of the Auvergne that should have gone to the Cantal, so as to keep his land under the same authority. His friendship with the Bishop of Rodez must have added weight to his arguments in favour of this territorial rearrangement. When we first drove there I was still new to the Aveyron and unaware of the subtle complexity of its geology and the mosaic-like landscape it had yielded. Since Laguiole was barely one hour away, I assumed we were on the western fringe of the Aubrac. A few months later I was corrected by Stéphanie Augeyre, then the head of the Maison de l'Aveyron in Paris and a native to the area, who stressed patriotically that what lay west of the river Truyère had nothing to do with the Aubrac. It was an altogether different entity, the Carladez, which once belonged to the lords of Carlat whose castle loomed forbiddingly on the Cantal side of the border, above a *mesa* (flat uplands) of black basalt. Later I discovered that west of the Truyère lie lava and basalt, while to the east lies granite.

The castle was the scene of bloody confrontations in the Middle Ages and of voluptuous pleasures during the hedonistic Renaissance. Marguerite de Valois spent a year here in 1585 during her 18-year exile from the Louvre, where her scandalous love life had caused a great deal of embarrassment. The tumultuous life story of the sexually insatiable queen was no news to me, having followed her trail for many years through various neighbourhoods of Paris with a mix of gossipy excitement and admiration, but stumbling upon her in these backwoods was a welcome surprise. Here, undaunted, she carried on with her Parisian ways and continued to entertain me. Indeed, no sooner had she landed at the Château de Carlat than she picked up a new *beau* among the locals — Athis — to whom she was about to surrender when the lords returned from hunting unexpectedly. In her haste to get dressed she donned her bodice back to front, leaving her generous bosom uncovered. Others in her place might have been flustered, but not the resourceful Margot, who grabbed the bouquet of flowers that Athis had brought her and stuck it in the compromising gap, thus starting a new fashion, known as the *barbarel*, which has remained the traditional costume of the women of the Auvergne to this day. Whether this story ever reached the ears of her husband Henri IV I know not, but it was he who ordered the demolition of the castle of Carlat, in 1604.

Colourful private lives apart, following his conversion to Catholicism and his accession to the throne of France, Henri IV set out to demolish the fortified bastions in the provinces fearing they might become Protestant strongholds, but was assassinated in 1610 before he could see his project through. He was succeeded by Louis XIII, whose minister, Richelieu, carried on his mission on a much larger scale. As the architect of absolutism, Richelieu was determined to eradicate any faction that might present a threat to the throne, and that included the Queen Mother Mary of Medici and her entourage.

I was puzzled that I had never heard of the Carladez and was relieved it wasn't mentioned on my Michelin map when I checked it again, which at least cleared me of the sin of doing a slapdash job (I have meanwhile learnt not to restrict myself to road maps). But Stéphanie was not blameless either, having failed to mention its neighbour, the Viadène, which is situated east of the Truyère and is even more likely to be overlooked, especially from a speeding car, as it rolls its green serenity among silvery rivers and blends imperceptibly into the western shoulder of the Aubrac. Jean-Pierre Viguier, the excellent chef and proprietor of Le Relais du Coustoubi at Campouriez, was no less patriotic about his Viadène than Stéphanie was about the Carladez :

Attention, il ne faut pas mélanger les torchons et les serviettes!

(Hang on, one must divide the sheep from the goats), he said with a twinkle.

He meant it also of the Aubrac, whose *Montagnols* or *Mountagnols* used to trade their cheese for the wine of the *Coustoubis*, the Viadène's winemakers (from *coustou* in *patois*, or *coteau* in French, meaning a hillside and *bi* for *vin* or wine). Verbal jousts pointed to the superiority of wine over cheese, some of which are attributed to a certain Joseph Vaylet, a *Coustoubi* naturally biased towards the former, whose rhymes have been lovingly preserved by Jean-Pierre in an album with old photos and postcards. Later, I read that the *Coustoubis'* territory was situated further south, closer to Entraygues in the Lot Valley, a warmer, sunnier area, pointed at reprovingly by the hardy *Montagnols* as conducive to idleness.

It was Monsieur Levadoux from the Cantal who took it upon himself to resurrect the old vineyards of the Lot Valley. The range of varieties in Entraygues specifically was astonishing, including several that could not be found anywhere else. It is believed that they had been brought on the Lot from the southwest, and accumulated over the years in Entraygues where all goods were unloaded because the river was not navigable beyond. In 1963 Levadoux invited over the Baron Le Roy, chairman of the Office International de Vins de Qualité and an amateur connoisseur of rare wines. By a miraculous stroke of luck a forty year old bottle of Le Fel had been unearthed and was offered him to taste. He must have liked it because in 1965 Entraygues-Le Fel was granted the VDQS (Vins Délimités de Qualité Supérieure) appellation. Entraygues-Le Fel was a tiny wine country at the time, barely 4 hectares.

Jean-Pierre serves the wines of his small vineyard in the restaurant, a cheerful, no-nonsense place much appreciated by locals, which is always a good sign. Occasionally, he picks up his accordion and tables and chairs are pushed aside to make room for the punctuated rhythms of a *bourrée*. There was a lot of music making in the villages in the old days, Jean-Pierre told me. People did not have the money to push their studies far, but there was a lot of talent around.

We arrived on a sunny late autumn day, and started off with an apéritif of homemade walnut wine. His wife Odette completed the pleasure with a *mise-en-bouche* (appetiser) of endives, walnut and sausage laid prettily on a slab of *lauze*, demonstrating that magical French flair for conjuring up stylishness out of a commonplace object. The words Bon Appetit scribbled at the bottom of the menu added a further touch of hospitality, and an invitation to tackle a succession of copious regional dishes, starting off with the jolly *assiette des Coustoubis*. A flavourful farm chicken came next, accompanied by a *truffade*, a variation on the theme of the *aligot* which Stéphanie had introduced me to as a speciality of the Carladez. Jean-Pierre, on the other hand, claimed it was a speciality of the Viadène, while I read it had originated in the Cantal. Go figure! I was given the same contradictory information regarding the origin of the *pounti* — a sweet-and-sour pudding with plums and herbs which the farmer's wife used to take over to her husband while he was making hay in the fields.

The Truyère marks the boundary between the Carladez and the Viadène at the bottom of wild gorges, winding its way south towards Entraygues where it meets the Lot. However, it lost some of its wilderness with the development of hydroelectricity in the 1930s. The steep declivity of its bed and the torrential volume of its waters could not go unnoticed, especially in an area that lagged behind the rest of the nation in terms of development — the river's days of untamed freedom were numbered. However, remnants of that wilderness have survived here and there, notably around the superlatively romantic site of Bez Bedène (from besses, birch trees; Bedène alludes perhaps to a Roman road that went over the bridge), which stands on a lonely promontory above the river Selves, surmounted by a 12th-century church tower with a picturesque open-timber roof.

An early reservoir was built in 1932 at Cadène, by Brommat, followed in 1933 by the stunning Art Deco underground power station at Brommat, compared by an eyewitness at the time to an immense Egyptian temple. The 105m-high concrete dam at Sarrans was the highest in France when it opened in 1934, creating a massive lake of 1,000 hectares, the largest on the river. The famous historian Amans-Alexis Monteil, author of the classic *Description du département de l'Aveiron (note the old spelling)*, would have been hard put to recognise the wild valley he depicted in 1800/1801. Despite the changes, the lake of Sarrans offers its own scenic beauty, highlighted by the Laussac peninsula, a popular resort complete with a picturesque village topped by a picture-postcard church. Even in Paris the opening of Brommat and Sarrans were considered major feats, important enough to prompt President Albert Lebrun to make the long journey to preside over the official inauguration. They also drew foreign workers to the area, predominantly Polish and Spanish, who often married locally, belying the notion of a hermetically closed up region prior to the early 1970s.

With World War II behind her, France set out to take the big leap forward. The regional Société des forces de la Truyère was superseded by the national EDF (French Electricity Company) and new dams and power stations increased the capacity of the hydroelectric system of the Truyère — Maury on the Selves (in the Viadène) in 1947, Couesque in 1950, Cambeyrac in 1957, Brommat II in 1974 and the pumped storage system of Montézic in 1982, generating 900 megawatts. That's as much as a nuclear station, which it is programmed from Paris to replace at two minutes' notice, in case of a breakdown. Its underground station is fed by two reservoirs, a lower one at Couesque and a more recent one at Montézic, above Couesque. The entrance to the station is hidden, like in a fairy tale, behind a walnut tree leading to a stunning star-studded vault where the entire cathedral of Notre-Dame could be fitted. Unfortunately, there are no visits for security reasons. All in all 1,706 million KW are generated by the 44km-long Aveyronnais section of the Truyère, controlled from Toulouse.

Just as a *Montagnol* is not a *Coustoubi*, an Auvergnat is by no means an Aveyronnais; except in the Carladez, where one is both, as confirmed by Claude Chauvet from the tourist office of main town Mur-de-Barrez. This attractive little *bourg* still sits within its medieval walls on top of a hill (Barrez meaning altitude), whose basalt-stone houses point to the volcanic soil of the Auvergne, its tall pitched roofs to snow-covered winters. In summer it is cheered up by flower boxes, while in winter the white slopes of the Cantal create a dramatic contrast with the black stone. In the weeks leading up to Christmas the miniature high street, where the shops have been lined up tightly since the Middle Ages, looks like a fairyland. It is a five-minute walk from the south gate to the site of the north gate, which was pulled down at the time of Louis XIII. The castle was demolished at the same time as part of Richelieu's policy of centralisation. Its stones were recycled to build the town's new houses, whilst the esplanade which marks its site provides a splendid outlook over the *lauze*-covered roofs of the town and the convent of Ste-Claire in the foreground, the summits of the Cantal in the offing, and the valley of the Bromme down below.

In 1643 Louis XIII made a clever move when, having seized the domain of Carlat from Spain, he handed it over to the Grimaldis of Monaco thus killing two birds (Spain and Carlat) with one stone, whilst gaining a willing ally on the Mediterranean shores. The massive defence tower that flanks the south gate and the square in front are known respectively as La Tour and La Place de Monaco. The café across the square was named, naturally, le Bar de Monaco. The Grimaldis lost their hold over the Carladez during the French Revolution, when it was incorporated into the new *département* of Aveyron as explained above. But some traditions die hard. Among the Prince's various titles listed in the Great Hall of the Grimaldi Palace in Monaco, I've been told, is that of Count of Carladez. Apparently too, the senior club members of Mur-de-Barrez are granted free admission to the museums of Monaco, in the name of the old alliance. Similarly, Claude Chauvet had no trouble obtaining an internship with the tourist office of Monaco when she applied from Mur. Incidentally, the south gate was allowed to survive because the assailants used to approach Mur from the north, notably the Protestants in 1578. Its empty site has been dubbed La Porte Berque, meaning 'gap' in Occitan.

Coming across St Thomas de Cantorbury (spelt the old French way) was a surprise. Although he had spent time in France there is no evidence that he ever travelled through Mur. Whilst trying to find out more, I discovered that he had actually been born to French parents, but nobody could explain to me why the borough's 12th- and 13th- century church is dedicated to him. Much of the church has been demolished and rebuilt since, notably by the Calvinists. Inside the church an unindentified recumbent figure has survived under the front keystone. Nobody knows whom it is supposed to represent, nor how and why it got to the ceiling, and no other church is known to house a recumbent figure in this bizarre lofty position, believed to be unique in the world.

When we first drove past Mur-de-Barrez in July 2003, it was too hot to even consider dragging ourselves out of the car, let alone go sightseeing. This was during the stupendously hot summer that took 15,000 lives in France. Driving north on the D904 all I had in mind was to get away from the heat, the further north the better — until we came across a signpost that pointed to a place I had never heard of — Valon. For no explicable reason I felt urged to take that road, pushing up steep twists and turns, past sundrenched remnants of vineyards and orchards, beneath a glaring sky.

I am glad that I listened to my better instinct, for at the end of the road, poised on top of a headland, was a toy-tiny village surmounted by the square tower of a medieval castle straight out of a story book. Around were breathtaking hills, and far below the Truyère carved for itself an idle loop of sapphire. Perhaps the place was too small to be eligible for '*un des plus beaux village de France*' status, (it didn't even have a village shop or a café, only a designer jeweller that catered for summer tourists), but it certainly deserved it. I was already fantasising about getting a holiday home there and trying to figure out if it was possible to build a swimming pool on such steep slopes. Obviously I would have first had to enquire whether any house was actually up for sale, which was an impossible mission since not the faintest hint of life was manifest, as if the village had been spellbound into deep slumber.

Even the owner of the van with the snacks and sodas seemed to have volatised in mid activitiy, his handwritten menu still displayed on the slate by the open counter. We hung around for a while under the shade of the walnut trees where he had parked his van, thinking he would be back any moment, but he never appeared and we ended up going into the little church, the only available shelter from the heat. To our astonishment, it was filled with wonderful bouquets of freshly cut flowers, an evident sign of very recent life; unless they had been arranged by the same fairy who had put the village to sleep. When I noticed the memorial plaque to the victims of the last two wars, the fairytale village of Valon materialised into reality and the sorrows that accompany it. The long list of casualties from the Great War included three young men aged 21, 23 and 30 who went by the name of Laporte, brothers perhaps.

Later I found out that the renowned Cardinal Jean Verdier, hailing from the neighbouring village of Lacroix Barrez, celebrated his first communion in the church of Valon. His father was the village innkeeper and blacksmith. He also kept a farm like everyone else, but the son was called to the church and became the socially committed Archbishop of Paris in the years leading to World War II. During a reception in Paris he was quoted to have declared, "I a little boy from the Rouergue, I who used to tend to the sheep, if I am now Cardinal of Paris, I owe it to my home village, to my mother." The churchman's quote also testifies to the fairly recent presence of sheep in the mountains of northern Aveyron. Cardinal Verdier was honoured by Lacroix Barrez with a bronze statue, and a small museum that can be visited by special arrangement.

There was still no sign of life round the van when we came out of the church. The castle was closed but there was a notice at the entrance that mentioned something about le Roi Titus. I wouldn't have had the energy to climb it at any event, no matter how rewarding the spectacular views afforded from the top.

We left Valon as we came, weary and listless, under the same glaring sky. I didn't think I would ever come back — it was so remote. Besides, although it was like an exquisite theatre set, there was little to occupy one there. But destiny decided otherwise and introduced me to Jean Laurens from nearby Vilherols, where his ancestors had settled around the year 1500. The family's early *château* was replaced in 1770 by the present one, where Jean's parents still live. The 18th-century outbuildings have been beautifully converted into three tastefully decorated *chambres d'hôtes* and one magnificent *gîte rural* featuring a huge fireplace in the living room. The traditional architecture, the old *lauzes* that cover the pitched roofs and the basalt walls have all been preserved, but inside everything has been updated to high standards and the *gîte* even has a spa. The summer *canicule* (heatwave) was forgotten when I arrived there in October. The grass had regenerated to its old green self, the leaves were beginning to turn, and in the distance, the blue ridge of the Cantal had received the first drifts of snow during the night.

A few weeks earlier, in Paris, I met Jean Lauren's daughter, Marie. She was inexhaustible about the Carladez and mentioned a gem of a lost hamlet I was on no account to miss when I stayed at Vilherols — Valon! She was just as surprised I had already discovered it, as I was to find out that the Château of Valon had once been in the hands of her family. It is also believed that an officer by the name of Laurens lived in Valon in the 16th century. Marie also mentioned some magnificent theme trails, les Sentiers de l'Imaginaire, the brainchild of an artist, Nadine Vignolo, who was doing cultural community work for the local authorities. She was given studio space in the chapel of the Château de Valon where she created children's activities around a character by the name of Le Roi Titus. It seemed I would be coming back to Valon after all.

I first met Nadine at Murols, a small basalt village once shared between livestock and villagers. This is where the Sentier du Feu et du Vent (the Fire and Wind trail) is situated, stemming from the village smithy which, under the guidance of Nadine, some local volunteers had restored and turned into a heritage museum, not unlike Capou's *'grenier'*. Except that Capou's is the depot of an impassioned collector, whereas Nadine sought to recreate a traditional way of life in its natural habitat. This was the home of the Seintinies, a ten-generation lineage of smithies going back to 1688 when the first Seintinies is known to have taken up the trade in nearby Cadilhac. The last Seintinies, Paul-Henri had no children and left the business to his brother Jean's sons, but they chose to move to Paris, in 1972, and that was the end of the smithy. Their father Jean, who has died since, was Mayor of Murols where his widow Simone still lives.

We were shown around by Solange who was self-consciously proud to act as a guide and spokesperson of a neat project carried out by ordinary villagers. The all-purpose living quarters, the old bread oven, the black iron cooking-pot over the fire place, the imperturbable grandfather clock that ticked away the years: every detail had been recreated with respect to traditions and authenticity. A loaf of bread lying on the big, bare dining table suggested the family would come in for dinner any moment, an ordinary family, just like Cardinal Verdier's, whose childhood home in Lacroix Barrez must have looked pretty much the same as the Seintinies' — quite some journey from here to the pulpit of Notre Dame! We then continued travelling into the past at Chez Marius, who is no longer among the living. His widow Renée has carried their pre-war, black-and-white film set of a place into the 21st century, blissfully unchanged. The dismal weather mingled atmospherically with the steam and smell of cooking, and with the din of the characteristic rolling staccato delivered in a jumble by the diners, all of whom were local, predominantly men. Monsieur le Maire René Vigne was there too, and bought everyone a *gentiane* which we drank off the no-nonsense counter, without the frills that had accompanied it at Michel Bras'.

It was still wet outside when we made our way to the Fire and Wind trail. An impressive iron dragon named Blaise stood at the entrance to the trail, symbolising the association of fire and metal going back to Hephaesthus (Vulcan). Nadine has an extensive knowledge of old myths and often weaves them into her projects. The dragon was made from scraps of old ploughshares by Albert, Roger, Roland, Léon, Solange, Michel, Martine, Evelyne, and Lulu, far from the limelights of Paris and New York that shone respectively on the likes of the late sculptors César and Arman who also used scrap materials in their art. Nadine and her team work behind the scenes. It is hard to imagine the amount of energy Nadine has invested in the project, negotiating with landowners, clearing the land, stripping it of barbed wire, laying out the trails, writing out tales to accompany each trail, staging them into plays, then guiding and directing the participants. For over and above the laying out of enchanting theme trails for the pleasure of visitors, it is the sense of fulfilment she has infused across the Carladez and the Viadène that makes Nadine's work so invaluable. As many as 10% of the community are now involved in one or several of her ventures, in their spare time and on a strictly volunteer basis.

The projects are not merely an end unto themselves but a catalyst for the revitalisation of the community. They are kept open-ended so as to encourage the participants to keep bringing in new ideas, to experiment and to uncover their dormant talent. Jacky is a good example. He has a sawmill and chops wood for a living, but as part of Nadine's projects, he designed and built the suspended bridge over the tumbling creeks in the Sentier du Bois Magique (The Magical Wood Trail) at Taussac and carved wood sculptures of the characters that appear in the tale Nadine wrote to accompany the stroll. So far only three out of the six trails intended have been completed because part of Nadine's wisdom is not to rush, but allow ideas the time to mature and follow the rhythm of nature.

Nadine studied the techniques of medieval illuminations at the Beaux Arts school of Anger. Several illuminations decorate her trails. I especially loved those along the Sentier de l'Eau (the Water Trail) at Brommat. She also teaches the technique at the Centre Européen in Conques, where an Introduction to Medieval Art programme is offered to school children from all over France. Her penchant for the Middle Ages extends to Arthurian knights and landscapes inhabited by hermits, woodchoppers, wolves, dragons, witches and elves. It must be said that in this northwestern strip of the Aveyron, the boundary between reality and fairyland oftentimes gets blurred. Go visit the ancient lime tree in Nigresserre by Thérondels; it has a massive gnarled trunk with a hollow the size of a home. Indeed, an old woman lived in the tree as recently as 1937. She even brought in a bed and a stove.

I walked the trails with Nadine at different times of year, treading on crackling rusty leaves sprinkled with chestnut and mushrooms in the autumn, past slender sparkling birches in the winter. One frosty morning we saw a pair of icy diamond pendants hanging from a rock which someone must have left behind for the attention of a giant princess. In early spring we were greeted by hosts of daffodils and, later, by the fragrance of white lilies of the valley. Was it a bunch of Nadine's elves that had unrolled a blue carpet of forget-me-nots in the glade by the water, or Puck who had laid a patch of moist moss midst the shady undergrowth in late July? The same question may have crossed Nadine's mind as she toyed with the idea of producing *A Midsummer Night's Dream* in the Sentier du Bois Magique (Magic Wood Trail). It would be an interactive experience involving both audience and players; Puck would cause confusion (in other words, the plot would progress) as the participants moved along the trail towards the little open-air theatre Nadine had created in the woods. There each lover would be paired with the appropriate partner and order would be restored.

Whilst waiting for Nadine to bring the project to fruition, I joined her party on a midsummer's night stroll which she had dubbed *soirée de contes* (evening of stories). Flashlights and lanterns helped us see the way as we walked through the dark woods of the Sentier du Bois Magique playing out the tale that accompanies it. A narrator dressed up as a tree was posted at the entrance to the trail and read out the prologue. His deep voice and rolling lilt sounded familiar and turned out to belong to Monsieur Pagés, the Mayor of Taussac. Various fairy-tale characters appeared along the way, the wicked witch of course, and the kindly woodchopper, who was the gardener Alain in real life. Walking next to me was Thérèse, the postwoman from Taussac, who turned out to be the sister of Solange from the smithy. Whilst listening to Françoise the pharmacist from Thérondels play a little piece on the violin, it occurred to me that, probably unwittingly, Nadine reproduced in real life *A Midsummer Night's Dream*'s play within the play. For weren't Monsieur Pagès, Françoise, and Alain the fellow creatures of Quince the Carpenter, Bottom the Weaver, or Snout the Tinker? Wasn't Nadine breathing back to life the old sense of self-realisation through communal creativity so often lost in contemporary society?

Incidentally, Thérondels is a lovely village, built around a women's abbey around the year 1000. Its 11th-century church merits a detour, as does the unmissable Chez Miquel, a three-generation hotel-restaurant where Jean-François's great cooking combines with Véronique's smile to ensure the guests get a taste of regional specialities in welcoming surroundings. Most rooms afford magnificent mountain views and the flowery garden comes with a good-size swimming pool.

The show Nadine put on at the Château de Valon was supposed to be the highlight of my visit. A feverish bustle prevailed around the castle where performers of all generations were applying the last touches of make-up on their faces. Costumes designed by Anaïs mingled with horses, goats and hens, a donkey, a pony, even a lama, and flamboyant hangings that coloured the scenery with a pageant-like merriment. Lots of tickets had been sold and the attendance was expected to be impressive, but dark purple clouds had gathered up north, the wind had begun to rise, and before we knew it the first bolt of lightning zigzagged across the dark sky. Then another and another, until all hell broke loose and the gates of heaven opened, pouring out gusts of wind and rolls of thunder so low, it felt as though any moment the sky would crash over Valon and wipe it out of existence. The sets in the courtyard were wrecked, Nadine's sweater and some of the hangings went flying over the mountain, a weighty slab of *lauze* had flown off Claudine's roof, who is from Millau in the south actually, but spends the summer months in the old family house beneath the *château*. Needless to say, the show had to be cancelled and everyone made their way home disappointed. Except me. Taking the audience ride, I watched the Shakespearean drama unleashed by the elements and allowed my fancy to fly me to Cawdor and confound the hollering of the wind with that of the three witches. Since Cawdor and Valon are practically contemporary, it was fairly easy for my imagination to make their damning prophecy to Macbeth resound through the flashing skies of Valon.

The next morning the curtain rose upon a scene of luminous serenity. The storm had moved elsewhere taking with it the wind and the clouds. Claudine's husband, Jacques, had turned up for the weekend and it was perfect weather to go out with him and be introduced to some of the villagers, 20 in all I found out from Roger Coudouel, rising to 30 in summer when Valon plays to a full house. Roger knows everything about Valon since his family have been farmers here for several generations. He is also town councillor in Lacroix Barrez and in summer takes part in Nadine's shows in the *château*. Félix Delfour and two other villagers were just leaving the communal bread oven ladened with several *fouaces* and fruit tarts they had finished baking for the village *brocante*. Jacques pointed to another stone oven, the *sécadou*, which had once been used for drying the chestnuts. There were plenty of chestnuts in the old days, and plenty of fruit orchards and vineyards.

Valon may have felt like Scotland the night before, but it actually looks south to the sunny Lot Valley. In the Middle Ages it held a strategic position between the Lot and the

Auvergne, hence its castle which was controlled by the Counts of Rodez. Today, farming has become a dying proposition and most of the houses have been turned into holiday homes. The octogenarian Renée Delmas has been renting the village presbytery for some 35 years. As I stepped into her delightfully countrified garden, it dawned on me that the fairy hands behind the wonderful bouquets of cut flowers I had noticed in the church on my first visit, two years earlier, must have been hers. Renée has a passion for all things English (as do Claudine and Jacques, by the way) and has brought into her wonderfully cosy interior a blend of French and English styles, the best of both worlds. She was inexhaustible about her long standing English friends from Somerset whom she had met on the car park of Valon some 20 years earlier.

There were English people in Valon even earlier. Jack Downie was working for the British Embassy in Paris and discovered Valon while touring with his wife and two boys in spring 1963. They bought a dilapidated farm in Prat, the hamlet down the road, and came back in early August to do it up. They were going to spend the month restoring the place, but on the day after their arrival Jack collapsed and died of a massive heart attack. Forty years later, all the old timers remember this tragedy. André Cabrefpine, a healer from Le Prat like his father and ancestors going back to the 16th century, recalls that the funeral was attended by a big crowd, including members of the Embassy in Paris, who gathered for mass in the church of Valon. It was his father who had provided the cart and pair of cows that carried the coffin uphill to the little cemetery of Valon. Like the vineyards and the orchards, like everything else, the cemetery rolls down the very steep hillside and looks out onto the beautiful hills across the valley. The family no longer comes over, the mother and one of the sons having moved to Australia, I was told. In a decade or two there will be no one left to report their story, but the odd passer-by who will chance upon Jack Downie's grave on some future visit is bound to be intrigued by the moving words inscribed there, just as I was before I got the story:

En cette terre accueillante de Valon
Gît Jack Downie
Mais dans nos coeurs il vit
Car nous pensons toujours à lui
L'amour parfait banit la crainte
21 September 1919 — 4 August 1963

The visitor might appreciate too that the Downies chose to express their grief in French as a mark of deference and courtesy to the host village. Should the visitor continue his wanderings to the cemetery of the village of Lapeyre in the Valley of the Sorgues in southern Aveyron, he may be even more surprised to stumble upon the grave of an English lady from much earlier times, namely Medora, the daughter of Lord Byron and his half sister Augusta. Today, the presence of Brits in rural France is commonplace. Jacques pointed to some isolated houses scattered on the hillside in the distance, one of which was owned by a solitary Englishman who apparently likes to paint by the Truyère. Another house belonged to a Russian choreographer. How on earth did *she* discover Valon? Nonetheless, at the time of writing the majority of the residents couldn't be more French. Among them on my last visit was a radiant Parisian enjoying a sunny retreat reclining in a deck chair in his garden, below the road to le Prat where Claudine and I were headed. From our vantage point we got a bird's-eye view of him that made him appear to be floating on his back in a nirvana position of bliss, described in French as *faire le vide*.

Coming from Valon, Entraygues seems like a lively metropolis, boasting roughly 1,400 residents. Lying 'between the waters' of the Lot and the Truyère, which meet here at right angles, it is the southern gateway to the Carladez and the Viadène. The Pont Notre Dame and Pont de Truyère, which span respectively the two rivers, were built in the 13th century and were the first bridges to connect the Rouergue and the Auvergne. The Pont de Truyère was even guarded by defence towers. Viewed from above, they seem to keep the *bourg* afloat in delicate balance as it drifts towards the granite hills that shelter it to the north, where vineyards and chestnut groves take over. The vineyards used to span the entire hillside, as well as the steep schist slopes of Le Fel west of the Truyère, covering more than 1,000 hectares before the phylloxera bug hit in the late 19th century. The chestnut groves grew on the northern slopes facing the Auvergne, to which still bears witness a stretch of land named La Châtaigneraie. They too were hit by some bug and dwindled like the vines.

Lying at the junction of the Lot and the ancient trading route to the Auvergne, Entraygues held a strategic position for commercial navigation going back to the Middle Ages and all the way down south to Bordeaux. Also during the 13th century, contemporary with the bridges, the Counts of Rodez fortified Entraygues and erected a castle which burnt down in the 17th century and was replaced by another, also now gone, except for two of its towers. Commercial activity culminated in the second half of the 18th century, when the flat-bottomed *gabarres* plied the Lot in ever larger numbers, carrying downstream cargoes of timber and barrel staves, alongside textile and leather goods from St Geniez and Espalion, further east, for export to America. In turn, a wealth of products from the New World colonies navigated upstream, catering for the local trading bourgeoisie that generated the valley's prosperity.

Norwegian cod also travelled upstream from Bordeaux, a much needed staple in a strictly Catholic area where fishing was rare, not because of any shortage – quite the contrary, the rivers teemed with fish – but because the farmers had no time to go fishing. The 'stockfish', as the cod was named, would be dried unsalted back in Norway, where it would have hung up in the open air strung by the tail, for up to twelve months, before being shipped to France. It would arrive in Bordeaux stiff as a board and then be immersed in the water and fixed to the stern of the boat for the eight-day duration of the journey upstream. By the time it was taken ashore at its destination, it was rehydrated and ready to be cooked. When potatoes appeared in the Rouergue in the second half of the 18th century, their marriage to the 'stockfish' birthed a comfort dish which became the *plat de résistance* of the colliers of nearby Decazeville when its coal mines opened in the 19th century — *estofinado* in Occitan. The rural inhabitants of the valley followed suit and made it their traditional Friday and Lent dish, to which they added walnut oil and hard boiled eggs before mashing everything together with a fork. A sprinkling of parsley and garlic, combined with the magic touch of a French housewife's hand, did the rest. And when reheated in the evening for dinner, it tasted even better.

Today, when back-to-roots comfort food is a highly prized commodity, the *estofinado* (indifferently referred to also as *stockfish*) is served at several respectable restaurants in western Aveyron, sometimes beyond the Lot Valley, and not necessarily at a low price. The fact that it is a seasonal dish (to be avoided in the summer) enhances its status as a culinary landmark on a back-to-nature pilgrimage.

I am always game for this much less demanding alternative to a hike to Compostela, but I require my stopping-place to be authentic and imbued in local colour, to which end I recruited Olivier and Thérèse from Najac, south of Villefranche-de-Rouergue, to be my guides (Always ask a 'foody' local before you look up your guidebook). Without a second of hesitation, Olivier uttered the name of some *auberge* I couldn't catch, in a village I had never heard of — Malville. Some background reading in anticipation of the outing suggested that the '*mal*' alluded to the Muslim invasion in the 8th century. Olivier made all the arrangements right away, and announced with his characteristic enthusiasm that Evelyne and co. were expecting us with great pleasure the following night. He couldn't have been better inspired! For here roots and nature are distributed in equal proportions, roots that go back to 1852, when Augustin Montbressous first opened this village *café-bar-restaurant-épicerie*, and nature by way of fresh produce supplied by nearby farms (notably the excellent organic *tomme* cheese, produced some fifteen minutes away by an offspring of the illustrious General de Boissieu, who also happened to be the son-in-law of the late President Charles de Gaulle).

Although the entire range of Aveyronnais specialities is honoured here, I preferred to go for their stockfish because a) that's what I had come for, and b) it was the only speciality of cultural and historical consequence I hadn't tasted yet. It was generous in quantity and excellent in quality, lovingly prepared by Tante Thérèse, Augustin's great granddaughter who had been in charge of the kitchen '*piano*' (oven) for 55 years. Thérèse is so much part of the furniture that she was even born on the premises, as was once customary. An old photo immortalises her in front of the house in her baby buggy. Her younger brother Michel and his wife Evelyne lent her a hand when needed. These three 'musketeers' were on the point of retiring when we visited and the restaurant has been taken over since by Vincent and Aurélie Marcillac. However, the family still lives upstairs and Thérèse is still helping in the kitchen, although no one can tell for how long for she is now in her 70s. And since Evelyne has not given up her position as town councillor, the emblematic tricolour *mai* (staff) is still displayed outside the restaurant. Vincent promises to preserve the authenticity and his clientele has not changed. The *épicerie* was already gone when I visited and Vincent also added several new dishes. Times do have to move on. If you make the journey specifically for the stockfish, be sure to order it over the phone the day before: 05 65 29 30 46

The arrival of the railway in 1859 was fatal to river life on the Lot. Within five to six decades the picturesque traffic of boats had petered out and altogether disappeared in 1926. Don't let old engravings and nostalgia tempt you into idealising those times, because navigation on the Lot can be a perilous exercise (rafting and kayaking enthusiasts take note), and many a boatman ended engulfed by its waters. Towing a boat upstream was usually the job of draft horses or donkeys, but over here it was often done by men, who would pull the boat by the neck, using a towing-collar by way of a yoke. The boatsmen on board would help them along by punting the boat forward with a pole or an oar. Further assistance was provided by the sails, when the winds were favourable, and a pretty sight it was.

Old pictures of their equally stocky Auvergnat neighbours, who were the water suppliers of Paris in pre-Haussmannian days, came to my mind. It required a robust constitution to climb up five or six storeys yoked to two buckets of water dangling down the shoulders, let alone carry a bathtub on one's back. A generation later their children went into the coal business as *charbognards* and then evolved into *cafétiers*. No doubt their stocky build pre-disposed the Aveyronnais to excel in the game of *quilles* (skittles), the main local sport. Annual championships mark the calendar year of village life and reach as far as Paris where they play against the Aveyronnais Parisian diaspora.

The arrival of the railway brought Bordeaux and Cahors closer too and toughened competition for the local viniculture, just as it did for Estaing, followed by the phylloxera bug that all but wiped out its vineyards a generation later — the same scenario as elsewhere. Gone were the days when yokes of oxen could be seen along the Auvergne Road, plodding their way uphill with barrel-laden carts towards Aurillac, where no respectable bourgeois meal was conceivable without an Entraygues or Le Fel wine. By the early 20th century all commercial production had ceased, but some vineyards were still cultivated for their fruit which gained a reputation as a laxative, thus turning Entraygues into a popular health resort. Hence the 'Anglo-Normand' style of some of its houses, much in vogue at the time in fashionable resorts.

The cure was completed by a drink of whey from Laguiole that must have increased the desired effect, at least according to old cartoons that depict the holiday-makers in the area of the loos, with their pants more often down than up. It seems they were no less health conscious than today's fitness-club and organic-food addicts, and liked to complement their outdoor leisure with a healthy meal, taken at l'Hôtel des Voyageurs, Au Pont de Truyère, or at Le Lion D'Or, still going strong, where Stéphanie and I dined on generous samples of *produits du terroir*. Locals, however, continued to make wine for their personal use, lovingly pampering their little vineyards which yielded a congenial, unpretentious wine, low in alcohol but pleasant enough to accompany a hearty meal of fresh produce, the kind of wine we were served by Jean-Pierre at the Relais des Coustoubis. During the *vendanges*, which would last up to three weeks, the village cellars would give off a pleasant smell of new wine. After six or seven days it would be ready to be drawn and everyone would do the rounds of the neighbours to compare notes, usually approvingly, '*Es pas missant!*' (it's not bad!), although it was also fun to tease one another in good spirits. But the main target of the banter were the *Montagnols*, who came down from their cheesemaking mountains to 'get their refill' for the year.

The new wine was served in all the inns and was accompanied by shelled walnut, just as it still is at the Relais des Coustoubis, and by *cabécou* (goat's cheese) wrapped in vine leaves. These point to an age-old cohabitation of vineyards and goats, which were completely at ease on the vertiginous slopes, nibbling freely on the readily available chestnut. They came in handy as suppliers of wine skins and dung, while the tender meat of the kids tasted delicious when cooked with sorrel in spring. Today, Laurent and Olivier Mousset from Le Fel, and Isabelle and Serge Broha from Viellevie (on the Cantal side of the border) keep goats and produce *cabécou* cheese alongside their wines.

In the 1980s, a new generation of enthusiasts set out to regenerate and expand their area's viticulture, the same trend as in neighbouring Estaing. The *coltadas* (terraces) were rebuilt, equipment and technical methods were modernised and the vineyards expanded to 22 hectares, shared by six independent vintners. Three are situated on the thin granite soil above Entraygues and are reputed in particular for their white wine, as was the case in the past, although they now produce reds and rosé as well. The white is produced exclusively of *chénin blanc*. It is an attractive dry wine, light gold with a fruity character. It accompanies well river fish, goat's cheese and *foie gras*, and more elaborate fish dishes once it has aged somewhat.

We visited Jean-Marc Viguier at Les Buis, 200 metres above Entraygues, close to the road to Aurillac. This used to be a mixed farming holding, with dairy cows, goats and chestnut groves, but Jean-Marc preferred to concentrate on wine. He also makes an excellent *crème de châtaigne* and *kir*, a nod of respect to the past. That said, Jean-Marc is a modern-day vintner, who uses up-to-date equipment, such as vats made of polyester rather than stainless steel, because, he claims, it is just as hygienic whilst no less permeable than wood. Yet, although scientific and technical progress allow him to control the tannin, for instance, he believes that much remains within the mysterious realm of intuition, on which he often relies when all is said and done. He can't be wrong if Michel Bras is one of his clients. There was certainly more poetry than science in his language —'*la vigne pleure*' (the vine weeps) when the suck descends to the root to protect the plant, or '*un petit vin de soif* ', an unpretentious modest wine, whose only ambition is to quench a fellow's thirst.

It is often one big family in the Aveyron, and Laurent and Olivier Mousset from Cassos by Le Fel are cousins of Jean-Marc's, whose retired father was happy to help his young nephews start out their own vineyard. Their aunt Marinette keeps a restaurant in the tiny village of Le Fel, one of those earthy basic places where the clock stopped ticking fifty years ago or more, just as it did Chez Marius at Murols. Unlike the Auberge du Fel next door, it has no terrace with a stunning view over the valley, but l'Auberge du Fel caters to tourists and is open only during high season, while Marinette is the daily home of local regulars with robust appetites, who enjoy washing down her homely cuisine with her nephews' wines. We started our lunch there with a mixed salad of fresh green leaves and chestnut tossed in fragrant walnut oil vinaigrette. The flavourful pigeon came with a side dish of roast potatoes, mushroom and parsley that were so comforting, it was impossible to turn down Marinette's second and third helpings, even though you knew the inevitable cheese tray (including her nephews' delicious *cabécou*) was yet to come. To our relief Marinette was kind enough not to frown upon us when when we left half the dessert untouched and split the rest between us. Marinette is a widow; she has worked hard all her life and feels it's time to sell her business and retire. So far she hasn't found a buyer, but once she does things will never be the same.

Auguste Abeil and Frédéric Fortveille are the other two vintners of Le Fel, arguably the most dramatic vine landscape in France. Even if you are not a wine person, do take the time to visit the hillside for the scenery is breathtaking. Detour, for instance, to the tiny, almost adjacent, Roussy on top of the hill, just a few minutes' drive from Auguste Abeil's winery at la Terrasse du Haut-Mindic, on the D527. I can't think of a more privileged position for the final stopping-place than its lofty churchyard and its panoramic view over the Lot Valley and Entraygues. It even beats Valon. Although the church dates only from the 19th century, it is attractive and merits a visit. It also benefits from good acoustics and is used on occasion as a venue for concerts.

The slopes of Le Fel are so steep that they must be terraced before they can be planted. Laurent Mousset was lucky to have Jean-Marc as a cousin to lend him a hand because it's a Herculean job to dig into the schist, and all the more so on this rugged terrain. It's a lunar, rocky landscape, but some claim it once produced the Aveyron's best wine. Auguste Abeil knew nothing about wine and just as little about the area, but he fell in love with it when he visited it from his home town Aurillac. When it was time to sell his successful business and retire, he thought that going into winegrowing might be a way of making a move here. With the typical naive daring of the blissfully unaware, he walked into the celebrated mega bookshop Gibert Jeune on the Boulevard St-Michel in Paris and picked up a basic handbook for beginners. This is how he became a *vigneron* in 1987. His first vintage was barely better than plonk, but one has to start somewhere, usually at the bottom. Eventually quality started improving, and significantly so in the last ten years. It's a busy life, following the annual rotation of the months, each with its specific task. Pruning must be done in February, the pegs changed in March, in April the vines must be tied to the pegs... and so on and so forth until the *vendanges*. In between the wine has to be drawn and bottled, then the bottles have to be labelled, and finally sold... There is never a dull moment.

Le Fel's wines are almost exclusively red. There is a small quantity of rosé but no whites. They are well rounded and velvety, often with a fruity bouquet. They suit local rustic dishes, *tripoux, potée auvergnate, charcuterie, estofinado*, and full bodied cheeses. Two varieties go into the red wine, the *fer servadou* which is native to south west France (of which more later), and *cabernet franc*. Auguste also mixes in a small percentage of *pinot noir*, while Frédéric Forveille from Méjanasserre prefers to add a bit of *cabernet sauvignon* to his reds.

When we arrived at Méjanasserre, the silence was so deep, you could almost hear it. I stood there for a while with closed eyes, inhaling the crisp air, soaking up the perfect sun and the faint touch of breeze. Although Méjanasserre means 'halfway up the hill', it felt like standing on one of the world's summits. Next to us, Frédéric played weathercock, his arms stretched alternately towards Conques ahead, Rodez to the left, the Cantal to the right, and Laguiole, behind us. We could not see any of them but it felt good to connect with these familiar landmarks from the elevated paradisical vantage point. Like some garden of Eden, Méjanasserre was even watered by its own spring, next to which stood an ancient Merovingian sarcophagus. It had been unearthed on the site, pointing possibly to an ancient cemetery, as good a place for your eternal rest as Roussy in terms of glorious scenery and pure air.

Frédéric's vines yield 25,000 bottles a year and honour some of the Aveyron's most reputable restaurants — Jean Luc

Fau's Goûts et Couleurs in Rodez, Nicole Fagegaltier's Au
Vieux Pont in storybook Belcastel, Isabelle Muylaert's Auguy
at Laguiole among them. He and his wife Véronique are
ecologically minded and keep everything as natural as possible.
He was excited about the 2005 vintage because the weather
conditions in the summer had been excellent, with warm days
and cool evenings, sprinkled by occasional gentle rain.
Consequently, he said, '*la vigne n'était pas stressée*'. So it wasn't
just Jean-Marc who related to his vines as if they were close
fellow beings. It's a French thing. And since a French *vigneron*
tends to be a man and *la vigne* happens to be of the feminine
gender grammatically, they might have been talking of a
beloved mistress.

Another piece of good news about Méjanasserre is that you
can stay there, for Véronique and Frédéric have added to their
winery a few *chambres d'hôtes* and *gîtes*. It's also a *ferme auberge*,
where you can just come for a meal. Whichever formula you
choose, you will enjoy every bit of its indoor and outdoor
nooks, to which Véronique has added an artistic touch in
many different ways, painting, sewing curtains and cushions,
upholstering, doing patchwork and ceramics, growing flowers
and herbs that get tossed into her salads. They are quite
delicious, as is the bread that is baked in their traditional oven,
out in the open for all to see. Chickens, geese, ducks, guinea-
fowl, everything is raised organically and in the fresh air, and
all the meat is roasted on a spit over the fire, including juicy
piglets. You can be served either in the rustic, woodsy
restaurant, or outside on the terrace, just above the vineyards.
You will be surrounded by greenery and flowers, by rambling
creepers and climbing roses, oblivious to the cares of the world.
Méjanasserre has got so much going for it that it has become

a trendy destination even among the high and the mighty, who will wind down here over lunch before winding up at Michel Bras for dinner. Remember to make your reservations well ahead of time and check the restaurant's opening days and hours as they vary according to the time of year.

Chapter 4

INTERLUDE: NEW VERSUS OLD

I met the first bunch of *néo*-Aveyronnais at the weekly market of Villefranche-de-Rouergue. Sylvie had offered to walk me through her favourite stalls before she went to work, so it had to be very early, a beautifully sunny Thursday morning in June, surprisingly cool and breezy after the oppressive heat of the past few weeks. Before hitting the town I detoured to the top of one of the surrounding hills for a panoramic view of the town's red-pantiled roofs, criss-crossed by a grid of narrow old streets — an oversized red checkerboard, where southwest France and the Middle Ages converged.

Rising from above the roofs on the eastern edge of the town square, the massive belfry-porch of the collegiate church of Notre Dame (familiarly referred to as La Collégiale) looked quaint with its dwarfish spire, suggesting the monument had never been completed. This is where the market is held, and when I arrived there a little later, and saw the belfry from street level, it looked familiar yet somewhat altered, like a face you'd seen before under different circumstances. What a great backdrop to the square! It added so much character to the old arcaded rows of houses that hemmed it in on all four sides. I could fancy the Capulets and Montagues playing out their age-old feud against its backdrop: perhaps by the big wrought-iron cross which enhanced the medieval feel, although Colette, with whom I visited it later, pointed out dismissively that it was only a 19th-century addition of little artistic value. It didn't bother me — I liked the way it stood there by the food stalls and the way the massive porch of the church portruded brazenly into the square. True, it wasn't in line with the rest of the arcade, but it created a reassuring sense of continuity between the market world of earthly goods and the Godly house of prayer, a sense of unity between the here and the hereafter.

The vendors had just put the finishing touches to their stalls and were posted under the festive waves of yellow parasols waiting for the curtain to rise. Many of the stalls were still in the shade at that early hour; those that were exposed to the sun looked even more ravishing, especially one makeshift stall decked with bunches of mixed flowers straight from my old English Nursery Rhyme books — you would never get foxgloves from a florist in Paris! At the stroke of eight the scene was set in motion and things began to liven up. I could see Sylvie making her way towards me: a handshake and a smile and we were off, wading with the flow of shoppers through a riot of fragrant hues and the clamour that was fast building up.

Eric Belin was standing next to a row of bottles of homemade fruit juices. His Parisian accent gave him away as an outsider, even though his grandparents were from the Aveyron. At any rate, they were from the north, and that's a different world altogether from western Aveyron, which is where Villefranche-de-Rouerge is situated, already in the Quercy. Besides, once you've moved away from the Aveyron, even if it's only one generation back, you've lost the status of a fully-fledged native. Only those who have remained on the soil continually can claim to belong to this category, someone like Gérard Carles, for instance, who speaks with the regional lilt and specialises in duck preparations - *foie gras, pâté, rillette, fritons, magret, cou farci*, and *confit...*

The Carles family farm is at nearby Monteils, 10 kilometres south of Villefranche, a pretty ride along the Aveyron river and through rural countryside. It was midday when we drove there, and other than the odd village or farmstead, a mix of old stone and red-roofed new bungalows, the occasional red-dotted cherry tree or clusters of grazing cattle, everything was intensely green under the blazing sun. At some point the farmland gave way to shady oak trees that followed the course of the river, but soon we were driving again past golden squares of corn fields, or green ones planted with maize as food for the ducks.

This is a small farming area, too small to keep its children unless they take the place of their parents, which is why Gérard's son Jacques had to leave the farm and try his luck elsewhere. He found work in a factory but was miserable and didn't last long. Yet his time there was instructive and generated the idea of turning the family farm into a business specialising in duck. His apprenticeship in the factory opened his eyes to the notion of economic productivity, the key to his success story. This he has coupled with quality obtained through a wizardly marriage of copper caldrons and an open fire, which yields deliciously flavourful products. Alongside these he also developed the concept of duck by-products, such as his Rouergat (the adjective of Rouergue) '*oulado*' (soup, in Occitan), a house speciality made of the bird's leftovers and garden vegetables which costs him next to nothing to produce. Another trick was to maximise the production by using up every bit of the bird, including its bones. Nothing gets wasted, everything is recycled as in nature; and the business is booming.

There were three busloads visiting the farm that day, some 150 tourists packed into the flowery courtyard like the parties in front of Paris's Notre Dame in high season. There we stood waiting in the blazing sun, inhaling the smell of a French farm mixed with those of lavender and roses. I wasn't sure what we were waiting for, but it turned out to be a tour of the farm's one-time cowshed, now a 'museum', which could only take one busload at a time. This is where you learn what happens to a duck in the different stages of production that will eventually land it on your plate, or fit it into a tin.

Upstairs the barn had been converted into a vast dining hall, where we were seated at three endlessly long strips of trestle tables, for an equally long meal. As elsewhere in southwest France, *foie gras* is the pride of the house, the result of 28 sessions of force feeding (twice daily for fourteen days), by which time the weight of the duck's liver will have increased from 120 to 400g, and the bird's life cycle will be terminated. Jacques is adamant that the process is painless (Dr Guillotin had said as much in support of the guillotine), and that the ducks actually love his maize concoctions and stretch their necks eagerly for more. It must be said in his defence that he feeds them with a spoon and is attentive to their comfort. He even strokes their necks gently whilst feeding them, the way you would a pet. Nevertheless, when their time has come he feels no emotional dilemma about killing and throwing them into the simmering caldron.

Adhering to the same philosophy, Henri Dardé, whose blue eyes couldn't be gentler, pampered his bull Pedro on his immaculately organic pastures for five full years, before sending him off to his close friend Gérard Garrigues from the 2-Michelin star le Pastel, in Toulouse. There Pedro simmered on a very low fire for several hours before being offered to Henri as a gourmet relish he was not about to forget. Yet Henri loved the bull, a rusty-coloured Salers who carried majestically his five tonnes of weight. Rumours that Pedro was destined to the abattoir had reached the local media who devoted a full page to this news item. An association in defence of Pedro was set up, urging Henri through compassionate letters to reconsider. Henri thought this was preposterous. Just because Pedro was taken up by the media doesn't change the laws of nature. From Henri's standpoint, cooking Pedro and enjoying eating him is an act of love and respect.

By the time we were through our *dégustation* of Rouergat *oulado, foie gras* salad, stuffed cabbage, stuffed potato, duck with olives and the very rich plum tart, I was in full empathy with the wretched birds and was wondering if the weight of my liver too had multiplied three-and-a-half fold. A couple of regional songs closed the event, served with a regional accent and a local *eau-de-vie*, and an announcement that farm products were available for purchase. Jacques is creative and entrepreneurial: by taking full advantage of the current fad for les *produits du terroir*, he has managed to turn *la France profonde* into a profitable commodity. And he does it with PR charm and self-deprecating humour, as he points to his potbelly and the rest of his fleshy body where plenty of duck savouries have transited over the years.

Eric Belin actually lives across the border, north of the Lot river, which falls already within the *département* of the Lot. Strictly speaking he is not even *néo*-Aveyronnais, but *néo-rural*, which applies indiscriminately to any rural area in France. Having studied agriculture, he knew he wanted to move out of the Paris area, but had no specific destination in mind and came down here by chance. Like Sylvie, he was part of the wave of the early 1970s youths who sought a healthy, back-to-nature lifestyle. Today he lives at St-Pedroux and sells his fruit juices directly on the market, rotating between Villefranche-de-Rouergue on Thursdays and Figeac (in the Lot) on Saturdays. His 12-year-old son Matthieu was selling his own grown berries, which he and his brother Simon had transplanted to the family garden from the nearby forest. They sure looked, smelt and tasted it!

I wondered why Matthieu wasn't at school on a Thursday morning, but Eric reminded me of the ongoing nationwide teachers' strike. But of course... We self-centred Parisians seem to forget that French life does not stop at the Boulevard Périphérique and that only 2 million people live within its boundaries, representing less than 4% of the population of metropolitan France. Since I am used to social protest being an integral part of the Parisian scene, I was surprised to see it played out against the backdrop of a colourful medieval market light years away.

As well as teachers, various groups of 'Greens' were also busying themselves among the stalls, and as the morning progressed a mix of political handouts, tourist brochures and commercial flyers accumulated in my bag. One of them caught my attention in particular: LE MONDE N'EST PAS UNE MARCHANDISE (THE WORLD IS NOT A PIECE OF MERCHANDISE)... which remains to be proved, but at least I was heartened that someone should try to do something about it. Followed an appeal to join a three-day gathering on the emblematic Larzac plateau in August 2003, ahead of and against the World Trade Organisation's meeting in Mexico scheduled for the following September. There was no signature on the pamphlet but it rang the familiar bell of the radical farmers' union, la Confédération Paysanne, whose Gallic resistance against the corporate world of *malbouffe* (junk food), is led by the above mentioned modern-day Asterix, the moustachioed José Bové.

Three days later, at dawn on Sunday the 22nd of June, when the sounds of the nationwide Fête de la Musique had barely faded out, a helicopter and a police force of 60 swooped down on a lonely sheep farm in the midst of the Larzac wilderness. In no time the place was sealed off, the stone house stormed, and the unsuspecting José Bové snatched from his sleep before he could see it coming, or count his sheep for that matter. The reason for his arrest was his destruction of genetically modified crops, for which he was given later a 10-month prison sentence. The operation was carried out with the usual French panache (I mean, really! Was it necessary to send out 60 armed policemen to catch one unarmed citizen in his sleep?). The same method, without the helicopter, was used to capture Cartouche, but then, Cartouche was the most notorious criminal and the terror of early 18th-century Paris.

Bové's supporters protested against his arrest with a continuous concert of loud chanting and metallic drumming outside his prison where they stood their ground in full forces throughout the night — one way of prolonging La Fête de la Musique. They vowed to persist until his release, rumoured to be staged on Bastille Day when President Jacques Chirac was expected to pardon their leader in the name of social peace. To everyone's surprise the French President turned out to be less magnanimous than expected and cut only four months of the sentence. Consequently, the metallic concert outside the prison walls resumed all the more loudly but fell upon deaf ears. Bent on making a statement, the authorities reiterated that the destruction of GMC was illegal and proceeded to arrest several of

José Bové's friends, to make their point. However, he was released the following August by a court order from Montpellier, which put an end to this childish arm wrestling. It was all about saving one's face: In France there are never any losers and no one ever makes mistakes. Despite another pending prison sentence, at the moment of writing José Bové is a presidential hopeful for the upcoming 2007 elections. Unrelenting on all fronts, although he identifies himself as '*paysan*', he has chosen this time to focus his campaign on the have-nots of urban society.

Patrick Legendre was selling his own honey at the stall next to Matthieu's berries. Patrick explained that he liked to follow the seasonal cycle of flowering, which is why he had on offer chestnut honey in profusion. I recalled the pale blossoms I had noticed on the chestnut trees whilst driving along the Aveyron a few days earlier, delicate from afar like scraps of rice paper. Patrick, too, came down south with the late 60s- and early 70s-wave of flower youths. They travelled here and there with no specific place in mind other than knowing that they wanted to leave the city. Eventually they arrived in the Lot valley, loved it and settled above the river by Loupiac, atop the limestone cliffs. Patrick adores it there. I imagine I would too judging by the name of his place — le Mas du Causse — evoking both a characterful traditional stone farmhouse (*mas*) and the thrilling semi-arid landscape of limestone (*causse*). The word '*mas*' is used all over southern France. Those in Provence, the ones with the rosy walls and red pantile roofs that look so pretty among the olive groves and lavender fields, are way beyond your average budget, but over here you may still come across something affordable, though certainly not for long. Patrick's place sounded heavenly and I hoped to have the opportunity some day to pay him a visit.

In early July, a week before my next scheduled trip, some friends came over for dinner in Paris, among them Emily from Dorset in England. On my computer screen at the time was the paragraph about Patrick, and a map of southwest France was stuck on the wall to help me along with the writing of this book. One thing led to another and before we knew it Emily and I were discussing the Aveyron where her family had had a holiday place going way back. Her grandmother Josephine Wilson, now in her 90s, had spent time there during the Occupation and remembered when the *résistance* blew up the Madeleine bridge on the Lot. Emily filled me in on her own childhood holidays in the Aveyron, playing with the neighbours' children. Her finger roamed on the map for a while, until she found what she was looking for and called me over,

- "There! That's the place! le Mas du Causse."

- "But these are the people I am just writing about!" I exclaimed.

Upon which, Emily rushed over to my computer and stared at the screen in disbelief.

I did eventually make it to the Mas du Causse. Thérèse drove me around the Quercy one afternoon, when we suddenly stumbled upon Loupiac accidentally. Not a soul was around, as usual, other than a superbly attractive young woman standing by an iron gate, to whom we turned for directions. Typically, she turned out to be Patrick's daugher, the very one Emily used to play with. Patrick served us tea under the shady trees in the garden and offered me a jar of his homemade honey. His charming wife, who is a talented and original painter, showed me some of her work in her next-door studio. They never regretted their move.

Sylvie continued my guided tour of the stalls. I felt a strong sense of community among the vendors, even though most were outsiders like Sylvie. Not just Eric with his vitamin-packed fruit juices, Patrick and his energising pollen, or Didier Vallet who picks his medicinal herbs directly on the meadows of the Aubrac. I met also Dominique Poisson from Normandy who sells arty jewellery, Jean-Louis and Eliette Chauliaguet who sell Provençal tablecloths, and many others who give the lie to the widespread notion that rural France is being deserted. True, the native children tend to seek a greater choice of opportunities in the city, but it's been a two-way traffic for the last thirty odd years, and while the young natives seek the excitement of the city, the newcomers get an equal kick from restoring dilapidated old farms.

Sylvie and Daniel's first home was a love-at-first-sight affair. They spotted it while driving outside Villefranche, on the way to Montauban. It wasn't much of a place, but it had a picturesque pigeon-house, and the bright red vine trumpets looked so pretty against the ochre walls and the blue wooden shutters! What more do you need when you are young and in love and spend all your time looking into each other's eyes? They first came here on holiday in the early 1970s, when the post-'68 generation would have none of the 'beach-potatoeing' on the Côte d'Azur, a vacuous way of spending one's holidays referred to as *vacances idiotes*. Ecologically-orientated holidays were the 'in' thing, away from the mobs on the polluted Mediterranean coast, and preferably with a purpose and substance (*vacances intelligentes*).

They tried summer skiing in the Alps and kayaking on the Ardèche, and eventually wound up in the Aveyron having heard of some association called Vacances Insolites (Alternative

Holidays), the brainchild of a local artist, Hervé Vernhes (Yes, the very same). They tried their hands at all the current fads — weaving, pottery, wood carving, silk painting — all part of the back-to-nature syndrome. It sounded so familiar! A smile came to my face as I recognised my own itinerary from that time. Confessing my own similar history, we chuckled at our past idealism. I had only given it one shot though, a fortnight of pottery classes on the hills of Provence, which my clumsy hands brought to a disgraceful conclusion. I still have stashed away somewhere in my kitchen two glazed would-be flower vases which shrank into ashtrays at the potter's wheel. Since nobody smokes in our household, they come in handy for serving appetisers but my pride was ruffled at the time, nipping in the bud any aspirations of dabbling further in arts and crafts.

Sylvie and Daniel loved the Aveyron straight away. They were also deep into ecology and craved a career change. Everything is simple when you are young and anything is more glamorous than a white-collar job, so Daniel trained to become a cabinet-maker. He has had other career changes since, each of which he believes has enriched his life. At present he is involved in alternative medicine, acupuncture and Japanese Reiki; he has even been to China on a training course. Many *néo*-Aveyronnais have branched out into new-age type activities. Those who have taken up agriculture did not branch into traditional livestock breeding, which has remained in the hands of the natives.

Whilst talking to Patrick I noticed a cluster of peasant women with live poultry, rabbits and free-range eggs in baskets lined up at their feet. They had no stalls, and no parasols to protect their wizened skin from the sun. Standing in full view in their dark nondescript dresses, their eyes deeply set in ageless faces, they looked like outlandish dark ghosts risen from another page of history. Strange how sometimes the most native of natives becomes an alien on his own soil. And yet it was these peasant women, not Patrick, not Eric, nor Didier, who were the 'real thing', the true aboriginals going back to the obscure beginning and perpetuating the universal division of roles in rural society, where the wife tends to the lighter chores of the farmyard and the farmer to the tougher job of handling the cattle.

My mind wandered back to the livestock market at Laissac where we'd been the year before with Georges and Odette — not to be missed if you want to inhale the true smells of *la France profonde*. Oh, it's much more than just the smells; it's the smells mixed with the fodder, the mud and the droppings, the mooing and the yelling, the jolting, the stumbling, the prodding of sticks and the confusion of hoofs as each herd pours out of its truck in a jumble, then dashes forth to the enclosure through a corridor of mobile barriers. This is the biggest livestock market in southern France and farmers and animals are driven here even from across the border. It is held every Tuesday and involves so many animals that it requires mindboggling speed and orchestration to manoeuvre the barriers and channel the surge of cattle without causing chaos. This is the Wild West-on-Aveyron, a stupendous spectacle worthy of a rodeo (and worth close to €1m of transactions per year), much of which I watched seated on one of the barriers.

It was fine so long as the cows' swaying tails did not brush against me, but when all of a sudden a herd of bulls gushed forth through the corridor in a torrential stampede, I remembered the famous bull running of Pamplona and made myself scarce as fast as I could, before shed, barriers, myself and all were carried away by their frenzied horns. That and the wet weather drove us to the Café du Fourail, the market's 'annex' where everyone meets. The place was packed, the din was extraordinary, and the *patron* Gérard Andrieu's wife navigated cheerfully and smoothly between the tables, serving everyone efficiently, a joke here, some banter there, treating all as her children. Suddenly I noticed that other than Odette and myself, she was the only woman around, the archetypal mother earth, the backbone and pillar of an all-male group and the soul sister of Hector's wife in that bouncing song by Georges Brassens.

Back in the market with Sylvie, the peasant women were still posted in the same position, mysterious and incongruously dark among the colourful stalls of modern times. When I asked Daniel how the natives and '*néos*' interacted, he confirmed my overall perception that people here are friendly in a matter-of-fact sort of way: there is no fawning, no 'commercial' smiles, but no hostility either. Yet beneath the surface there are undertones that tell a different story. There is a certain intimacy into which a '*néo*' will never be admitted; and in any case, as Daniel had pointed out, the very fact that they eat different food puts a limit on how far the friendship might go. A *néo*'s daily menu reminds me of what the Californian Alice Waters has on offer at her restaurant Chez Panisse or in her cookery books. It hardly includes *fritons, aligot, tête de veau* or *tripoux*, except on special occasions. With such different eating habits and philosophies, the two groups are unlikely to gather round the same table on a regular basis. Besides, how can you feel as intimate with a recent acquaintance as you would with someone who's been part of your family circle for generations?

The segregation begins as soon as you open your mouth and your accent gives you away as an outsider. The gap widens across suspiciously raised brows as you are about to sign the purchase deed of your new home and you present your official papers to the local *notaire*: It transpires that your wife was born in Lille, that the two of you got married in the Ardèche, so why do you live in the Aveyron? That's odd. Why did you have to move around? We natives are born here, grow up here, get married to our neighbours' daughters, and die here. Those of us who move away remain 'cousins' by virtue of blood, but it won't be quite the same once they leave. They too begin to be perceived as outsiders, and certainly so will their children. After a while, if they are successful, the feelings towards them turn ambivalent, as they become a source of both pride and envy.

What about foreigners? Oh, they are the furthest removed from the native nucleus; they move on the outermost circle, further out than the *néo*-Aveyronnais who after all are French. It's a very subtle hierarchy, not always perceptible behind friendly faces. There's nothing hypocritical about it, nothing personal, no ill feelings — it's just the way it it. When I asked Monsieur Bouyssières, Mayor of Najac, how he felt about the English living here, he answered meditatively, '*ce sont des êtres humains*' (they're also human beings). Others complained that the English were causing prices of property to rise. But then, the locals are the first to profit by asking those prices.

The *néo*-Aveyronnais also cause prices to rise, but more moderately, because their purchasing power is much lower than the Brits'. On the other hand, they are an asset to the local economy into which they inject new blood, unlike most foreign residents who are not in a position to do so, if only because their French isn't good enough usually. *La France profonde*, too old to adjust to a fast-changing world, should count her blessings because, for all we know, the starry-eyed flower children may prove to be her link into the future and a buffer against the assaults of a global, corporate economy.

Sylvie and Daniel now live outside Villefranche, by the river Aveyron which, in this section, carves its way through a gorge. They call it '*la Vallée heureuse*' ('The Happy Valley'), and if you continue a little further beyond their house, you can even take a dip in the river or a swim. The house is set against the cliffs and has a long strip of garden that leaps from the river up the tiered slope that was once covered with vines. Villefranche was the Aveyron's largest wine country before the phylloxera bug ravaged its vineyards in the 1880s. They were never replanted here because the development of the railway made it easier to be supplied by Cahors, Bordeaux and the Languedoc.

Daniel looks after the vegetables and Sylvie after the flowers, but for much of the time the two of them have to join forces in a never-ending battle against the invading forest. To me, on my brief visit, the unkempt thicket of oak, ash, maple and others looked utterly romantic. But I don't have to deal with it on a daily basis, as do Sylvie and Daniel, which was why they hadn't got round yet to planting fruit trees. But even without the fruit trees it felt Edenic in the early hours of the morning, when we took our breakfast facing the river. The sound of the nearby waterfall, the occasional dialogue between a couple of birds, and the crowing of the neighbour's rooster is all the noise you are likely to get as you lick your spoon clean discreetly, because it would be a crime to let Sylvie's golden peach-and-ginger jam get wasted in the dishwasher. I say 'you' because Sylvie and Daniel let the top room of their house. It is spacious and quiet, and looks out to the Aveyron. The spot where you can have a swim is just a few minutes upstream.

Chapter 5

THE SEAT OF THE GODS

They say one is as happy as God in France. It sounds even better in French —*heureux comme Dieu en France.* Where exactly in France they do not specify, but I suspect it must be in the Aveyron, since it holds the national record for longevity, or so I've been told. If you wish to narrow down your quest further and seek the very heart of divine bliss, head for Najac, a 30-minute drive along the gorges of the Aveyron due south from Villefranche-de-Rouergues. By rail it takes 15 minutes, a fun and scenic ride in and out of 9 tunnels and over 7 bridges well worth the experience, the perfect way to disembark at Najac's sleepy little station that has been standing its ground since 1853.

Jacques Mazières, from the Belle Rive hotel opposite the station, still remembers the avalanche of pigs that used to stream down the hill past the establishment on market day. Everything travelled by train in those days — people, animals and goods. The market was held in upper Najac, opposite what is now the hotel l'Oustal du Barry. Jacques's great grandfather started the business to accommodate passengers when the railway arrived here. Consequently he named it l'Auberge de la Gare, which then became Café de la Gare, and later still Hôtel de la Gare. When a new clientele of holiday-makers started travelling to Najac in the summer, one of its British residents and an acquaintance of Jacques suggested that visitors might be put off by the proximity of the railway implied by the name, and thought it would be commercially wise to change to Le Belle Rive, evoking instead the beauty of the surrounding river banks.

As elsewhere in Najac, business peaks in summer and plunges into hibernation in winter. A sizeable swimming pool and tennis courts give it the feel of a resort, a far cry from those market days, when the restaurant was packed with farmers and with the bustle and din of their conversations. Jacques recalls that each farmer was thoughtfully offered by his grandparents a bundle of hay for his pig as a freebie.

Najac was big time pig land. The animals were nourished on chestnuts and left to enjoy the great outdoor air much of the year, which gave the meat a particular flavour. The *jambon de Najac* enjoyed quite a reputation and was already appreciated in the 16th century by the likes of Rabelais. Apparently, President Pompidou made sure to have some stocked at the Palais de l'Elysée, his presidential residence. Jacques's grandfather decided to get himself into the ham business to supplement his income. He would buy it fresh, prepare it, then sell it mainly locally, but also to a couple of outlets in Paris. In those days, the goods would travel by train till the end of the rail track where they were relayed by a horse-drawn cart. These belonged to the SERNAM, France's major freight transport company to this day, into whose hands I entrusted several of my house moves over the years. Today, of course, they use trucks. Jacques brought out the family album and showed me an old faded photo of a horse being given the priest's benediction before setting off with its loaded cart...

Here, as elsewhere, the killing of the pig was a big event that involved the entire community. It would usually take place in January or February. When the work was done everyone would enjoy grandmother's succulent *astet*, a regional speciality still served at the Belle Rive, a good enough reason alone to stop at their restaurant. It is made of the boned middle loin with its fillet, stuffed with a freshly mixed *persillade* (chopped parsley and garlic). The roast is wrapped in a lacy *crépine* (pork fat), then left to sit in cool temperature for several days, before being put in the oven to roast on a spit. When it comes out after an hour and a half, it is imbued with a heavenly flavour, but it is equally tasty eaten cold accompanied by *ailloli* (a garlic-based mayonnaise). Grandmother's *astet* was a way of saying 'thank you' to all those who had helped turn the animal into *jambon, paté, rillettes, fritons* and other such delicacies. Just like at Jacques Carles' duck farm, nothing is wasted, as confirmed by Odette who watched her father kill the pigs every winter in her childhood village of Montrozier.

Odette remembers how she used to help with the various preparations, notably the ham. This was done by the *cantou*, the characteristic fireplace large enough for people to sit in. The ham would first be covered with ashes and then left to dry for an entire year, dangling from a hook. The choice pieces of the pork would be offered as gifts to the village priest and minister, to the two schoolmasters who taught respectively in the state- and church-run schools, to the postman, and to the nuns. Monsieur le Maire was excluded from the list, as were the village doctor and the *notaire* who belonged to a different social class, usually referred to as *notables*, although in Montrozier, according to Odette, only the landlords of the *château* were defined as such. These happen to be the offspring of the industrialist and philanthropist Maurice Fenaille, a friend of Rodin's and a patron of the Louvre among other museums. He also founded the Musée Fenaille in Rodez, where works of art from the Rouergue are on display on beautiful premises, starting with a superb collection of Celtic menhir statues, the largest in France.

Today, there are strict regulations and all animals must be killed in an abattoir, but the traditional killing by bleeding is still carried out privately by some. One of these, the sparkling 83-year-old Georges Souyri, whose "R's" roll out of his mouth like a drill, was sincerely disappointed that I was leaving the next evening and would be missing the opportunity to watch him in action the following week. I reassured him that being a spineless city dweller, I very much doubted that I would have enjoyed the occasion, especially having visited the Musée des Traditions du Sud Aveyron, by Cornus, where village life in the early 20th century is created through a variety of scenes which include the killing of a pig. The poor creature and its three executioners were so true to life that the scene made my stomach turn, which is the greatest compliment to Yves and Agnès Calvetti, the dreamers, founders and owners of the museum, whose only resources are their passion for their project and their amazing talent. Despite their restricted means, their museum can hold a candle to Madame Tussaud's in London or the Musée Grévin in Paris. Nestling on the pastoral hills of southern Aveyron, it is set up in a beautifully converted *bergerie* (sheepfold), a worthwhile destination even for those travelling without children.

Because my chance meeting with the Aveyron has brought me into contact with rural life, the food chain is often on my mind. No matter what locals claim, I find it hard to believe that when a pig is held down with its feet tied up and is about to be killed, it is less scared than a prisoner about to be executed. No doubt I am a hypocrite, since I do relish all the specialities mentioned above and have never considered becoming a vegetarian. This does not stop me from feeling uncomfortable about my own contradictions and the intrinsic perversity that is part and parcel of living.

Henri Dardé's mother, another old-timer from *la France profonde*, had no such inner struggles when she grabbed the older of her two roosters, turned it upside down, tied up its feet, stuffed it into a wooden funnel with its head sticking out, then chopped it off the way you would grind coffee in an old-fashioned grinder. It took several seconds, which seemed an eternity, before I registered the sinister drama that had just been played out on the silver screen. I think it eventually clicked when I sensed everyone around me collectively hold their breath. This was in the Latin Quarter and we were watching *La Vie comme elle va*, which won its director, Jean-Henri Meunier, several awards including one at the film festival of Los Angeles. When Simone Dardé's dog lapped the oozing blood of the slain rooster with evident pleasure, and we, the frozen audience, started to cringe, she had the good idea of creating unintentional comic relief by stating that this way he wouldn't pester the other one anymore! No doubt about that! Her comment, uttered in absolute earnest, provoked a general uproar of laughter in the cinema.

It was early evening by the time Georges Souyri took us round the flowery garden of his farm at La Roque, sitting on one of the hills surrounding Najac. It was a blessed moment: the sun having just begun to withdraw, the air was bracing and a cloud of aroma rose from his patch of chives. Facing us in the distance, the houses of Najac closed ranks at the foot of its studpendous château, the ultimate medieval perched village. The wrinkles on Georges's face were like the rings on the trunk of a tree, beautiful, dignified and charged with the wisdom of a long life of communion with nature. Everything else about him exuded the vitality of inexhaustible youth combined with

109

the serene contentment of autumnal years. I contemplated whether his farm might not be the very spot that inspired the saying *heureux comme Dieu en France*.

Najac's railway station lives to the same seasonal rhythm as the Belle Rive. Except for the summer months, when traffic intensifies somewhat, Arnaud Barre, the *chef de gare*, spends much of the day dozing in his office, comfortably settled by the stove with his feet on the desk. In between he makes himself a cup of coffee, sells the odd train ticket, cleans the window panes after a fashion, and throws an occasional bucketful of water over the red geranium in the window boxes — just enough to allow the flowers to make it through the summer (last time I saw them, however, it looked as though Arnaud had given up on watering them). It's not Arnaud's fault if Najac receives little traffic and leaves him idle. The nightly Carmaux-Paris stops here at 10.45pm, by which time the station is deserted and Arnaud is fast asleep in his own bed, all the more so as he will have to be up in time to meet the 6.30am Paris-Carmaux the next morning. At least in theory. When I arrived there once in late August, the station was locked and there was no sign of Arnaud. I gather his presence is optional. The train leaves Paris's Gare d'Austerlitz at 10.24pm, and if you can put up with sharing a shortish night with other travellers in a sleeper, it's a great start for a *France profonde* experience because, without any transition, you are snatched from the noise and fumes of Paris and catapulted into rural exoticism at the other end.

Occasionally, those alighting here may notice Arnaud's relaxed, lackadaisical manner and begin to wonder about their own senseless lives in the harassing city. The odd one might even have fantasies about trying an alternative route. If he or she were to push as far as the Mairie, up in the village, and take a look through the past censuses, they would discover that Najac holds the secret to an enviable quality of life. For it transpires from those figures that it's not just the Aveyron, but Najac in particular, that holds some impressive records of longevity. When I first visited Najac, several of its residents were over 95. The late Céline who had once worked as *secrétaire de Mairie* was 104 when she made a remarkable appearance in Jean-Henri Meunier's film. The village is led by France's senior and veteran mayor, the above-mentioned Hubert Bouyssières, who is 87 and has been in office uninterruptedly since 1946, after spending World War II in the Resistance, which he abstains from mentioning. Heroes are often silent.

On every other topic, however, Monsieur le Maire is quite loquacious. He is also a solid cook, judging by the impressive dinner that accompanied our first meeting, which he served me at one of the children's tables in the school *cantine*, located in the Mairie. Actually, the Ecole de la République and the private Catholic school share the same space; the low number of children in Najac does not warrant two canteens. Nor two schools either, for that matter. However, in a country that perceives the separation between church and state as fundamental to the fulfillment of the Revolutionary principles of equality and liberty, offering the citizen the choice between state-run and church-run schools is perceived as a fundamental right. They are referred to significantly as *l'Ecole républicaine* (or *de la République*) and *l'Ecole libre*.

Rows of empty coat pegs were nailed to the *cantine* walls at child height, suggesting a lively bustle at other times of day, and probably a different kind of menu from the one I was served by Monsieur le Maire, which was an uninterrupted flow of *jambon, saucisson, pâté, foie gras, confit de canard, plateau de fromage, tarte aux fruits*, and plenty of red wine. When we finally paused, Monsieur Bouyssières disappeared briefly and returned with a saxophone and a beaming face which soon combined into a flow of French oldies and other favourite tunes, leaping up and down together with his dancing fingers. Eventually he put down his sax and treated me to an outpour of old French love songs. As his twinkling eyes looked into mine, they seemed to suggest that we outsiders were more than just tolerated '*êtres humains*' but were actually most welcome. As a matter of fact, Monsieur Bouyssières was among the first Aveyronnais to encourage tourism and took an audacious step back in 1976, when he opened a holiday camp in Najac, catering predominantly to the Dutch. When the villagers protested against his initiative, he ignored them and even established a direct railway line between Najac and Amsterdam. I enquired whether it hadn't been a tough battle, but he just shrugged his shoulders philosophically, '*bof! les chiens aboient, la caravane passe.*'

I was struck by Najac's quick air as soon as I got out of the car on my first visit. When I started browsing through the pages of its history, I found out that Najac had always been famous for its healthy air. Even in the Middle Ages, when the whole of Europe was being decimated by the plague, Najac stood on its rock unaffected. In 1458 the Seneschal of Rouergue wished to transfer his seat from plague-ridden Villefranche to Najac, offering the town a golden opportunity to boost its economy and political status. Najac's Consuls, however, spent their time arguing over petty logistics and the project never materialised. In 1490 Louis XI transferred the Seneschal's seat to Rodez, relegating Najac to the fringes of history owing to a lack of vision on the part of its leaders. The plague did break out in Najac eventually, but only once, in the 17th century.

Whether it is the healthy air or the overall quality of life that attracted them, a good number of outsiders have settled in Najac in recent years. Some arrived here by chance, fell under the spell or 'caught the bug', kept coming back and eventually made the jump. Today they are fully-fledged Najacois, often young parents, which is very good news for an ageing village. Thérèse, a nurse from the Gard who arrived here in poor health is now reborn and blossoming. Stéphane and Stéphanie came from Paris and set up an internet company in conjunction with the village bookshop. Isabelle Aronovitz, also a Parisian, is in charge of the *château* and is a knowledgeable and exciting guide. Olivier the village pharmacist — and sunshine personified — is the one Aveyronnais among them, although he too is an outsider, born and bred in the cathedral city of Rodez.

Jean-Henri Meunier and Katlène arrived here in 1996, when Kenji was six and Mensah was nine months old. Their flat in Paris near the Buttes-Chaumont was a small rented place, but with property in the area selling for FF 15,000 per m² at the time, becoming a home owner in Paris was unthinkable. Over here they were offered a 2,500m² patch of paradise for FF 1.2 per m², which came with a Brigadoon-like view of the *château*, and the silver morning mist around it as a further bonus. The ruins that came with the plot of land have meanwhile been restored into an atomospheric, woodsy home, hanging with excellent paintings, acquired from friends and acquaintances. Sign of the times — Jean-Henri and Katlène are entirely French. The foreign names they've given their children reflect their openness to other cultures.

Henri Sauzeau, a neighbour and a close friend of the Meuniers, has a different story to tell about Najac. Admittedly, times were different when he arrived here in 1954 without a penny to his name. A few months earlier, on Christmas Eve 1953, he was thrown out of his native, warring Indo-China with just one hour's notice. The people of Najac — an insular community in those days — did not welcome the 'Chinaman', heedless of the fact that he was as French as any of them and descended from a noble family in the Poitou. China or no China, fifty years ago even a French Poitevin was a stranger in the remote cul-de-sac of Najac. Let alone a Brit! Yet by the late 1960s history was gathering speed and our planet was beginning to shrink. It was not the people of Najac who were expanding their horizons (other than their Mayor), but the outside world who came to them, thanks notably to BBC Bristol, whose wonderful 75-minute coverage of Najac's village life in 1972 was soon followed by the first British harbingers. As many as 78 houses in Najac and its outskirts (the *commune*) are now owned by UK nationals, 9 by Dutch, 3 by Belgians, 1 by Swiss, 1 by Danes, 1 by Germans, and even 1 by Americans. This makes a total of 94 houses, an impressive figure considering the overall number of its inhabitants, 744 according to the last census, in 1999.

Italian-born Lorena too arrived here in the late 1960s and was hardly more welcome than Henri Sauzeau, but she carried on with her business unperturbed when the villagers called her '*l'omelette*'. Her trattoria restaurant, Il Cappello, with a wonderful outdoor eating space in the leafy garden, serves the kind of crunchy pizzas we used to enjoy in Italy back in the late 1950s. And unlike most restaurants in the Aveyron, she stays open late at night and all year round. No doubt Najac has opened up since her arrival. At the Four du Pain Suspendu, under recent British ownership, locals gather for theme dinners that honour the world's diversity of culinary traditions. Even Burn's Night was celebrated here in January 2007, with the backing of a few local Scots. Apparently the chef of the Belle Rive likes to drop in for the homemade cakes which owners Peter and Bridget Dickson serve with their afternoon tea.

Despite the new blood, Najac remains an inconvenient cul-de-sac, bypassed by fast-speed trains. The Paris-Carmaux night train is threatened with closure and locals intend to put up a resistance, should this be implemented. The line may well be unprofitable, but it will be a terrible shame if the pleasure of alighting at Najac's sleepy little station soon after dawn is denied holiday makers.

Najac had a more privileged position in Gallo-Roman times, close to the major road that connected Segodunum (Rodez) and Divona (Cahors). Although no archeological clues have been unearthed to confirm the presence of Romans, names ending with 'ac' point to a Roman heritage (as names ending with 'jouls' are of Celtic origin). Besides, several of the area's medieval roads can actually be traced back to the Roman occupation, such as Najac-Rodez via Souloumiac (now La Fouillade) and Rieupeyroux. In all probability, too, the beautiful medieval bridge of St-Blaise which spans the Serène, south of Najac, stands on the site of an older Roman one that connected the two sections of a secondary road joining the well-known Cahors-Albi route further south. Some thousand years later the pilgrimage to Compostela set Europe in motion. Travelling through the Rouergue, the *Via Podiensis* headed west beyond Conques, towards Cahors and Moissac, whilst the less travelled *Cami de l'Espanhia* made its way south to Najac, where pilgrims found shelter at the Hôpital St-Jacques, under the tutelage of the Dômerie of Aubrac. Heading south beyond Najac over the bridge of St-Blaise, the road turned west past Varen and St-Antonin (now in the *departement* of the Tarn), and continued on to the Garonne Valley, where it turned south once more.

Lou Cami de l'Espanhia is hardly remembered by the modern pilgrim, and never mentioned on tourist brochures, and yet the connection between Najac and Conques goes all the way back to the fateful year of 866, when the monk Ariviscus (or Arosnide), who stole the relics of St Foy from Agen, made home with his trophy by way of Najac, which lay on the only existing road between Agen and Conques. Although Conques was the main beneficiary of the robbery, Najac enjoyed some of the windfalls. It is interesting that the first written mention of Najac is to be found in the *Livre des miracles de Ste Foy de Conques*, which is in fact a history of Conques written between the 9th and 11th centuries.

The story reports that one of Najac's lords was captured and chained in a dark den under the careful watch of seven jailers. Since Ste Foy's 'speciality' was to work miracles in favour of unjustly taken prisoners, she responded to the lord's prayers and appeared before him. Although he couldn't see her in the darkness of the cell, he heard her voice urging him to break loose of the chains. At first he was skeptical, but since he had nothing to lose he thought he might as well give it a try, and to his surprise found himself unfettered and free to take to the nearby woods before his jailers had time to notice his escape. Protected by the thicket and the night, he made his way to Conques where he offered his broken chains to the revered saint before retracing his steps to Najac. Among the extraordinary jumble of scenes on the Last Judgement tympanum of Conques, the keen observer will spot a carving of Ste Foy in action, severing the chains of a fortunate prisoner. Although she is mostly associated with Conques, she was just as fervently worshipped in Najac into the 19th century.

Today the historical connection between Najac and Conques (and Aubrac, for that matter) is forgotten; nor does the modern pilgrim pass through *lou Cami de l'Espanhia* and Najac. But the people of Najac do celebrate the famous fouace, which they believe originated in their village, although it may well have been introduced to Najac by travelling pilgrims coming from Aubrac. Be that as it may, come St Bartholomew's Day, in late August, a gigantic 40-kilo *fouace* makes its way down the village aboard a decorated float surrounded by cheery music bands, a merry occasion that closes at night with a traditional *bal-musette*.

Bearing in mind that the heyday of the Compostela pilgrimage was over by the 13th century, the majority of pilgrims who passed through Najac did not see its emblematic *château* but an earlier more modest construction over which the present 13th-century *château* was rebuilt. The red limestone of its lower parts and of the square tower belong to the older castle and contrast with the grey schist that was used the second time round to make it more resistant. Rising out of the lofty granite rock at the edge of a promontory, it affords breathtaking views extending as far as the Pyrénées on a clear day. It also provides Najac with that crowning picture-postcard setting that has won

117

it the '*un des plus beaux villages de France*' designation. Way below, the loop of the Aveyron acts as a moat on three of its sides. To the modern-day traveller this translates into the pleasure of a magnificent panorama; to its one-time occupants it offered a unique strategic position, flanked by the hillside on the one side and at the same time leaving no room for a battering ram in front of its gate. Thus it stood against the skyline, erect, proud and impregnable. Only treachery and famine might have rendered it vulnerable, but the threat of treachery was removed by an ingenious design that made it impossible to infiltrate unnoticed. The height of the steps, their angle at each landing, the height of the ceilings, the positioning of the loopholes were all ingeniously designed so as to thwart any would-be assailant.

The castle is now owned privately by Monsieur de Montalivet, who took upon himself to bring it back to life, together with the nearby splendid Cistercian Abbey of Loc-Dieu. Besides the horrendous costs incurred by Monsieur de Montalivet, it must have been a daredevil exercise for those who carried out the restoration suspended above a vertiginous void. Happily, it has only been partially restored and retains the romantic poetry conferred on all ruins by the erosion of time. More such ruins can be seen at Peyrusse-le-Roc, an easy outing from Najac, past Villefranche-de-Rouergue and Villeneuve, then on along the D40 towards Naussac. The D87, to your right before Naussac, will take you to the drowsy little village which crowns the hilltop with its roseate hues (hence Peyrusse, red stone).

Nothing in the village itself hints at the presence of a ghost town on the back flank of the hill, the remnants of a sizeable medieval town of 3,000 inhabitants, comparable to Conques and Najac. So when, with no forewarning, the spectres of old Petrucia* launched the stupendous ruins of its lower castle out of the wooded precipice, I was all but knocked over in disbelief. Further enchantment was provided by ivy-wrapped vestiges nestling along the steep path amidst a makeshift arrangement of crosses meant as a recreation of the stations of the cross. It was a strenuous climb that led back to the village, past a second castle, confirming the former glory of Peyrusse.

Later, I found out that the town had shifted hands between the Houses of Aquitaine and Toulouse before falling into those of France. There was even a leper hospital down in the valley, and a sizable church, and a synagogue too, tucked discreetly in the rock like some pirate's den. Later still I found out about a blossoming economy drawing a handsome revenue for two hundred years from the nearby silver and lead mines. When the mines were exhausted in the 14th century, Peyrusse had nothing to offer its people other than small-scale farming. Rapid decline followed, as it did in Conques once the momentum of the pilgrimage subsided.

It was during a heatwave in early July that I first came to Peyrusse, while touring with Sylvie. It was late in the afternoon but the sun was still pounding at us mercilessly, forcing us into the cool dark shelter of the village church. My attention was drawn to a series of wall paintings and the carvings on the wooden altar. They seemed to bear the distinct stamp of the same bold and sensitive hand, combining the incisiveness of primitive art with gentle roundness and a dreamy expression. The artist's name was unfamiliar to me as yet: Hervé Vernhes... but Sylvie's eyes brightened with recognition. This was the

---

* The ancient name of Peyrusse-le-Roc

man behind the arts-and-crafts holidays that first brought her and Daniel to the Aveyron.

It was nearly six o'clock when we came out of the church, but the sun was still blazing ruthlessly and the empty square was in a state of torpor. There was no sign of life other than an invisible hammering sound somewhere. Without really thinking about it, I started walking in its direction like some wound up mechanical doll. Perhaps it was simple curiosity, although I am inclined to believe I was led there by some mysterious necessity. And sure enough there he was, with his grandfatherly face, seated in the shade of an ancient wall above the precipitous valley, chiselling a block of stone with his powerful hands. An acquaintance, disciple or fan was standing next to him loosely engaged in a conversation. I joined in timidly, a sentence here, a question there, when all of a sudden the church bell barged in peremptorily to mark the seventh hour. Beyond was silence and hills.

On the opposite side of the valley lay Hervé Vernhes's childhood farm, where his brother still lives. Twice daily the boy would drag his wooden *sabots* between home and school, down one steep slope and up the other, through the stony soil and hitherto unearthed ruins of ancient Petrucia. Who remembers today, and who will remember in the future, that it was Hervé's idea to bring Petrucia back to the living? Who will remember the outdoor theatre he created among the ruins, thanks to which Peyrusse was alive with crowds of visitors every summer? That was in the 1970s when Sylvie met him, before the premature passing of his beloved Francine who had created the costumes for their productions. Hervé Vernhes belongs to the brotherhood of sacred anonymity, whose members have deposited a tiny legacy of emotions in the stone of the Rouergue, be it on menhir statues, a cross, a church, or elsewhere, then carried their names into oblivion upon departure. I have yet to visit the Château de Gironde above the Lot valley, where Hervé claims to have left his best preserved work (he complained to me about the dampness in the church of Aubrac). Old Petrucia might have been excavated anyway, but it is thanks to Hervé that I discovered it that evening.

Sylvie had an errand to tend to and left me with Hervé for a while. Towards the end of the conversation he urged me to go and see the old ruins, promising me a uniquely romantic scenery, and walked me down the dusty path to the beginning of the site. We parted ways at the foot of the upper castle, after which I continued downhill, weaving my way through the stations of the cross in the reverse, then up the ladder of the sheer Roc del Taluc for a breathtaking view in company of the two surviving square towers of the one-time mighty lower castle. Evening was falling fast as I hurried past the synagogue, then the church and the hospital. By the time I reached the bottom of the valley, the shadows of night had crept out of the wooded banks of the Audierne and got the better of the sun.

Unlike Peyrusse, the *château* of Najac was in perfectly good order up until the French Revolution. It was not the wind or the rain that brought about its ruin, but the people of Najac themselves who plundered it throughout the 19th century, using its stones to build their own homes, with the blessing of the *château*'s new proprietor.

Like Peyrusse, Najac was eyed by all, perhaps even more so because of its unique strategic position. Competition was rife in the Rouergue between the Counts of Toulouse and the

Bishops of Rodez, but in Najac it was Raymond IV of Toulouse who had the upper hand, making it the seat of the local administration when he bought it in 1076. However, it seems that Najac was lost to the English in the 12th century, when much of western France went to Henry Plantagenet, together with its fair lady, Eleanor. Her son Richard Lionheart is reported to have had a meeting in Najac with the King of Aragon.

The Counts of Toulouse were soon back, but by the middle of the 13th century a new peril loomed in the distant north — the House of France. Patiently, the Queen Mother Blanche de Castille set out to spin a web in which Toulouse would eventually be entangled, then squashed. Using the threads of matrimony, she married Alphonse de Poitiers, her younger son and brother of Louis IX (St Louis), to Jeanne, the only child and daughter of Raymond VII of Toulouse. The 1229 Meaux-Paris Treaty stipulated that should Jeanne survive the Count but die childless, the domain of Toulouse would go to France. In other words, the treaty recognized *de facto* the suzerainty of the French crown. The fate of Toulouse was sealed: It was only a matter of a couple of moves before he would be checkmated.

Alphonse was now the next in line to inherit both domain and title, which occurred in 1249, upon the death of his father-in-law, Raymond VII. The invaluable *château* of Najac, sitting on its elevated promontory, was part of the deal. Some 2,000 men were brought over from all over the kingdom of France to rebuild the castle in a style exported from the north, which helped reinforce the new political order. Among the features that strike the modern visitor are the 6.8m-long loopholes that could be used simultaneously by two or three archers, the longest in Europe. Alphonse de Poitiers spared no effort to intimidate his foes. The sculpted heads of St Louis, Alphonse de Poitiers and Jeanne set in the corbels on the ground level of the keep may add a pleasing decorative touch to the overall austere architecture, but they should first be read as a political statement. They corroborate in the stone the definitive merger between the two houses, to the benefit of the French Crown.

The struggle over the coveted region of south west France was at the root of its phenomenal urban development during the 13th and the better part of the 14th centuries. Some 600 'new towns' (*bastides*) were built, 300 of which have survived on an area extending from the foothills of the Pyrenees to the Massif Central, corresponding to 14 of today's *départements*. In the Aveyron this occurred only in the western part, where the disputed territory lay. As each protagonist tried to extend his own domain at the expense of his neighbour, he would found a new *bastide* on or as close as possible to the boundary he had in mind. Furthermore, by securing the prosperity of the *bastides*, their founders gained the support of their new settlers, which in turn reinforced their position *vis-à-vis* the local lords, the other rivalling force to be reckoned with. To complete the manoeuvre, they shifted the administrative and judiciary apparatus to the *bastide*, thus keeping the local lords under their thumb. What better way of securing their own popularity than by allowing a plaintiff to win a case against his local lord?

Raymond VII of Toulouse set the tone in 1222, when he built Cordes (now in the Tarn), close to Najac, which would later also become a *bastide*. In the Aveyron, the first *bastide* he built was Villeneuve, in 1231, which he envisaged as a defiant outpost on the far north confines of his domain, beyond which the determined Blanche de Castille lay in wait. Both attempts were admirable but futile, for without a male heir, his line was in its terminal phase.

Villeneuve took sixteen years to complete, providing a magnificent example of the characteristic *bastide* layout, with its north-south, east-west grid, which far from originating in America goes back to the Roman oppidum, perhaps even earlier. Similarly to the North American avenues, the warp of the city's fabric was made up of wider arteries for the passage of carts (*voies charettières*), crossed at right angles by narrower pedestrian alleys, the weft so to speak. Lining them were blocks of houses of equal size, providing from above the pleasing checkerboard effect which I had first viewed in Villefranche-de-Rouergue. The carriage-roads led to the public square, the hub of the town where everything and everyone converged. The beautifully preserved arcades (*couverts*) of La Place de Conques at Villeneuve, like those of Villefranche, were intended for the protection of wares. Close to 800 years later, they provided blissful protection to me, during the record temperatures of 2003.

The very attractive church of St-Sepulcre predates the founding of the *bastide* in its Romanesque parts. The 11th-century façade provides an example of the Romanesque style at its purest. Like the mother church in Jerusalem, the shape of a Greek cross was applied to the floor plan initially, but when Villeneuve expanded after the founding of the *bastide*, the church was enlarged in the southern Gothic style prevalent at the time and the present nave was substituted for the Greek cross. The new church, dedicated to St Pierre and St Paul, houses a cycle of wall paintings depicting the Compostela pilgrimage, which points to a secondary pilgrim route that travelled through Villeneuve. The paintings date from the early 14th century, by which time the pilgrimage had lost some of its momentum.

Raymond VII also provided a hospital for the inhabitants of Villeneuve. A Latin inscription has survived on one of its sculpted stones and reads: "Raymond, Count, gives this place to God and to the poor." His good intentions, however, were to no avail. In 1249, only three years after the completion of Villeneuve, he was gone (perhaps from poisoning) and superseded smoothly by his son-in-law Alphonse, according to the arrangement stipulated in the Meaux-Paris Treaty. It would be another 22 years before Alphonse and Jeanne died, both in 1271, following which the domain of Toulouse fell into the lap of the kingdom of France. Needless to say, the circumstances of Jeanne's death were never elucidated.

In 1252, barely three years after Raymond VII's passing, Alphonse set out to build his own *bastide*, Villefranche-de-Rouergue. Choosing the northern bank of the Aveyron, Villefranche was meant to defend the border with English-ruled Aquitaine, the other major player in these parts. But it was also meant as a display of power at the doorstep of Najac, the rebellious neighbour 24km to the south, whose inhabitants had been incited by the local lords to mourn the passing of Raymond VII, although he had died in the remote town of Millau. Two hundred people, including the town's officials, had gathered on the public square of Najac, crying, "We are all dead because the Lord Count is dead." Furthermore, Najac's flirtation with the Cathari heresy, no matter how mild, presented a political threat to Alphonse, for over and above their religious dissension, the Cathari were fighting for the preservation of an independent Occitania in southern France, with the House of Toulouse at its head. This is why the Meaux-Paris Treaty had tied the ending of the Crusade against the Albigenians (the Cathari) with the marriage of the Count's daughter Jeanne to Louis IX's brother Alphonse de Poitiers and the above mentioned arrangement. Moreover, several Occitanian estates were ceded to the French Crown as part of the package.

The area that now came under the jurisdiction of Alphonse had been trampled and bled by successive waves of crusaders, often no better than blood-seeking ruffians. First those headed for the Holy Land, then those led by Simon de Montfort against the Albigenians, who were hardly more civilised. Opinions vary as to whether Simon de Montfort actually took the castle of Najac, although it is believed he did take Peyrusse. After his death at the siege of Toulouse, on 25 June 1218, apparently by the hand of a woman who threw a stone at him, his son Amaury continued the holy war of extermination of the Cathari with the blessing of both King and Pope. Raymond VII having sided with the Cathari, their annihilation contributed to weakening his position. He should have known better, for his father Raymond VI had been excommunicated by the Pope for supporting the heresy. Although the Cathari considered themselves Christians, the Pope would not sanction their doctrine of Dualism, which placed God and Satan on an equal footing as the two forces governing the universe. The Pope was at least as alarmed at the prospect of losing a considerable income, since the Cathari refused to pay the tithe.

Alphonse's Villefranche was meant to steal the show from Najac and become the new administrative seat of the province. It outstripped Najac in size and was intended to become a thriving economic hub, hence the choice of its site at a prominent junction of both rivers and roads and in the vicinity of silver and copper mines. For besides their political and strategic role, the *bastides* were built as a socio-economic venture at a time of phenomenal and, as yet, unexplained population explosion, which the Black Plague would take care of the following century... Legions of homeless vagrants roamed and plundered the devastated countryside, constituting a source of instability and insecurity. An incentive was needed that would be attractive enough to coax them into bartering the freedom procured by anarchy for the constraints of a social code. The *bastide* with its promise of economic prosperity was meant to play that role.

Alphonse offered to enfranchise the willing new citizens of Villefranche as stated in its name, and went as far as to grant them the privilege of property ownership. Remarkably egalitarian in spirit, the *bastide* was divided up into equal allotments (another reason why the grid layout proved convenient), doubled by a second allotment on the periphery of town to be used as kitchen gardens. 50% of the proceeds went to Alphonse, as did the local taxes. In other words, the *bastide* venture benefited everyone, both its new citizens and its founder, who recouped his initial investment in no time and turned it into a handsome profit.

Further profits were derived from the taxes levied on wares traded by outsiders, which the *bastide*'s residents were exempted from (as also reflected in the name 'Villefranche'). This privilege too was an effective incentive to lure the shifting population back to town, where they were also granted exemption from the tax on the making of bread — *banalité* — (hence the *four banal*, the old village ovens you may come across during your meanderings). In return, the new citizens had to comply with the regulations of the Charter of Customs. It was reinforced by the four Consuls, elected once a year by the male heads of each household.

The Charter dealt with every aspect of local life, from the hygenic supervision of animals and meat to adultery, which was viewed as disruptive to the public order. In order for a charge of adultery to be filed against a male offender, he would have to be caught with his pants down by at least two of the Consul's agents. Other than being fined, the culprits would be made to run in the nude through the streets of the *bastide*, which was obviously an embarrassment, but at least it showed a more egalitarian spirit than the one prevailing in hell where, if we go by the tympanum of Conques, the adulterous female alone was exhibited topless. Prostitution, on the other hand, was handled with characteristic ambivalence, as an evil necessary to the social order. Thus, provision was made for a loophole by way of a bordello inside the *bastide*, but at a discreet location. However, once the women had rendered their daily services, they were chased out of town for the night like pariahs.

Contrary to Villefranche, the *bastides* of Villeneuve and Najac were grafted onto existing towns, clustering around and protected by a church (*sauveté*) in the case of Villeneuve, and a *château* (*castrum*) in the case of Najac. The rugged topography of Najac did not lend itself to a grid fabric, and a ribbon development was laid out instead along the promontory's crest. Only the section of the high street that opens up into a small plateau was wide enough to accomodate a triangular market place where the old fountain still stands. Having panted my way up the hill many a time, I can understand why Alphonse de Poitiers chose to let Najac be superseded by Villefranche, where shopping is so much more convenient (other than finding a parking space...). Alphonse's main concern in Najac was political and strategic, rather than economic, which is why he focused on the rebuilding of the *château* as a preventive measure against further rebellious attempts.

The new construction and its stupendous height were designed to serve as an omnipresent reminder of his invincible power and an unequivocal warning not to mess with him. Building began in 1253, barely a year after Villefranche. It was an ambitious project, embellished by unexpected dainty touches, such as the curly-headed cherubs in the Gothic chapel situated in the keep, or its leafy carvings inspired by the surrounding vegetation of oak and chestnut. And since Najac had been involved with the Cathari heresy, two representatives of the Inquisition arrived here in 1258, to negotiate some form of retribution. They belonged to the Dominican Order which had been established by the Inquisistion specifically to extirpate the Cathari heresy.

In comparison with what your average victim of the Inquisition had to endure well into the 19th century, Najac escaped quite lightly, mainly with fines and some sort of 'community work' on behalf of the church. Several sinners were ordered to make a pilgrimage to various destinations, including Rodez, Rocamadour, Compostela, St-Denis north of Paris, Rome, and as far as Jerusalem in one case. Having recently travelled to Rocamadour, I can think of much worse punishments, especially as it is so close by. Only one citizen, Hug Paraire, was sentenced to be burnt at the stake, probably to set an example because he was one of the town's four Consuls.

The rest of the town got away with collective penance and was made to pay for the construction of a new church that was vast enough to hold the entire congregation of Najac — 4,000 at its peak. From now on there would be only one faith, observed by all, in one House of God, at least so until the 16th century when Najac, like the rest of the Aveyron, had to contend with the alarming spread of the Reformation. Incidentally, the basilica of the Sacré Coeur in Paris was also built as an expiatory monument, the offenders there being both the Paris bourgeoisie who had erected a temple of sin in the Palais Garnier Opera House and the working classes who had committed an even greater sin by rioting against that very same bourgeoisie which represented the social order. Both in Paris and in Najac gigantism was the order of the day for all to see, be humbled and embraced by.

The Knights Templar would not come off so lightly, Philip the Fair having schemed to wipe out the Order and lay hands on their wealth. All the Templars of the Rouergue were brought to Najac in 1307 and thrown into the *château*'s prison, there to await their sham trial and perish by fire. Few escaped.

The church of St-Jean still stands below the castle, but the town has since shrunk to the size of a village, and the number of regular churchgoers has dwindled in recent years. Although the Aveyron is deeply steeped in Catholicism, its younger residents attend mass sporadically, as do the French in general. Saturday evening mass is still celebrated here weekly, but Sunday mass is celebrated in rotation with other villages, except in July and August, when Najac receives the surplus of 30,000 holidaymakers, some of whom like to attend mass. The rest of the time the church is kept locked to prevent burglaries under the committed care of black-haired, black-eyed Guy Tourette, a proud Najacois from father to son, as he likes to stress at the beginning of the tour. Erect and solid like the granite of the *château*'s rock, his thundering voice resonates in forceful staccato through the austere edifice as he tells its story to visitors, alas, only in French. He is so much at one with the surroundings that I would have never guessed he'd been abroad, let alone in Africa, where his military career had taken him. He is one of those Aveyronnais with such a marked identity that they seem sealed off from the outside world. Yet, scratch a little beneath the surface of their rocky soil, talk to them about their life story, and you will be surprised how many of them have actually tasted other parts of the world before returning to harbour, because there is no place like home. All the more so when home happens to be the residence of the gods.

Chapter 6

INTERLUDE: OLD VERSUS NEW

Not in my wildest dreams would I have imagined Myriam working for the insurance company Axa. Her raven-black hair and charcoal eyes burnt with the same aboriginal fire as those of Sébastien Persec and Guy Tourette, with an added hint of mysticism. She evoked a straight-haired, more contained version of Gina Lollobrigida in Christian-Jaque's 1952 swashbuckler *Fanfan la Tulipe*, drawing cards outside her caravan (Later I found out that this very scene was shot in the Averyon, at La Couvertoirade of which more later). Myriam's simple rustic house, standing amidst the jumble of an unmanicured garden in the middle of nowhere seemed just right for a would-be gypsy. It turned out that my intuition had not been misguided and that she had indeed been immersed in astrology and fortunetelling since her childhood, and also paints in her spare time. Assuming her job at Axa's was just her bread and butter, I was surprised she actually enjoyed working in finance. She may be steeped in the esoteric and the archaic, but she is no less connected to the economic and political reality of today. In her younger days, she had worked as an air hostess because she wanted to travel the world. In other words, she embodies that distinctive fusion between the mystery of ancientness and down-to-earth modernity I come across so often in the Aveyron.

Whilst driving through the Aubrac during the searing *canicule* of July 2003, my heart went out to the pathetic-looking cattle that scraped for food on the desolate yellow

earth that bore no trace whatsoever of the little patch of
Connemara I remembered from earlier visits. Suddenly I
noticed a huge dark mass, crouching inert on the parched
ground. I cannot say why it made me start with revulsion and
sent a mysterious charge of terror down my spine. I hadn't
even yet realised that the primeval-looking shape was a bull,
very much alive. Myriam was not in the least surprised by my
reaction, which corroborated her notion that the bull is
emblematic of the untameable forces of nature onto which our
collective psyche projects its fears. Seen in this light, the
bullfight is magnified into a sacred and sacrificial *pas de deux*,
danced significantly on a circular stage and ending, hopefully,
in the cathartic death of the animal. To me, this translated into
simple mathematics: 6 dead bulls per session, 6 sessions per
week, 15 weeks per year, make a total of 90 dead bulls per year
in Nîmes alone, where Myriam was born and bred, although
she is a pure Aveyronnaise. But in Myriam's paintings the
contrasting mysterious, mighty darkness of the bull and the
vivid red mantle of the matador symbolise the eternal
dichotomy between shadow and light.

How far a cry from the world created by earthy Christine,
who splashes on her canvas thick layers of fiery hues inspired by
the luminous landscape of her native Causse Comtal, outside
the spectacular village of Bozouls. Perched above a red chasm
famously dubbed '*le trou de Bozouls*' ('the Hole of Bozouls'),
the village stretches along its promontory at the end of which
an exquisite pink-stone Romanesque church has been standing
precariously since the 12th century. Its slanting pillars create
an astonishing effect, but point to the fact that they all but
collapsed due to the weight of the *lauze* tiles of its roof. A
stronger wooden framework and a lighter roof were provided in

the 17th century. Undeterred by the periodical floodings of the Dourdou, some of the villagers have taken up residence at the bottom of the 'hole', among them an American couple from California, who, to my surprise, had already bought their house back in the 1980s, when even fewer foreigners knew the area.

Christine went to school in Bozouls, but lived on a farm outside the village, where her family had lived off the land of the plateau for an unknown number of generations. She too had travelled the world, and the Gioacometti-like female silhouettes that inhabit her paintings were inspired by a trip to Africa. But it was the red-and-black explosion of energy that accompanied her depiction of New York that I was most taken with, astonished that someone from a remote rural area could be so at one with the vibrations of the ultimate metropolis.

I spent several days with Christine and her family in Talou, an old converted farmhouse surrounded by empty countryside. The only two other farms there, a couple of miles apart, belong respectively to her mother Marie and to Uncle Paulou. Talou now has a heavenly swimming pool where I swam late one afternoon, blissfully by myself because everyone had gone off to visit Conques. With no-one to distract me, I had all the leisure to take in the quasi abstract surrounding landscape, the stark fields and meadows, the sparse bushes and lone tree standing out against the clear sky, above all, the radiant light that Christine transposes to both her paintings and to her everyday life. At Talou, even a routine meal becomes a celebration of colour and light, which a few ordinary flowers picked off a bush help to enhance; or just a bunch of leaves put together on a napkin. Christine has the gift of turning something commonplace into an artistic display. Whilst we gathered under the pergola by the pool for our Sunday dinner, it was hard to believe that not so long ago, the adjoining bright kitchen, now stocked with Ikea utensils, had been the living quarters of the farm's pigs and chickens.

The juicy roast duck had been prepared and brought over by Christine's mother Marie. As soon as I saw it I had an uncomfortable feeling that it was one of the ducks I had seen waddling and quacking in her farmyard a couple of days earlier. Well obviously. Marie was not keeping ducks as an ornament. She explained that she killed them herself, with the same sort of funnel used by Simone Dardé from Najac. It may not be a pretty sight, but it's practical and quick, and besides, that's the way it's done in the countryside. Her brother Paulou accepts bullfighting just as readily: after all, the bull is given a chance to fight for his life and survive, which is a fairer deal than being led to the abattoir where no escape is possible. Myriam agrees, although of late she has shifted to painting the bulls of the Aubrac, so as not to upset certain sensitivities. Uncannily, she is following in the footsteps of her prehistoric ancestors who painted the auroch bull on the prehistoric cave walls of western France. A true Aveyronnais can never let go of the past. Note that one spectacular prehistoric cave is situated at Foissac, in western Aveyron, but it has no wall paintings.

The home of Myriam's ancestors, in the middle of nowhere and way back like Christine's, is situated on the plateau of Montbazen, just outside Goutrens. It is a quintessentially rural area, a few minutes' drive from the farm of Farrebique, the subject of Georges Rouquier's iconic film on rural life shot in 1945— *Farrebique Or The Four Seasons*. At that turning point of history, the film awakened the Aveyronnais' sense of identity and drew their Parisian community to the Opera House, where

▲ Espalion ©Patrice Geniez

©Patrice Geniez ▼

Fête de la St Fleuret, Estaing
©Patrice Geniez

▲ Conques, revealed ©Régine Combal, OT Conques

Conques at closer quarters ©OT Conques ▼

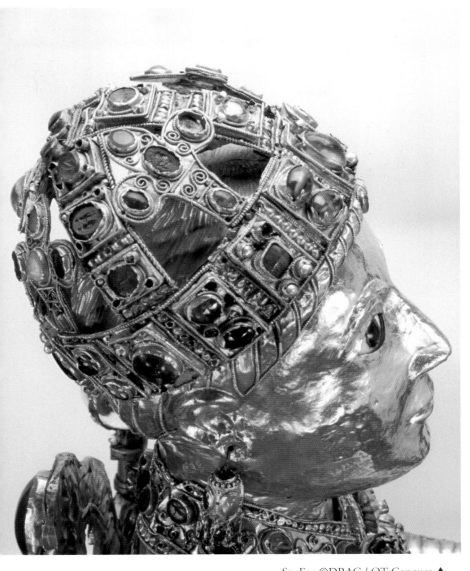

Ste Foy ©DRAC / OT Conques ▲

◄ Fête de la Ste Foy, Conques ©Thirza Vallois

Najac ©Philippe Larroque

▲ Valon ©Pierre Soisson

Blaise the Dragon ©Pierre Soisson ▼

Toulouse-Lautrec's nursery at the Château du Bosc
©Thirza Vallois

▲ Fête de la St Bourrou, Marcillac ©Thirza Vallois

Fête de la Fouace, Najac ©Thirza Vallois ▼

Market Day at Villefranche-de-Rouergue ©Giovanni Bertolissio

©Thirza Vallois ▼

▲ ©Thirza Vallois

Hubert Bouyssières, ▶
Monsieur le Maire of Najac
©Thirza Vallois

©Patrice Geniez ▼

▲ *Miséricordes*, Rodez Cathedral ©Thirza Vallois ▼

▲ The wine country by the Château de Panat ©Patrice Geniez

Philippe Teulier's father tending to the vines ©Patrice Geniez ▼

▲ Fête de la St Bourrou, Marcillac ©Patrice Geniez ▼

it ran for a record period of three months. The film was awarded the *prix de la critique internationale* at the 1946 Cannes Festival and the *Grand Prix du Cinéma Français*. The legendary Marcel Carné (director of *Les Enfants du paradis*) said that he came out of the screening 'shattered' and found the powerful lyricism of the spring scene particularly compelling. Indeed, the combination of black-and-white images and voiceover that portray nature's rebirth is a cinematic landmark :

> "*The torpor of winter has ceased; germination has begun; all the might of nature, contained within the earth for months, is now released. Life returns; the blood quickens in the arteries; the suck rises; the blood of men beats harder and harder; nature's buds burst open; finally, the walnut's little catkins herald the arrival of spring...*"

As the scene unfolds, the voiceover matches the camera's close-ups to better capture the throbbing of nature, the sprouting of new life, and finally the build-up of the season of love; the bees and the ladybirds; the swelling of buds, the opening of curved petals to the sun, the mating of sweet nectar and golden pollen. When finally all of nature pulsates in unison with the promise of rebirth, Henri's proposal to La Fabrette under the leafless tree the previous autumn is fulfilled against the dazzling blossoms of spring. Even if your French is non-existent, this spring scene alone merits a detour to the town of Rignac, where the local supermarket carries the videos and DVDs of the film.

Georges Rouquier chose Farrebique for his film because the owners were his cousins, which made it easier for him to spend a year on the farm and film the cycle of the four seasons. He first spent time there when he was three years old, during World War I, after his father had been killed in Verdun and his aunt and uncle took him in. In 1983, he returned to Farrebique once more to record its evolution over the intervening forty years. His second film also won him a prestigious prize, *le Prix special du Jury*, this time at the Venice Film Festival. The sequel was named *Biquefarre*, after the next-door farm that was sold off ten years earlier and torn down because, like in Najac and Conques, and everywhere in the Aveyron, the stones of the old farmhouse were recycled.

Life had changed dramatically by then: the ever-present team of oxen of the early film had given way to a tractor and in 1974 the younger brother —10-year-old Raymondou back in 1945 and now the head of the family — built a new charmless, modern bungalow next to the old farmhouse, the likes of which have proliferated since all over the Aveyron. Thank goodness he did not pull down the old stone farmhouse, even though nobody lives there any more and it is now merely a spectral memorial. But as long as it stands there is hope it may be brought back to life some day. When it was built in the 19th century, it had one storey. Later, Raymondou's grandfather added the upstairs where the entire household lived, sharing the same all-purpose living quarters which were reached through the external flight of steps, as was customary. There was a mud floor, no running water, no electricity and a single fireplace to keep everyone warm. Additional heat was provided by the animals, which spent the cold months downstairs, a makeshift substitute to underfloor heating during those harsh pre-global-warming winters.

By 1983, Farrebique had long been subject to the intrusion of the constant ringing of the telephone and the rattling of *deux-chevaux* cars which plied the surrounding country roads, repeatedly incorporated into the soundtrack of Rouquier's second film. One still attended mass in one's Sunday's best, but it seems that nobody gathered for evening prayers anymore, as had been daily practice in 1945. The solo part back then was performed by Grandmother, whose Rs drilled from her fast-moving lips as she told her beads, a continuous, unintelligible gurgle that bore not the faintest resemblance to French, nor to any variety of Occitan I am familiar with. Listening to Christine and her mother, who grew up in the same place, I was surprised how much people's accents had altered within one generation. Other things too had changed by 1983. Europe was groping its way towards unification and even the remote Aveyron was subjected to the laws of world markets. During a heated coversation about preferential meat tariffs between Britain and New Zealand, the more recent foe of the last several wars (read Germany) was swapped for the atavistic one — *'Ces salauds d'Anglais!'* ('These English bastards')— blurted by one of the farmers as a incontrovertible self-evidence. Small-scale farming was no longer viable in an economy bent on scrapping national borders. Money interests were creeping their way into the hidden corners of rural France, reshaping mentalities, sometimes poisoning relationships between hitherto steadfast friends. Land was becoming a profit-generating commodity and Biquefarre was coveted by profit-seeking predators. The early innocence was lost; man had lost his harmony with the seasons. The children continued to leave: Maria had retired to a convent in the earlier film, Marcel went to medical school in the second one.

It is a commonplace belief that rural France attempted its first leap into modernity only in the 1950s. As a matter of fact, the Aveyron had a mining infrastructure and a railway network back in the 19th century, as explained later, and agricultural machinery had been introduced in the 1930s, as were the hydroelectrical installations on the Truyère. The process of modernisation was embryonic at that stage, but if it hadn't been for World War II, it would have intensified and snowballed. When the Germans marched on the Aveyron in 1942, 8-year-old Jacques Moulay happened to be helping his grandmother push her cartful uphill. Watching the occupation army stamp its booted feet past him is a vision he is not likely to forget, even though the long-term economic repercussions of the Occupation escaped him at that young age.

By requisitioning their new machinery, the Germans forced the farmers to return to the old agrarian methods, setting rural France back by twenty to thirty years. Fortunately, the old discarded plough and cart were still lying around in the fields, or rusting away in some shed, and could be yoked once more to the oxen. The only sign of modernity in the earlier film was the arrival of electricity on the farm, to which, typically, the conservative Monsieur Rouquier had been opposed. Just as typically, it was his forward-looking wife that was determined to have it installed — it was so much more convenient than the old oil lamps. Needless to say, she ended up having her way.

In July 2003, it was my turn to visit Farrebique. Myriam drove me there from Valady, in the wine country of Marcillac, past the red sandstone village of Clairvaux. It was late afternoon, and when we reached the viewpoint of La Croix de Bel we got out of the car to soak up the patchwork scenery of vineyards, red hills and checkered green and yellow fields that reached out to the horizon. Here and there clusters of houses and farmsteads added variety to the picture; elsewhere sprinkles of golden buttercups embellished the green meadows. Occasionally the twitter of an unseen bird interrupted the silence, and a drift of undefinable fragrance distracted me from my daydreaming.

Eventually we started talking. Myriam spoke of ancestral roots, of her people's attachment to the land, and of the importance of being buried in the family tomb, the crucible where the passer-by of a moment is prolonged into infinity. In her family one still buys burial grants in perpetuity, a practice which city dwellers gave up decades ago. Her great aunts were still around in the late 1960s, when she was a little girl, and had carried over from the late 19th century the customs, dress, speech and manner of their own childhood. She remembered the winter gatherings round the *cantou*, the household's all-purpose single room with its mud floor, like the one in *Farrebique*; and the family's washing being taken to the river... also like in *Farrebique*, and all over rural France, as I witnessed myself in spring 1968, when we took a few days' break from the Latin Quarter's barricades and travelled in the Auvergne. Odette and her sister Denise told me about how they had to help their mother wash the sheets in the Aveyron which flows through Montrozier. We were in the kitchen at Las Canals, where they had been busying themselves since early morning, whilst the teenage generation sprawled in front of the television in the adjacent living/dining room, watching the Tour de France. There was no such thing as a 'couch potato' when Denise and Odette were growing up; everyone had to chip in with the constant stream of chores described in *Farrebique*.

We reached Farrebique by way of a narrow country road that wasn't even marked on my map, but was gloriously shaded by a bower of chestnut trees on the far edge of what felt like the world's end. Raymondou Rouquier greeted us with a shy smile, and with the weight of 60 additional years since the film was shot in 1946. Although he was younger than his sisters, as the only son the farm passed on to him, as was customary. It was hoped the girls would find a husband, for otherwise they would have to go into a convent or into service. In the film, Grandfather entrusts the boy with the task of turning Farrebique into, '*la plus belle ferme du pays*', but although Raymondou had managed to make ends meet and adjust to changing times, he was unable to fulfill Grandfather's dreams of glory. The sheep had to be done away with, because dairy cows are more productive, and no one rears pigs anymore, although the memory of those times is still vivid and prompted him to shift the conversation to the various pork specialities of the Aveyron. Within seconds his reserve was gone, and by the time he got to *fritons* (which, he explained with evident relish, are particularly delicious when seasoned with parsley and garlic), he had become quite unrecognisably animated. The wonderful thing about the French is that they can triple their gastronomic ecstasy through the processes of anticipation and recollection.

Although Farrebique did not become an award-winning venture, standards of living have risen for everyone since Grandfather's days. In the old days, the farmhouse was shared by all three generations (lower life expectancy made it unlikely for four generations to live under the same roof simultaneously), and the notion of privacy was an unheard of luxury. Today, every nucleus family aspires to own its independent living unit, and at the time of my visit, Raymondou's son Florent and his wife Muriel were adding another bungalow to the farm. Incidentally, Muriel was the

142

child minder of Myriam's little boy, which is how I was first introduced to Farrebique.

Life moves on and the Rouquiers now shop at the small supermarket in nearby Rignac, which sells copies of the films. The traditional stone *four banal* (bread oven) from the earlier film has long fallen out of use and today they buy their bread at the *boulangerie*. But some customs die hard in rural Aveyron: Raymondou's kitchen is still reminiscent of the all-purpose living quarters of yore, with its big table standing right in the centre, where we sat through the afternoon. Sure, the *cantou* has been replaced by electrical appliances, but the oilcloth with its flowery pattern and the unmistakable smell of the French countryside threw me several decades back.

As the afternoon drew on, Raymondou offered us drinks with a home-made *fouace* that had already been sliced into, confirming that it was a basic staple in people's homes. As we leapt merrily from topic to topic, the touchy subject of the British proliferation in the Aveyron came up, as it does without fail every time I am introduced to an old-timer (sometimes to not-so-old-timers too). Raymondou was tactful however, inserting cautious preliminaries between comments, such as "apparently", "I've heard that", "it seems that". This helped tone down the overall message, which implied that the Brits were causing prices to rocket, and that "apparently" too, to my surprise, '*les Anglais sont riches!*' I was cautious too when I proceeded gently to rectify his facts putting the blame on the law of supply and demand and on the higher cost of living in Britain. By sticking strictly to economics, I hoped to remain on neutral ground and diffuse emotional arguments. Whether Raymondou believed me or not I know not, but he listened dutifully and never once contradicted me. What was said behind my back later I know not either, but the impassioned *cri du coeur* — '*ces salauds d'Anglais!*' —, blurted spontaneously in *Biquefarre*, is still ringing in my ears.

Hervé Vernhes and Jacques Moulay, on the other hand, like the idea that the Brits are moving in, because they are restoring old houses and saving the regional heritage. They also approve when they turn their houses into *chambres d'hôtes* or *gîtes ruraux*, because it's good for tourism. But then, Hervé is an artist who spends his winter months near Paris and Jacques lived in Canada for many years. Raymondou visited Paris only once in his entire life, and in general ventures outside his little part of the Aveyron only on very rare brief organised tours.

Most of Raymondou's school mates, like himself, remained in the area and married locally. The old generation has died out by now, and that includes those we see in the film. One is much more aware of departures in a small place. Little by little one notices that the dead are taking up more and more space in the screenplay of one's life, filling up the village graveyard, making demands on one's memory, and increasing one's usage of the *passé imparfait* (past imperfect tense). At least the influx of outsiders ensures these communities survive, albeit in a different guise, even though the survivors may feel dispossessed.

Georges Rouquier has also joined the dead by now. He died in 1989, but there is talk of building a museum in his name and in honour of *Farrebique* in Goutrens, where the family name is listed in the telephone directory five times. This is quite a prominent position for a village of 430 inhabitants. One of the Rouquiers, Gilbert, was Mayor of Goutrens, whilst the present Mayor, René Garabuau, is married to the only remaining Rouquier from the demolished Biquefarre. Among those behind the project of the museum is an American fan of

Georges's, William Glicher of Maryland, who worked as a consultant for *Biquefarre* in 1983 and, like so many outsiders, caught the Aveyronnais bug. Uncannily, another person who worked on the film was my very close friend and upstairs neighbour, Baba. I remember her some twenty years ago going away for three months to shoot a documentary about a farm "somewhere" in France. Little did the two of us suspect that twenty years later I would be writing a book about the same remote area, let alone visit Farrebique. Raymondou remembered nostalgically "the attractive young assistant director", who is still attractive, I confirmed, but like Raymondou is more than twenty years older and a grandmother of two...

Today, the days when the first electric bulb brought light to the cowshed of Farrebique are history. Electricity is now a source of aggravation in Goutrens rather than a sign of progress, a threat to the environment in the shape of high-voltage pylons that nobody wants. Interestingly, another American from Maryland, John Herman, got involved in the protest movement and sent a letter to the Prefect of the Aveyron, expressing the hope that the Aveyron would not go the way of the US, where economic development and industrial growth are given priority over nature, history and quality of life. It seems that the Aveyron has ceased to be a strictly Aveyronnais affair. It also seems that its natives are becoming resigned to this new reality: in July 2004 when I came back to Farrebique, Raymondou told me that Florent and Muriel were toying with the idea of restoring the old farmhouse and converting it into *chambres d'hôtes* or *gîtes ruraux*... Were they emulating the Brits?

145

Rignac now has a pretty swimming pool, adjoining the camp site. The young woman who gave me directions to the swimming pool had never heard of Farrebique, neither the place nor the film, although her father, to whom I spoke later, knew both as a matter of course. Today, this is no longer a close-knit community and people across the generations don't necessarily know one another even if they shop at the same local supermarket. But coincidentally, the stranger who was lounging by the pool next to me turned out to live in Paris, a couple of blocks away from me. Myriam picked me up and as we left Rignac she pointed at Raymondou who was driving past us and who, she said, is now the president of the local senior club. There was no such thing as a senior club when he was 10 years old, and it's the last thing his grandfather could have imagined.

Chapter 7

THE LORD, HIS HOUSE AND HIS VINEYARDS

For a remote, provincial town of 26,367 habitants (53,785 if you count the suburbs), the dimensions of Rodez Cathedral are very impressive — 107m by 37m by 30m, as against Paris Notre Dame which measures 130m by 48m by 35m. Both cathedrals stand on the site of earlier Romanesque basilicas. The Parisian monument was levelled deliberately to make room for a more fashionable Gothic one and enhance the political prestige of its new bishop, Maurice de Sully. Construction began in 1163 and continued for close to two hundred years. In the case of Rodez, the Romanesque edifice collapsed accidentally on the night of the 16th and 17th of February 1276, and nobody knows why. The people of Rodez must have been shocked by the accident, all the more so since their basilica had been standing for hundreds of years. The vestiges that have survived point to a monument of great splendour with a Last Judgement tympanum that was in no way inferior to the one in Conques.

The cornerstone of the new cathedral was laid a few months later on what is now the eastern side of the edifice from where construction progressed westward, in the prevailing Gothic style, emulating the new vogue in the north. On today's scale the new project could be equated with the Paris Grands Travaux of the 1980s and 1990s, let's say, the Louvre Pyramid, the Arche de la Défense and the Bibliothèque de France put together. But the construction of Rodez Cathedral stretched over three hundred years rather than two decades, stalled by plagues, famines and wars, and came under the supervision of 18 successive bishops. One might argue that its construction has never really ended, because the brittle nature of its red sandstone requires perpetual restoration.

Needless to say the scheme required the raising of tremendous funds, towards which the parishioners were all too willing to contribute, since their investment would be set off against their sins on the Day of Reckoning and secure them safe entry into Paradise. They were equally willing to lend their flesh, sweat and muscles to the gigantic job of digging nine-metre foundations into the rock upon which the cathedral stands like a spectacular beacon above the city. On the other hand, few volunteered to level the steep slope that led to the worksite, now Avenue Victor Hugo. An astute Consul is said to have resorted to throwing handfuls of gold coins up in the air, free for all to grab on a first come, first served basis. It seems that everyone made a dash for the slope and from then on there was no shortage of hands. It is also said that an immense cemetery once lay on the hilly site of the cathedral, containing the remains of thousands of inhabitants. Some say it was an artificial hill, created by cartfuls of earth brought here from elsewhere; others say there was once a lake under the hill; others still claim it was a volcano.

Owing to the bellicose times, the cathedral's western façade was incorporated into the city rampart, which is why the building must be entered from the north or the south rather than the traditional west. It also accounts for the fortified, austere aspect of the monument, though counterbalanced by the ornate, 87m-tall square bellfry, the tallest in France. It was built in the 16th century under the initiative of François d'Estaing, then Bishop of Rodez, to replace the previous tower that was burnt down in 1510, and took some fifteen years to complete. It is topped by a statue of the Virgin who seems to offer her spiritual protection to the inhabitants of Rodez. They, in turn, have taken advantage of her lofty position and concealed the city's lightning conductor in her crown.

Despite the flamboyant belfry and the luminous red sandstone of the ubiquitous cathedral, Rodez has retained an austere aspect, particularly on a grey day. Don't expect animated night life here. And if you want a proper dinner after 9pm, only Gilbert Bastide at the Bowling du Rouergue, (pronounce it 'booling' or you won't be understood) in the suburb of Onet-le-Château will open his establishment to you at any time of night. The setting of a bowling alley may not sound engaging, but the experience is well worth the extra mile, for the players couldn't be more local and the food comes directly from the *terroir*, fresh, flavourful and plentiful.

I happened to dine there with Georges and Odette on the night of a championship. The cooking smells drifting from the kitchen stimulated my appetite as soon as we walked in, and a good thing too, because having been brought over by friends of Gilbert, I was entitled to endless rounds of drinks and triple portions of every dish — *charcuterie, foie gras*, a juicy chunk of Aubrac steak, comforting *aligot*, and a beautiful tray of non-pasteurised unctuous cheeses. The walnut oil vinaigrette poured over fresh green leaves from the garden helped wash down the feast and make room for a divine fruit tart. Since the night was a celebration and I was there as a friend of friends, I was also granted repeated encores of a fiery *cabrette*, stamped and twirled by four dancers especially in my honour. This was followed at the end of the night by a quartet of accordions led by Gilbert, as a final gift.

The Saturday morning market helps enliven Rodez with the bounty of the Aveyron and neighbouring *départements*. It is held at Place de la Cité, at the foot of the cathedral. A smaller farmers' market is held simultaneously at the Place du Bourg, where it also takes place on Wednesdays. It is peopled with storybook characters from old-time Rouergue who offer for sale the fresh produce of their kitchen gardens and farmyards — basketfuls of eggs, poultry and rabbits, just like in Villefranche. The market is set against the picturesque backdrop of medieval and Renaissance burgess houses, some of which have kept their upper floors jettied outward, a way of saving on ground tax in olden days.

In medieval times all markets and fairs were held at the Place du Bourg. Goods arrived here from as far off as Spain, Italy, Flanders and Holland testifying to the prominence of Rodez as a commercial junction. They came under the authority of the Count of Rodez who ruled over the *bourg* and consequently over its square. The Place de la Cité, on the other hand, came under the rivalling authority of the bishopric. The two sections of town were separated by a wall which ran roughly level with today's rue Marie. During the French Revolution the guillotine was set up here, but after a while the residents began to be bothered by the stench and blood and demanded its removal to the periphery. Only the neighbourhood's gardeners were sorry at having to give up this excellent fertiliser. The same scenario occurred in Paris, when locals put pressure to have the guillotine moved from Place de la Révolution (now Concorde) to the Bastille, then further out to Place du Trône Renversé (now Nation). Incidentally, the authorities distributed one guillotine per *département*, which made a total of 84 guillotines operating on French territory, inclusive of Paris.

Despite ongoing power struggles between bishop and count, who also had to reckon with the authority of the consuls, the church held indisputable sway over the man of the Middle Ages. And in provincial Rodez this continued till very recently. After all, it was the Bishop of Rodez, St Amans, who converted the Rouergue to Christianity in the 4th century, helped along by a set of miracles, as related in the tapestry hanging in the church of St-Amans that bears his name. The cathedral's massive dimensions were in themselves emblematic of the paramount authority of the church whilst, on a practical level, they allowed the incorporation of the street life of Rodez within the cathedral walls, thus keeping the parishioners under the watchful eye, and thumb, of the ecclesiastical establishment.

Bringing one's victuals inside the church was a given, as were the random comings-and-goings of pigs, whose presence in Rodez was encouraged by the consuls on a time-slot basis, because they made excellent refuse collectors, ridding the streets in no time of the rubbish and excrement thrown out of the windows. Strict regulations, however, required them to be removed as soon as their job was done, failing which they would have their feet chopped off as a dissuasive measure. Although animals were denied the possession of a soul, they were not exempt of civic and moral responsibility and in extreme cases were brought to trial, notably in 14th-century Conques where a pig was charged with the killing of a newborn babe. All the fellow pigs of the village were rounded up and made to attend the trial and the execution that followed.

And just as street life was extended inside the cathedral, allowance was made for inroads into the adjoining cemetery, the city's only public garden, shared by the dead and the living, among them the city's prostitutes. The cohabitation of the

151

living and the dead was extended to the cathedral too, the prestigious members of society lying buried underneath the feet of their living counterparts (when heating was installed in the cathedral, some hundred skeletons were uncovered underground). The only problem with the dead was that every so often they would have some account to settle with the living and come back to haunt them, especially on the Day of the Dead (1st November). The tolling of the church bell was supposed to help shoo them away.

I am not quite sure whether any of them were invisibly present at la Bastide-l'Evêque when we visited it last 1st November, but there was not much sign of the living either in the village. Yet the church bell tolled away energetically under a surprisingly bright blue sky which, pleasing as it was, rather spoilt the intended effect. Due to the chaotic changes in recent weather patterns, the soggy grey misery normally associated with '*un temps de la Toussaint*' (All Saints Day weather), which is in fact the preceding 31st October, can accompany just as readily the month of May in Napa Valley, California, where I am writing at this very moment, facing a dreary mix of English rain and Scottish fog. That morning at la Bastide-l'Evêque, the sun seemed totally out of place as it dabbed the old stone with a delicate blush and coated the roof *lauzes* with a silvery varnish. It shone just as brightly over Najac cemetery later in the afternoon, and likewise over the cemetery of Rodez, when I visited it the following December. How can you expect the dead to prosper under such inappropriate conditions? Worse! On the night of October 31st, I spotted a handful of children in Najac, hovering about against the backdrop of its formidable castle dressed up as Halloween skeletons and witches. What on earth has happened to French traditions and national pride! They have gone the way of nature's seasons.

Undaunted by the bright sun and the decline of his congregation, the vigorous, animated Père Pélissou, the village priest who has since passed away, headed towards his church for the celebration of mass in shabby *charenteuses* (woollen slippers), that might have seemed unsuited for the solemn occasion, yet were true to the spirit of Christianity. Gone are the days of the black cassock. Gone are the days when the female villagers turned up for the Toussaint mass in their new black winter garments and hats, which would be replaced by new more colourful summer outfits and straw hats come Easter. Except for one woman from the village of Manhac in the Ségala, who appeared in a new hat not twice but several times a year, as reported by Colette, the superb guide from Villefranche-de-Rouergue who spent her childhood in Manhac and who, like everyone else, knew the woman in question. Apparently, the new hat signalled each time to the amused congregation the termination of her husband's most recent liaison, which she alone had not been privy to. The new headgear was her husband's offering, intended to absolve his sins in a more original way, you will agree, than the conventional bouquet of flowers.

Our own presence at La Bastide-l'Evêque on the Day of the Dead was purely coincidental, our main business being a visit to the tilt mill which a bunch of enthusiastic retirees had built from scratch to house an old tilt hammer (*martinet*) received by one late Monsieur Marre in lieu of wages, because his boss had run out of money. A good story that led to the resurrection of the copper industry that had once flourished in La Bastide-l'Evêque, at least as a museum.

Founded by the Bishop of Rodez Raymond of Calmont d'Olt to challenge Villefranche-de-Rouergue, la Bastide-l'Evêque never really took off, but the characteristic grid layout of its streets can still be detected in the village. Only the copper industry made a name for itself, taking advantage of the Lézert river where 13 tilt hammers operated along a stretch of 5km, working for a clientele from all over Europe. Villefranche, on the other hand, specialised in the making of pots and pans, which were then sold on the market. In his *Description du département de l'Aveiron*, mentioned earlier, Alexis Monteil reports that when approaching Villefranche, one could hear the town before one could see it because of the racket produced by the hammers, smiths and pewter potters. The reconstructed forge, complete with an attractive roof of hand-hewn *lauzes*, was built entirely by retired devotees and makes an unexpected pretty sight in the midst of bucolic surroundings of meadows, bright flowers, birdsong, and the lively sound of the Lézert. It seems unlikely that any of the village dead were lounging there on that morning of 1st November, which had more the air of a cheerful early spring than of grizzly autumn.

Inside Rodez Cathedral, delightful insights into medieval life are supplied by the wood carvings on the oak tip-up seats in the choir, the work of André Sulpice who came from Bourges. These are known as *miséricordes* (mercy) because they allowed the church dignitaries to rest on their brackets at prayer time while seeming to be standing, as was the rule. You will need the help of an expert to decipher the meaning of these astonishing scenes, and if you wonder how such pagan themes were tolerated on Godly premises, note that it made perfect sense,

154

since the brackets were to accommodate the churchmen's buttocks — adorning them with Christian themes would have been perceived as blasphemous.

Echoing the above-mentioned harlots who loitered in the adjoining cemetery, a coquettish, vamp-like mermaid teases the beholder from one of the seats by displaying her impudent bosom. Her equivocal smile is reflected in her mirror, whilst she combs lasciviously her long mane of hair. The perilous stories of the Iliad were not unknown to the medieval man, including that of the deadly misfortune that befell the seafarer who chanced upon an aquatic *femme fatale*. The eternal matrimonial power struggle between husband and wife is played out facetiously as the two of them are depicted grabbing at a pair of pants. Another pair of pants is seen slipping down the behind of an artisan, supposed to be André Sulpice, a tongue-in-cheek way of signing his work even more mischievous than Alfred Hitchcock's brief appearances in some of his films. A more provocative posterior is displayed defiantly by a contortionist, in the spirit of Carnival, the one time during the year when the world was turned upside down and all licence was permitted, the better to keep the people under the thumb of the church the rest of the year.

Another extraordinary scene shows a chimney bellows being blown into the strategic spot by a fellow citizen. The scene is actually more innocent than meets the eye, and conveys the ancient belief that the spirit of a virtuous man leaves his body through the mouth with his final breath, whilst the spirit of a sinner departs through the other side. The blowing of the bellows is meant to facilitate its exit, as exemplified also by a strange *farandole*, still danced today in several villages in Southern Aveyron on their patron saint's *fête*. At St-Sever-du-

Moustier, for example, it is performed in front of the church on the Monday that follows 15th August, the Holy Day of Assumption; at the Hospitalet-du-Larzac it happens on the third Sunday of July.

Dressed in white nightgowns and caps, their faces smeared with red and black make-up, the villagers stand behind one another in a circle, holding a chimney bellows in both hands. As the band strikes the first notes, everyone starts marching, singing along to the music the Occitan lyrics of *La Buffatière*. At the first beat of the refrain everyone pauses with their right foot in front, then bends over and blows the bellows in the direction of the posterior of the dancer in front, singing in unison, '*Et buffosi al traou, et buffosi al traou*' ('And blow it in the hole, blow it in the hole'). Once done, everyone turns about and repeats the same motions in the direction of the other neighbour's posterior. Then off they go, singing the next rhyme, and so on and so forth, the entire round lasting about an hour. Nobody knows when or where the Buffatière was first danced, but the dancers' smeared faces and fancy dress suggest it must have been part of the Carnival.

Only the cathedral canons and the consuls had access to the choir section, which was separated from the nave by a rood (*jubé*). This added mystery to the chancel and enhanced its sacred atmosphere, and thereby the prestige and power of the church. This also meant that the common man never got to see the exquisite carvings on the *miséricordes*, so there was no need to worry they might lead him astray. Incidentally, André Sulpice worked in Villefranche-de-Rouergue as well and carved similar *miséricordes* both in the choir of the Collégiale church and the old Chartreuse (Carthusian monastery), which is now part of the town's hospital but can be visited. No one knows what brought André Sulpice to the Rouergue.

The grip of the church over Rodez only began to relax in recent decades. Not so long ago, interminable files of black-gowned *séminaristes* were still part of the cityscape, as recorded in old photos, and by the wonderful writer of the *Paris populaire*, Francis Carco, whom I was surprised to chance upon whilst leafing through the literary pages of the Rouergue, where he had spent part of his childhood. In *A Voix basse*, written in 1938, he describes the strong gusts of wind that flapped the *séminaristes'* cassocks as they filed down the hill on their bi-weekly exercise. Unlike left-leaning Villefranche-de-Rouerge, Rodez was a stronghold of provincial, uptight conservatism. Locals from Villefranche tell me that this is still the case, as mirrored by the two daily newspapers of the two towns, respectively *Le Villefranchois* and *Centre Presse*.

Come September, the Ruthénois* bourgeoisie would pack up their homes and shift their quarters to the rolling red hills of the Vallon de Marcillac (also referred to as Rougier), lying a little further north. Once more, thanks are due to Alexis Monteil who enabled me to travel back in time through his depiction of those annual migrants, so ladened with victuals and possessions that, "as they pass you on the road, you might think they were on their way to found a new colony." For several weeks the valley of the Cruau and the villages of Cougousse, Grandcombe and Valady were home to their Gargantuan dinners, partaken in old stone dwellings that went by such names as Paradis and Versailles, against the backdrop

---

* Inhabitant of Rodez

of song-filled *vendanges*... There is still a tiny hamlet in the Cruau Valley named Petit Versailles. Some houses were pink, some were honey-coloured, others were red, some lay low at the bottom of a dale, others flaunted their proud pitched roofs and turrets on top of a hill. All nestled in a profusion of leafy greenery, which, as the season progressed, veered little by little to yellow, then rust and gold, before deepening into flamboyant crimson.

I am not quite sure why I am using the past tense because not much has changed since — the Château de Panat, and those of Muret and Pruines still flaunt their beauty, not to mention Georges and Odette's Las Canals, named after its profusion of springs, which was built by the Dominicans in the 18th century and later became the property of the Bonnal, a prominent Ruthénois family. The village of St-Austremoine is still snuggling amongst the vineyards, and the little Romanesque church of St-Jean-le-Froid is still perched above the village of Gipoulou, above all else, in a heaven of bracing air and fragrance sweet. We found the church locked, but just as we were about to give up and walk away, its keeper, an elderly villager with a saintly face, appeared out of nowhere, trudging towards us up the lane with a huge key like St Peter's and opened for us the door of this gem. Heaven extended further into hill views that swept 360 degrees into eternity and was kissed by a faint breeze that smoothed our way into nirvana. I wonder if the hilltop of St-Jean-le-Froid is where the Aveyron tourist board got the inspiration for its advertising catch phrase, L'AVEYRON — RETROUVER LA SERENITE. This is how Georges feels about the spot as he comes here for solitary meditation when he has to make an important decision.

The Romanesque church of St-Austremoine has also survived unchanged, and its key is also kept by one of the neighbours. The first time I went there I didn't bother to enquire, because I was intent on making the most of the first sunny afternoon of my stay and headed instead to the waterfall of La Roque by Fontcoussergues. For the next hour or so I made my way among the vineyards of the Route du Vin, not once meeting a living soul. The route ended at Salles-la-Source, a spectacular three-tiered village of ancient cave-dwellers, carved out of a sheer cliff of lime, already on the Causse Comtal. If you drive along the scenic D27, you will be able to appreciate the contrasting yellow stretches of the Causse and the green and red hills of the Vallon on either side of the road. Prehistoric presence here is confirmed by the spectacular number of dolmens in the vicinity — 253.

Salles-la-Source once had five castles, built by the Counts of Rodez after whom this stretch of *causses* is named 'Comtal'. The 12th-century Château of St-Paul still stands flanked by its picturesque towers, as does the 15th-century Château des Ondes complete with its corner towers. The village also used to have three churches, though only two have survived. The older one, St-Paul, also dating from the 15th century, has a remarkable octogonal belltower and houses a poignant 11th-century wooden Christ. The former village spinning mill, a reminder that sheep breeding was the prime activity on the lime plateaux, is now home to the Musée du Rouergue, devoted to the area's old crafts and trades — the wool industry in the Causses Comtal and winemaking in the Rougier. Salle-la-Source is home to a spring of the Créneau river (hence '*source*'), which swells into a buoyant 20m waterfall after wet spells, plunging into a pool of emerald luster when I arrived there together with the afternoon sun. On rare occasions in the heart of winter, when temperatures drop below freezing, the waterfall metamorphoses into icicle stalactites and glints in the sun as though encrusted with diamonds.

Eventually I did get around to visiting the church of St-Austremoine. It too has an old wooden Christ, dating from the 12th century and still covered with polychrome painting, but it is best known for its 15th-century cross, La Croix des Vignerons, richly carved with vine leaves and grapes. Winegrowing in the Vallon goes much further back, at least to the 9th century and the foundation of Conques a few miles further north, as confirmed by donations and purchasing deeds. Some date it back to Roman times, but there is no archaeological evidence to support this theory. The main feature of Vallon in Roman times was its position at the junction of trade routes. The elevated position of Segodunum (as Rodez was then known) on top of a hill added a strategic asset, furthering its development as a centre of commerce. Having amassed considerable wealth through the distribution of the wines of Languedoc to the hinterland, the merchants of Segodunum lobbied against the development of a local viticulture which would have affected their monopoly.

As Christianity gained momentum with the approaching of the year 1000, however, viticulture was promoted by monastic communities, notably by Conques, because, as the emblem of Christ's blood, wine was an essential element of the Christian ritual. In Conques wine was also offered to the pilgrim as a mark of hospitality; and since Conques was an off-shoot of the mother abbey of Cluny, Burgundian varieties were introduced here rather than those of the southwest. This is the story according to one theory, but there is another version that tells a different story:

It would appear that before the successful robbery of the relics of Ste Foy from Agen, Conques had coveted the much more prestigious relics of St Vincent, the patron of winegrowers. Today his name is associated with Montmartre in Paris, whose cemetery is named after him, as well as the street running along the vineyard and celebrated in a famous old song, *Rue Saint-Vincent*. Back in the 6th century, however, it was on the Left Bank of Paris that St Vincent was honoured by King Childibert, when he built there a new abbey close to the river Seine, since renamed after St Germain. To mark the prestige of the new abbey, Childibert placed there the saint's tunic which he had brought back from Zaragoza in Spain. Furthermore, he picked St-Vincent abbey for his burial site, where he was eventually laid surrounded by vineyards (where the renowned cafés les Deux Magots, le Flore, and the no less illustrious Brasserie Lipp, started by Marcelin Cazès, stand today).

Conques wanted more than the saint's tunic. It had its eye on all his relics and sent out the monk Audalde to take possession of them and bring them back. Alas, he was caught, tortured, then driven away, and returned to Conques empty handed. He was hardly better received by his own congregation who turned him away for his failure, but he had his revenge the second time round, when he did manage to carry off the relics and offered them instead to Castres (now in the Tarn). By good fortune, Conques had word of the presence of the relics of a lesser St Vincent in Pompéjac, near Agen, and dispatched Arosnide (or Ariviscus) to fetch them. It was during his mission that he noticed the relics of Ste Foy, the robbery of which was narrated earlier.

Agen too had been a famous wine country, whose prosperity came to an end only in the 17th century, when Bordeaux shut its port to the wines of Agen so as to secure for itself a monopoly in England. So Agen swapped its vineyards for plum orchards and its wines for prunes. The *pruneaux d'Agen* are renowned to this very day. It is reported that when Arosnide carried off the relics of Ste Foy, he added to his booty some graftings of *mansois*, the variety of southwest France. If this is true, then Marcillac wine has nothing to do with a Burgundian variety unless both varieties were cultivated in Conques.

The general name of the variety is *fer servadou*, but in each area it goes by a different name (*mansois* being applied only to the Vallon), pointing to the wealth of *patois* (dialects) of the Occitan language. In those days every little *canton* (district) had its own dialect and nobody spoke French. Apparently, when Napoleon decided to set up in the nursery of the Luxembourg Gardens a collection of all the varieties grown in the Empire, the Prefect appointed at Villefranche was at a loss, having received 72 samples with different names, many of which were in fact identical.

The turn of the first Millennium led to a surge of mysticism and religious fervour — of which the pilgrimage to Compostela was one manifestation, making the fortunes of Conques. It was a shame the abbey couldn't get hold of the relics of St Vincent of Zaragoza, but those of Ste Foy had plenty going for them too — martyrdom, youth, femininity and virginity were a potent combination. Donations of land began to flow in from the neighbouring valleys. Some donors renounced their earthly possessions altogether — another way of gaining access to Paradise — allowing the abbey's vineyards to expand. The rising military power of the lords helped accelerate the process in a more coercive manner. The dispossessed inhabitants toiled and turned the rugged and partially marshy Vallon into a lovely wine country, while the taxes levied upon them in addition to their hard work further increased the prosperity of both abbey and lords. In the 13th century, when the star of Conques and of some of the lords began to wane, the bourgeoisie of Rodez leased some of the vineyards and sublet them to the peasants.

The quality and renown of Marcillac wines were on a par with those of Bordeaux, Gaillac, Cahors and Cyprus inducing the inhabitants of the Vallon to devote themselves exclusively to winegrowing. This created an endemic problem of overproduction which persisted throughout the centuries, all too familiar at this present time of fierce competition from the New World. Furthermore, the plantation of vineyards to the exclusion of corn exposed the area to the peril of famine. Charles IX addressed this issue back in the 16th century, allowing no more than a third of the land to be planted with vines, but over all, despite the ups and downs of history, the Vallon continued to produce quality wines until the 19th century. The clientele remained local, however, owing to competition from Le Fel and Bordeaux on the one hand, and to the Vallon's geographical confinement on the other — climbing up the *saumada de vin* (the wine summits) on a mule-drawn cart was a foolhardy feat and one many producers preferred to pass on.

It took the initiative of one man to completely overturn the situation. During his term of office as Ambassador to London under Louis 18th, the Duke of Decaze was impressed by the

Industrial Revolution in progress in England and decided to promote the industrialisation of France. Of all places, he set his eyes on the remote 'Black Country' of Aveyron, on the north-western fringe of the Vallon, where he opened collieries in 1826, coupled with the building of a company town, Decazeville. Steelworks complemented the mining industry in neighbouring Aubin, where all the rail tracks of France were manufactured. It is ironic that the entire transportation infrastructure of 19th-century France took its origin in the most remote backwaters of rural Aveyron, making Aubin in a way the spearhead of the French Industrial Revolution.

Not that the local inhabitants benefited from any of this. Like elsewhere in France and Europe, the road to industrialisation was paved with economic and social convulsions, suffering and sacrifice, and fierce outbursts of violent protest that would later be echoed in Emile Zola's *Germinal*, the most tragic episodes of which were inspired by real-life Decazeville. In the Revolutionary Calendar, Germinal corresponded to the month of March when life begins to germinate, as does the action in Zola's novel. But Zola also had in mind the germination of social awareness among the colliers, rather than the idyllic germination of life promised by a benevolent nature.

The reality faced by the Ségala peasantry, among whom many of Decazeville's colliers were recruited on a seasonal basis, consisted in scraping the surface of the meagre soil for chestnut and rye (*seigle*, hence Ségala), the only staples available to nourish these 'black bellies', as the peasants were nicknamed. The saying went that when flying over the Ségala, the crows turned on their backs so as not to see the poverty of its people. Plunging into the black burning inferno of the coal pits was hardly a more felicitous alternative. The wine of nearby Vallon could have served as an antidote to their misery, provided it was cheap. Note that the soil of the Ségala has since been supplemented with chalk and manure and rid of its acidity. As a result, the Ségala is now a land of plenty, whose soil is among the richest in southern France and not cheap to buy. Its days of destitution are but a bad memory, as they are in Decazeville, where new precision industries have taken the place of the old coal pits, most of which closed down in 1966, despite the tough strike of 1962.

The tourist office organises visits to the open mine La Découverte, which only closed in 2001. It is a spectacular amphitheatre revealing alternate strata of black coal and light-coloured rock. The origin of the coal was a tropical forest that covered the area in a remote chapter of its prehistory, as explained in the very interesting geology museum of Decazeville, which shed light not just on my own mortality but on the programmed mortality of our planet. It also revealed the omnipresence and resistance of insects such as dragonflies and crickets that, unlike almost all other species, didn't evolve over a stretch of 400 million years. The low-lying area that became Decazeville received the tropical river deposits which over time turned into peat, then coal.

The most unexpected treasure I came across in Decazeville were fourteen oil paintings of the stations of the cross inside the church of Notre Dame, the work of the symbolist painter Gustave Moreau, who later became the teacher of both Henri Matisse and Georges Rouault, and a determining source of inspiration to André Breton. It was the painter Eugène Fromentin who had recommended Moreau to François Cabrol, the son of the co-founder of Decazeville and a savvy art lover. Since few visit

Moreau's wonderful museum in Paris, I was not surprised that none of my Aveyronnais friends seemed to know about his paintings in Decazeville. For whatever reason, Moreau refused to sign them and therefore the identity of the artist remained a mystery till 1964, although Marcel Proust did know about them and mentioned them in his unfinished novel *Jean Santeuil*. Definitely take the time to go into the church. You won't fail to be struck by the dreamlike poetry that haloes Christ and by the moving harmony of the composition and colours, which are reminiscent of the Italian school of religious art. Indeed, Moreau painted the series on his return journey from Italy where he had studied the great masters.

From the outset the Duke of Decaze had sought to establish a link between Decazeville and the Vallon viniculture. As chairman of the Marcillac winegrowers' committee, he had vested interests in both ventures. The arrival of the railway provided him with a golden opportunity to create a direct line between the Vallon and Decazeville, which inevitably was detrimental to the quality of its wines. When the vineyards were replanted after the phylloxera episode of the 1880s, the winegrowers chose to target the proletarian mass market with cheap plonk. Many of the new vineyards were planted by the miners themselves to supplement their income. Understandably, after working long hours in the coal pits, they had no inclination or energy to climb up to the higher terraces which yielded grapes of a superior quality. But even the lower tiers of the Vallon were pretty steep and hard to work; not to mention the hardships brought about by an uncooperative climate, the recurrent frosts in spring, and the perpetual fight against erosion.

The phylloxera bug had been wreaking ruin on French soil for quite a while before it penetrated the Aveyron through the gorges of the Dourbie, down south, coming from the Cévennes. It started off by swooping on a pocket-size vineyard in Nant, a little *bourg* at the meeting point of the Dourbie and the Durzon, which the Benedictine monks had turned into an Eden of orchards and vineyards in the 10th century. I knew nothing about this tragic page of history when we visited Nant in September 2004, driving east through the Dourbie gorges coming from Millau. It was a beautiful morning and the river was a transparent stillness of jade, sheltered from the sun by an arching screen of foliage. To the north, the luminous hills of the Causse Noir offered us the exquisite sight of the odd perched village, notably the gem of St-Véran, a village of cave-dwellers in older times, where the occasional cave has been wonderfully updated and adapted to modern living, a far cry from those olden times when evil spirits, werewolves, and other howling demons were believed to prowl the rugged wilderness through the long winter months. Admittedly, these homes are a bit dark inside, but in summer they are delightfully cool and environmentally friendly, since there is no need for air conditioning.

The best part of that day awaited us at the Auberge du Roc Banut in the village of La Roque Ste-Marguerite, where we settled underneath two spreading chestnut trees for a rustic lunch of *pascadou* (a thick local pancake that will see you through the entire day) and a simple fresh green salad tossed in a walnut oil vinaigrette. The pleasure included a nice *pichet* (jug) of Côte de Millau and an *addition* (bill) that barely amounted to a handful of euros. Beneath us the Dourbie drifted gently to Millau, offering a variety of water sports activities to energetic youths who, in all likelihood, had never heard of the phylloxera bug and who, like me, would have been hard pushed to believe that it was through this bucolic valley of plenty that the seed of so much human misery had made its insidious entry into the Aveyron before launching its full-scale attack on the entire *département*.

In those days, when French society was polarised between science and religion, republic and church, the poor winegrowers didn't know which way to turn. After playing ostrich for a while, rather than take the necessary steps to eradicate the bug, they resorted to erecting phylloxera crosses, one of which still stands on top of the hill of Monclès (close to Sénergues, between St-Cyprien and Lunel). After all, this was what their ancestors had been doing all along to shoo off the Evil one. Clearly the phylloxera bug was the same old Devil under a new microscopic guise. The crosses became pilgrimage destinations, where the devout would implore God to protect the harvest.

Occasionally the congregation would rail against the 'phylloxerised' Republic, the felon responsible for their affliction. Some believed France had been chastised for having gone republican, which was hardly better than being a heathen. Under such extreme circumstances, it is not surprising that even St Bourrou, the patron of the burgeoning vines, turned a deaf ear to the winegrowers' pleas. Today, under happier circumstances, the saint is celebrated on Pentecost Sunday at the church of Notre Dame de Fontcourrieu by Marcillac, a happy, colourful pilgrimage which you wouldn't want to miss, should you be wandering across the Aveyron on that weekend.

As a last resort, the *curé* of Marcillac led his congregation to Lourdes, to the exasperation of the scientific community, but even that didn't help. Overnight the Ruthénois bourgeoisie packed up and returned to town, abandoning their lovely country seats. The villagers too abandoned their homes in great numbers, setting out on the long journey of no return, to Paris, California or Argentina.

All was not lost, however, for when the vineyards were replanted, the *mansois* grafted well and was easy to propagate and preserve for better times. But worse calamities than phylloxera were yet to come, notably the wholesale slaughter of World War I, as recorded on every village war memorial, the 1929 Wall Street Crash, the German Occupation, the crisis in the mining industry after the Liberation, and the terrible frost of winter 1956 which destroyed between 80 and 90 % of the vineyards. The situation was so critical that the United Nations offered financial aid to this 'underdeveloped' area, but the locals were ruffled at being regarded as '*sous-développés*' and turned down the offer.

The closure of the Decazeville mines was expected to signal the death blow of the Vallon's vineyards; instead it turned out to be a blessing in disguise, forcing the winegrowers to recognise that only quality wine could save their viticulture. This was a daunting prospect, but also an opportunity to resurrect the old vineyards. Yet it was one thing to diagnose the patient's ailment and come up with the right prescription; to actually take the bull by the horns and do something about it required boldness and stamina.

Nine winegrowers took up the challenge in 1962 and set up a cooperative in a barn in Valady, a brave step since they had no commercial experience. They focused on creating a Marcillac identity based on its *terroir*. Few wines merit this more than Marcillac does, because thanks to the perfect natural symbiosis between the *mansois* variety and the red soil of the Vallon, Marcillac is the only pure variety wine and therefore the ultimate *vin de terroir*. It is rich in iron and tannin, which gives it a distinctive *goût du terroir*, much appreciated by the amateur in this age of homogenising globalisation. Recognition came in 1965, when Marcillac was awarded a VDQS (Vin De Qualité Supérieure) status, followed in 1990 by the sought after AOC (Appélation d'Origine Contrôlée), which guaranteed the authenticity of a wine's geographical origin. Earthy, dark and bright, the wine is often enhanced by blackcurrant and raspberry flavours, which I was pleasantly surprised to detect when I nibbled on bunches of garnet-coloured grapes that teased me from the roadside at St-Austremoine one golden October afternoon after the rain, when the sky had finally cleared and the countryside gleamed in glorious shades of vermilion and amber.

Today the Marcillac Cooperative is doing well, with 40 members, not counting the 11 independents who work in the Vallon. I visited two of them on a couple of occasions — Philippe Teulier and Jean-Luc Matha, having first been introduced to their wines at Michel Bras', which is no small recommendation. Philippe's natural reserve combined with his scientific expertise intimidated me at first, but when we moved on to the cellar for the main business of wine tasting, he loosened up in no time. It reminded me of a field trip to the vineyards of the Sancerrois during my student days, when, after day-long tedious presentations, everyone, including our venerable Sorbonne professors, gathered at massive long tables to imbibe endless bottles of Sancerre to bawdy songs and banter, true to the *gaulois* spirit. As Philippe proceeded to uncork the first bottle of Sangre de Pais, his ordinary *cuvée* which costs under €4, breaths were held in anticipation of the popping sound of the cork. A mischievous twinkle accompanied that holy moment, the same twinkle that Jean-Pierre Marc had shared with me in Estaing.

Fun aside, Philippe is a serious oenologist who chose to perfect the knowledge handed down to him by his father and grandfather at the renowned School of Oenology in Montpellier. When he returned home, he updated the family's cellar. His special Cuvée Vieille Vigne, yielded by the higher terraces, was awarded the Prix de l'Excellence by the Minister of Agriculture in 2005 and 2006 as the best wine of southwest France. This is all the more remarkable as the evaluation is determined by the number of points accumulated over a period of five years so as to guarantee a consistency in quality.

Big, bubbly Jean-Luc Matha was a picture of radiant openness right away. A pair of jovial eyes set in a rosy face and a fabulous black moustache made him look like Dionysus reincarnated in a Gallic version. In other words, *il portait son métier sur la figure* (he wore his trade on his face). He is also one of those 'salt of the earth' poets scattered across the Aveyron countryside, and greeted me with the key to the Celtic name of his little red-stone village Bruéjouls — 'a glade of heather'. '*Joul*' is the Celtic suffix for 'place', he explained, as 'ac' is to Roman settlements. Another poet, I forget who it was, once told me that Valady, where the Marcillac cooperative is situated, stands for '*val à dieux*', valley of the gods, which the more prosaically inclined have refuted.

Whoever has it right, there is no denying that both Philippe and Jean-Luc live in paradise, Philippe high above, at the

Domaine du Cros by Goutrens, with breathtaking views over the surrounding hills and the valley, Jean-Luc nestling down below among bright geranium (the heather must have gone the way of the Celts), and underneath a shady pergola of rambling vines where the large family table had been set for the traditional Sunday get-together, when we arrived there on a sunny summer morning. When we came back that same evening for a wine tasting, the tablecloth had been removed and the family had been replaced by friends. Jean-Luc uncorked his vintages, along with a dark Syrah from the Ardèche brought by a friend from out of town. It was explored with the adventurous curiosity and excitement of a newly discovered continent, generating an animated evaluation of the newcomer in which eveyrone participated with epicurean delight.

When I returned to Jean-Luc the following October to take part in the harvest, I was working my way along a row of vines next to a woman who had recently moved to the Aveyron from Nice with her nine-year-old son. Like so many others, she had fallen in love with the Vallon on a previous holiday. I wondered if it had been a wise idea to uproot a child from the Mediterranean coast, let alone his school and friends, but she reassured me that the boy had summed up his new environment as, '*Maman, ici c'est le paradis!*'

A man harvesting next to the woman brought me back to earth. As soon as he found out about my British connection, he went into a confrontational mode and lashed out with a belligerent tirade about the world's sad state of affairs due to Anglo-Saxon hegemony led by Uncle Sam, with England in tow. I would not have been taken aback by such a harangue down south, on the territory of José Bové, nor in certain pockets of rural Aveyron where Bové enjoys a considerable following. But somehow I imagined the Vallon as conservatively bourgeois, perhaps because of its history and proximity to Rodez, perhaps because most of the people I had so far met there belonged to such circles.

Visitors to France are not always aware to what extent French society is steeped in politics. Politics are as natural an ingredient at the dinner table as the appreciation of the food and wine being served. This is counterbalanced by the safety-valve of racy bantering and gossip that tend to be incorporated into the latter stages of the dinner, often accompanying the cheese or the *digestif*, preventing the evening from ending with the bitter aftertaste of a political argument. Thank heavens, no political discussions interfered with our lunch break at Jean-Luc's *vendanges*, a Gargantuan array of comfort dishes prepared by his wife, Françoise, and her friend, Aline. Françoise also looks after the family's wonderful vaulted gift shop, where the best regional products — *foie gras, tripoux, confits, etc* — are sold alongside Jean-Luc's wines and other regional *apéritifs* including *rascalous*, a pleasing blend of wine and walnut. Our lunch was washed down generously by wine, leaving us somewhat lighter and higher in spirits by the end of the meal, as reflected by the frequent outbursts of laughter and giggles that arose from among the vines throughout the afternoon. They were much more enjoyable than the morning's political tirade.

It was Philippe's great-grandfather who had assembled and replanted the family vineyards after the phylloxera calamity, a brave decision when most of the winegrowers had given up and went to seek a living elsewhere. With his 26 hectares of vineyards, Philippe owns roughly 13% of the production, making him the largest independent vintner of Marcillac, followed by Jean-Luc who owns 16 hectares and 8 to 9 % of the production. Owing to the endemic problem of overproduction, the expansion of vineyards on French territory is forbidden as a general rule, which is sad for small appellations like Marcillac because the demand cannot be met.

Most of Philippe's vineyards climb up the steep terraced red slopes facing the southwest sun. They were bathed in a splendid glow when we arrived there at twilight from nearby Goutrens, on the other side of which lies Farrebique, and another world. Philippe has astutely taken advantage of the steep slope to avoid disturbing the grapes through upward pumping. The grapes arrive at the top level of the wine press, where de-stemming takes place. The juice then runs into stainless steel vats for vinification, at 30° to 32°, for 15 to 20 days for Lo Sang del Païs, 25 to 30 days for the special Vieille Vigne. The wine then flows to the cellar, another level down, where fermentation is completed in the old wooden casks Philippe has inherited from his great-grandfather. Fortunately, there is still a cooper living in nearby red-stoned Clairvaux, who can provide him with spare parts when needed. Lo Sang del Païs remains in the old casks for six months, but the Vieille Vigne is left to ferment for a total of 18 months.

Jean-Luc also leaves his more special vintage, *Peïrase* (*Pierre fine* in *patois*), to ferment for 18 months, but he uses only one old wooden cask that holds up to 7,000 litres. *Peïrase* is the name of the *terroir* of one of his vineyards, just under three hectares, where Nature has worked a miracle by blending brittle, permeable limestone into the dense red soil of the valley, thus making it more airy, which benefits the vines. The bits of limestone also reflect the sunlight onto the vines like mirrors securing them the heat they need, whilst letting the water filter underground, so there is no need to worry about droughts — Jean-Luc will tell you that it is the *terroir* that creates the wine rather than the variety. The *Peïrase* vines are between 60 and 90 years old.

In the old days everything was done by hand, from the building of the retaining walls to prevent erosion to the tending of the vines. The hillsides were too steep for ploughs and oxen. When the earth was washed down by storms the men had to carry it back uphill in baskets, the same way they carried the harvest. Today the rows are more spaced out and some of the work can be done by small tractors, though the picking is still done by hand. The grapes are still carried to the press on strong manly shoulders, but the handsome wicker baskets have been relegated to heritage museums and replaced by plastic ones. I was therefore thrilled to discover that Jean-Luc still crushes some of his grapes by foot, the old way.

Initially I had intended to harvest at Philippe's too, but when after the first session at Jean-Luc's I found I had to lie in bed doubled up and could hardly straighten up my aching back the next morning, I reduced my ambitions to the more realistic and enjoyable goal of attending the traditional end of the harvest dinner, *la soûlarde*. The jolly name (from *soûlard* meaning drunkard) suggested a repeat of my early Sancerrois experience in my Sorbonne student days, but to my surprise everyone was as sober and well behaved as a cherub. Perhaps harvesting on the steep slopes of Le Cros for two weeks had exhausted them all. Oddly, it was the usually introverted Philippe who was the life of the party that night, no less beaming and bubbly than his friend Jean-Luc Matha had been down in the valley.

Chapter 8

A BRIDGE IN THE MAKING

On 9 December 2003, Air France flight no. AF 5681 deposited us at Rodez-Marcillac airport at 9:20 am after a 55-minute flight from Orly Ouest, south of Paris. This was my first bird's-eye view of the Aveyron, enhanced by an unusually crystal clear sky for that time of year. A week earlier I had been flying over vast, empty stretches of Canada and the United States on my way to San Francisco. The Aveyron looked like a miniature model, dotted with toy-like villages and farmsteads which belied the eternal complaints about the French countryside being deserted. It's all relative, but compared to the North American continent the Aveyron seemed heavily populated. in America you fly for what seems like forever before the landscape changes, while here, over the mountains of central France, it changes every few minutes — in no time the snow-capped mountains gave way to the Lot, replaced in turn by the limestone plateau of the Causse Comtal, and finally Rodez with the square tower of her ubiquitous cathedral.

A beaming Georges and Odette were waiting for us at the small airport which reminded me of how flying used to be during my childhood. Before hitting the road, Georges led the way to a quick coffee in the snack bar, where I met Thomas Roberts, the Irish Managing Director of the airport. Well, I'll be darned—an Irishman at the head of a French airport! It turned out he'd been on the job for the past 14 years. So he was even more of an Aveyron veteran than Georges, who had been involved with the Aveyron only since meeting Odette seven years before, and who was just as taken aback by this quiet revolution as I was. With a twinkle in their eyes they compared notes on their shared condition as *néo*-Aveyronnais, and were amused by the fact that they were both wearing identical old-fashioned checked shirts, which would have better suited the tweedy atmosphere of a country pub on the other side of the Channel than the Gallic airport of Rodez-Marcillac.

Once in the car all Irish traces vanished instantaneously, replaced for a brief moment by the Cathedral of Rodez rising proudly in the distance, above its city, against a somewhat hazy sky. Within minutes the outskirts of Rodez went the way of Ireland and we were speeding south towards an ever brighter sky that hinted at the Mediterranean lying hidden in the distance. Soon the honey-coloured hills of the Lévézou filed past us, giving me the urge to leave the car and gallop on horseback among their oak and pine— well, perhaps some other time... Today we were in a tunnel-vision mode, heading for a rendezvous with history in the making: the inauguration of the seven piers of the Millau Viaduct, soon to become the world's tallest bridge. Designed by Lord Norman Foster, the 2.5km steel deck would span the river Tarn by the summer and provide the Clermont-Ferrand — Béziers A75 motorway with its last missing link.

When we visited the bridge in the afternoon, our hosts pointed at the future Viaduct's northern abutment, where the deck had just begun to sprout out of the rugged hillside, projecting into the void like a diving board over an Olympic swimming pool. Except that it was overhanging a chasm 200 metres deep, and would hang 270 metres above the river bed once completed. Soon it would begin to emerge from the southern abutment too, and all being well the two sides would be joined in July 2004. My mind wandered to the famous handshake of the French and the English when the two sides of the Channel tunnel were joined. If the Millau Viaduct had been built close to one of the world's urban centres, the completion of the deck might have enjoyed similar media coverage, but then, the Tarn does not flow between Paris and London.

Coming from the north we had to pass through Millau, a small town of 21,339 inhabitants, lying on the right bank of the capricious Tarn, which travels to Millau from the north. After leaving behind its world-renowned gorges (in the neighbouring Lozère), it receives the water of the Jonte, and further south, that of the Dourbie, just before it makes a 90° turn into the town. It was a wise precaution to have built Millau at a safe distance from the river bed and spare it occasional floodings, most recently in autumn 2003. The Jonte and the Dourbie also carve their way through splendid gorges, but by the time the Dourbie joins forces with the Tarn at the gateway to Millau, the steep cliffs have melted into gentle slopes and open up into a basin where the town sits pleasantly between the spurs of the Lévezou to the north and those of the Larzac to the south.

A bright red billboard, stamped with the familiar McDonald's golden arches, stood by the roadside for the attention of motorists. Additional directions to the famous eaterie were provided by the message —TOUT DROIT (straight on)— in case it might be missed. Unwittingly perhaps, the message also underlined who had emerged the winner in 1999, when the then new McDonald's was dismantled by anti-globalisation protesters. I noticed no trace of the battle scene in the sleepy, provincial-looking town, however, whose red-tiled roofs and wooden shutters exuded the characteristic air of southern France, even in wintertime when the leafless plane trees looked somewhat lonesome. I assumed there would be clusters of *pétanque* players underneath their shady branches in warmer seasons.

It required a lot of imagination to picture the town in summer, when its notorious 13km bumper-to-bumper bottleneck is reported to be the worst *point noir* on the holiday roadmap of France. The new Viaduct, erected west of Millau, would divert holiday traffic from the town and eliminate the congestion, but opponents to the project were worried that at the same time it would deprive Millau of some of its business. Supporters of the bridge, among them the enthusiastic Mayor Jacques Godfrain, argued that, on the contrary, it would become a magnet to new economic ventures, over and above being a tourist attraction. Time will tell.

For technical reasons our visit was delayed to the afternoon, which was fine with us, since the gap was filled at once with a fabulous lunch. Everyone rushed back to the car with the juvenile excitement of school children freshly informed that their classes had been cancelled. Within seconds we were back on the road, driving along the D992 in the direction of Albi, headed for the 12th-century Château de Creissels. It happened spontaneously, with no preliminary drawn-out consultations: French food lovers don't need guidebooks. They know. Set discreetly among lovely grounds and venerable trees, the *château* has preserved its crenellated square tower and a wonderful vaulted hall with chunky stripped stone, now the establishment's restaurant. You would have expected Georges and Odette and the other two members of the party (one of whom was also a restaurateur) to be blasé about the intake of food, but the French never are. They enjoy each meal with renewed relish and fresh curiosity. Every item was discussed approvingly, notes were compared, and after a *dégustation* of a variety of Roquefort, washed down by an excellent Côtes de Millau Cave Montrozier, we finished off with a delicious *flaune*, a ewe-milk based pudding sprinkled with a hint of orange blossoms, and left the table satiated and in high spirits.

The early winter sun had begun to recline over the Viaduct worksite, setting the hills on fire. Beneath, the river Tarn meandered lazily like a ribbon of jade. Jutting against a winter sports' blue sky, the bright red support towers and stupendous red and white cranes looked like a gigantic Meccano set. I took endless shots of them from every possible angle, having been informed they might all be scrapped by my next visit, certainly so at the end of the project, by which time the bridge would stand out in its subdued whiteness against the grand landscape. Even the elevators would be done away with and access for maintenance and repairs would be gained through spiral staircases concealed inside the piers. This would be quite a climb in the case of P2, the tallest of the seven piers, which measured at present 245m. Once topped by its pylon it would measure 343m and surpass by 23m the Eiffel Tower. When we were allowed into P2, we were astonished to discover a stupendous hollow vast enough to contain a concert hall, or a cathedral... Yet from a distance it looked as slender as a forked needle.

The history that is being made outside Millau, however, goes way beyond a breakthrough in civil engineering. Boosting the economy of a small provincial town and smoothing holiday traffic would not have justified a €320 million investment. Mainly, the Viaduct will contribute to bringing together northern and southern Europe, which will open up and benefit the Aveyron. A century earlier Paul Bodin connected Albi and Rodez with a revolutionary metal railway viaduct over the river Viaur using the same truss design Gustave Eiffel and his associates had used for the Eiffel Tower. His state-of-the-art construction is still admired today.

Then, as now, the project led to a controversy, supported and opposed by the same arguments as those put forth today over the Millau Viaduct. In 1999 an additional road viaduct was built over the Viaur, a stunning piece of pre-stressed concrete, rising 106m above the river bed. Joining the two sections of the double-lane N88, it completed the connection between Lyon and Toulouse and contributed to the future integration of the Aveyron into the overall road network of Europe. Several other smaller viaducts have been erected in the Aveyron in the last few decades, initially to satisfy local needs, although eventually they too will be incorporated into the map of trans-Europe connections. In view of its pivotal position at the gateway to southwest Europe, and because today's technology can challenge a rugged terrain by leaping above it, the Aveyron is unlikely to remain for long a secret enclave.

It was certainly no secret to the Romans who, undaunted by its ruggedness, cut a network of roads through the province, among them the Segodunum (Rodez) — Condatomagos (Millau) road, which joined the *Via Domitia*, the east-west axis connecting Italy and Spain along the seashore, thus bringing together the Celtic north and the Mediterranean south. Not unlike today's European Union, Rome focused on improving communications so as to facilitate commercial exchanges and open up new markets for its industries. This benefited Millau, whose natural resources of clay, water and wood were ideal for the development of a flourishing pottery industry, which peaked in the middle of the 1st century A.D. but declined after a hundred years.

During its heyday, the colossal kilns at the Graufesenque (now an archeological site open to the public), could take up to 40,000 pots in one firing. Millions of pieces were turned out in Millau, mainly for export, some of which were excavated in Pompeii, others found on the shores of the Black Sea, in Mauritania, Afghanistan, and even as far as in India. If you are unhappy about the homogeneity of today's goods and services, Gap or Starbuck's, note that the same assembly-line uniformity prevailed in the Roman Empire, when every household, east, west, north and south, ate out of the same red earthenware dishes, most of which came out of the kilns of the Graufesenque. In other words, this was the Ikea of the Roman Empire. Note too that if Rome chose to shift the industry to the remote town of Millau, it was due to the much cheaper labour available there, what in modern terminology is known as 'outsourcing'.

A thousand years later, globalism was at the root of the Templars' prosperity too. Once defeated by the Muslims in 1291, and consequently dislodged from the Holy Land, where they had initially established a military order for the protection of Christian pilgrims to Jerusalem, they withdrew to Cyprus and set up their headquarters in Limasol. Before long they had spread all over Christian Europe, establishing no fewer than 7,050 strongholds, perhaps 9,000 (the figures vary depending on sources) over an area extending as far as Ireland to the west, Denmark to the north, Spain to the south, and Armenia to the east... In France, their main stronghold was in the Marais neighbourhood of Paris.

Their territorial possessions, largely acquired through donations, generated further wealth thanks to their advanced methods of farming and efficient management, while their geographical dispersion led to the development of communications and financial exchange, thus laying the foundation for an international banking system engendering further wealth. A hardy lot, they settled in the Rouergue and thereabouts, notably on the Larzac which, according to one romantic hypothesis, appealed to them because of its resemblance to the arid wilderness of Palestine. This pleasant tale doesn't stand up to scrutiny. The Larzac at the time looked very different from today. Much of it was covered with thick forests of beech and mature oak which the Templars and others set out to clear in order to make room for sheep farming, preceding the English by a good five hundred years. The clearing of the forests had actually begun on a small scale some 4,000 to 5,000 years earlier, but it was the Templars, and later the Hospitallers who superseded them, who really transformed the Larzac into pastureland. The odd forest could still be seen on the Larzac in the 18th and 19th centuries, and even now the forest reasserts itself in no time, if the sheep are removed from the pastures.

One of the more significant donors of land to the Templars was the King of Aragon, who became Viscount of Millau through marriage, a title that granted him the ownership of part of the plateau. By allying himself with the mighty knights, he hoped to destabilise his neighbour and rival, the Count of Toulouse. The esoteric mist veiling the Order of the Temple and its so-called treasure is sheer fabrication. As a matter of fact, few orders were as transparent as the Temple whose Rule was entirely written down and is available for all to read. In the Holy Land they were soldiers. On the Larzac they were farmers with no more than a handful of knights at their head. Their main activity was sheep farming, complemented by growing cereals for their horses (according to the inventory drawn up by the royal commissioners at the time of their dissolution they had only 35 horses, mules and donkeys).

It is another romantic notion to imagine a historical connection between their site at La Cavalerie and today's military camp, which was set up in 1903. The fact that they didn't fortify their settlements further proves this point. Most of the walls we see today, as well as other remains, are the legacy of the rivalling Order of the Hospitallers, who had also been established in the Holy Land to offer hospitality to pilgrims, and who were granted the Templars' possessions after their annihilation by Philippe the Fair in the early 14th century. The command posts of the Larzac were fortified only in the middle of the 15th century because of the insecurity prevalent in the wake of the Hundred Years' War. The only uninterrupted historical thread at La Cavalerie was the ancient route connecting the Larzac and the Mediterranean via the hilly pass of Le Pas de l'Escalette (in the neighbouring Hérault). The findings of Celtic, perhaps even Phoenician, pottery along that route date it back at least to the 5th or 6th century B.C. The road came in handy for the Templars who shipped their cereals and horses from the Mediterranean coast of France to the east.

We had several hours to kill between our visit to the Viaduct and the inauguration of its piers that night. Georges, who always knows how to make the best of any situation, offered to give me a brief taster of a Templars' command post. That's when I first heard of the Templar connection to the Larzac. He couldn't have come up with a more exciting suggestion, especially because it came to me as a total surprise, and moreover the weather was so radiant. But it was almost sunset by then, and night steals in fast at that time of year. Would we get there in time? I had a touch of *déjà vu* as I found myself speeding through an exhilarating Wild West landscape, under an ever-darkening fuchsia sky, trying to keep apace with the sun. It felt as though I was fated to keep chasing the solar body across the Aveyron and always to lose the race by a hairsbreadth.

The sky had deepened into purple and was about to cloak us in darkness, but good fortune granted us a full moon that night, and what we lost in terms of golden brilliance was largely compensated for by a silver mystery as we careered through the empty landscape. All of a sudden the black outlines of a fortified storybook village stood out like a shadow against the coming night —La Couvertoirade— a strange name, becoming its moonlit theatre set. Further lighting was provided inside the gate by hazy amber haloes hanging from lampposts along the narrow, cobbled streets. I would have gladly spent the rest of the evening wandering through the village, but my party being French, their inner clock began to remind them that it was *l'heure de l'apéritif,* which made them restless, especially Georges. I thought he was out of his mind to expect to find an open café in this otherworldly ghost town which had clearly shut down for the winter. If it had any life at all, it could only be during the tourist season.

However, Georges was not in the least concerned and led us through chilly, deserted crannies and past lightless windows. Suddenly, the silence was broken by the ringing of myriads of bells streaming down the slope in a jumble, together with a huge bleating surge of white fleece. It was a vision out of a bottomless past, that of the Knights Templar, the Biblical Patriarchs, and much further back, since a sheep-breeding population is known to have made its way here from the Mediterranean some 150,000 years ago. Obviously there would have been no pastoral jingling of bells during paleolithic times, but visually it seemed as though little had changed. Like my friends, the sheep too had a clock that made them stampede to the fold in close ranks, a rolling avalanche out of which emerged the dark silhouette of a solitary shepherd. Standing erect against the night, he poured out to the stray ewes a melody I had heard before, '*beni, beni, beni, beni, beeeeni...*'.

My! It sounded just like Capou on the *estives* of the Aubrac the past October, as if this shepherd was sending him back his echo, all the way from southern Aveyron to the far north. While listening to the shepherd, I recalled how the cows had quit their grazing and rushed to Capou, sensing that summer was over and expecting him to lead them back down to the valley. I was surprised to hear a shepherd on the fringe of the Mediterranean and a cowherd on the Irish- or Icelandic-looking fringe of the Auvergne singing out the same melodious phrase in Occitan, suggesting that the common heritage of southern France overrides its geographical diversity and local differences. Certainly so in rural areas where, despite shades and variations, even between two neighbouring valleys, the *langue d'oc* was everyone's native language until a generation or two ago. Capou's school teacher in Soulages encouraged its use, which is why Capou is completely bilingual. On the other hand, in his wife's school, in the neighbouring village of Huparlac, its use was severely reprimanded, in line with national guidelines at the time. Consequently, Capou's wife has practically no knowledge of her ancestors' tongue. Today's attitudes have changed and the *langue d'oc* is taught in schools as an option, just like English, Spanish or other languages. After a twenty-year struggle, nearby St-Affrique became the first town in the Midi-Pyrénées region where the language is taught all the way from nursery school to *baccalauréat* level. 12% of the town's pupils are now bilingual.

Foreigners are often amused by the French proclamation '*Ça n'existe pas!*' launched defiantly at the customer when one doesn't feel like putting oneself out. Not so Georges, who never gives up when he has an idea in mind, and who was determined to find an open café. Dragging our feet, we trailed behind him on what seemed to be a wild goose chase when suddenly we found ourselves gaping in disbelief at a door flung open across the street, looking into a cheerful lit up tavern, complete with a table laden with goodies. It felt like Goldilocks standing at the doorway of the house of the Three Bears, except that the pallid disk of the moon overhanging the deserted village exuded an atmosphere of a ghost story rather than a sylvan fairy tale.

The tavern was indeed closed for the season, but by an extraordinary coincidence Annick Chaudron had invited friends over for a game of Scrabble and thought she might as well keep the premises open for the unlikely visitor, like ourselves. A quick look around suggested that she and her expected company belonged to the 1970s back-to-nature category of *néo*-Aveyronnais. The towered medieval rampart of La Couvertoirade, and its age-old stone houses with their picturesque flights of steps and upper sun-rooms, would not have failed to appeal to the artistically inclined among them. Annick had prepared a wide variety of drinks, but having come in from the cold night, there was a unanimous preference for her aromatic hot wine, which provided us with the right fuel before heading back to the Viaduct for a prolonged, outdoor party at the foot of its piers.

I expected the celebration to be no more than a casual event, but it turned out to be both spectacular and emotionally charged. For one, most of the team who had been involved in the construction of the piers were leaving now that their phase of the job was finished. Tonight was their farewell party, an in-house occasion with friends, relatives and a limited number of media people. It began with a flow of champagne and the usual speeches, which can be tedious, but not so tonight when clearly everyone present was moved and proud to have taken part in the making of history.

When the speeches were done, we gathered by the piers. Above us, the full moon seemed to look upon us like the ancient wise man who has seen it all. The silence of anticipation prevailed when out of the chilly night came an eerie, electronic sound evoking the future, like a science-fiction soundtrack (of course space is not about the future, it only feels like the future from our limited anthropocentric perspective, because our journey into space has barely started). Standing that night by the Viaduct felt like expanding into the infinite future in contrast with the return to genesis which I had experienced on the Aubrac at the beginning of my quest. Perhaps my quest was about bridging the two, as purported by the invisible voice that proclaimed man's epic story into the void of the night? Starting from the ancient Pyramids and alternating with the ever expanding music, the voice reported man's successive architectural and engineering feats through the ages, before blending into a spectacular laser light show which ended in a grand finale of sparkling bouquets of fireworks. When the story reached the birth date of the Millau Viaduct —10 October 2001— I was struck by the coincidence: exactly one month after Sept 11. I was actually in the Aveyron at the time, on my first visit to Georges and Odette, and more specifically in Conques on that day, miles away from the Millau Viaduct, of which I knew nothing except that Georges had mentioned that a fantastic bridge would be built in the Aveyron in the near future. Making a mental note of these dates, the Twin Towers and the Millau Viaduct became inseparable in my mind, emblematic like the mythological phoenix of the never-ending cycle of construction, destruction, reconstruction, and so forth. In its midst, man, the indomitable, starts all over again each time, Sisyphus-like, against all odds and no matter what.

Chapter 9

ROQUEFORT, THE 'KING OF CHEESES'

It was mid-winter the next time I was back in Southern Aveyron for a visit to the Roquefort caves during the ripening season of their cheeses. Expecting the countryside to be at its gloomiest and its dullest grey, I was pleasantly surprised when we reached the foothills of the Lévézou and found them all covered in snow. It was twilight but night is quick to follow at that time of year and before long a dark purple sky hung over the deceptively still, empty hills. The first snow drifts rose out of the roadside so timidly I barely noticed them, but gradually they picked up momentum and started swelling up, twirling and whirling and spurting white powder like strange silent ghosts in a dance choreographed by Lois Fuller. A strong wind was blowing, but I was too engrossed in this unusual ballet to give it much thought. It was only once we got to Hugues' home in Tournemire, and Mathilde greeted us with an expression of relief, that I realised how icy and slippery the road must have been and why we hadn't driven past a single car on our way. Visions of pilgrims wading their way through the snows of the Aubrac, of village doctors doing the same on horseback in the night, of Sébastien Persec's grandfather getting lost in his own farmyard, came to my mind. The harsh days of the past are always round the corner in the Aveyron, as if the visible signs of progress have touched only its surface, because nature here is doggedly unpliant.

To get to Tournemire we had to drive through Roquefort — a few, grey, uninspiring houses extending in a ribbon along the

D23 by the river Soulzon, at the foot of the cave-ridden cliffs of Combalou. It was night time by then and the cliffs were bathed in soft, amber floodlights like a proud city monument. Trust the French to add a touch of elegance to whatever they can lay their hands on, even when it's a rocky ridge of a plateau lost in a remote rural sheepland. Except that come to think of it, Roquefort *is* a national monument, not only the backbone and trademark of the Aveyron's economy, providing a livelihood to 10,000 people (over 1,600 on site) and pleasure to over 200,000 tourists annually, without doubt the Aveyron's most famous commodity worldwide.

Hughes and Mathilde were great hosts and refuelled me with an *aperitif* and a solid meal which we finished off with an assortment of local cheeses, Roqueforts and others, accompanied by a very acceptable Côtes de Millau. This was the first time I had met Mathilde, who treated me as informally as my American hosts would do, belying the widely spread notion about the French being sticklers for etiquette. France is changing, fast, like the rest of the world, and the Averyon is no exception, whose 'expat' residents contribute to bringing it closer to the outside world. Mathilde for instance is a Parisian cellist, born and bred in the Latin Quarter. Hughes, who runs several local magazines, is from the neighbouring *département* of the Cantal.

The wind moved elsewhere during the night, sweeping away the mist and the clouds. It was under a radiant blue sky that I rediscovered the Larzac the next morning, buried at that early hour beneath a blanket of rosy snow, in superb contrast with the silver mystery of my earlier visit. Once more eternity prevailed, not the cosmic timelessness of my previous visit which the night alone can convey, not the happening of Creation as I experienced it on the Aubrac, but an awesome sense of having landed at the dawn of life. It felt as if Hugues and I were the first intruders on the hitherto pristine earth, the first to interrupt the silence and mark the crunchy powder with our footprints. There was no sign of life around, no sheep, even though you knew they couldn't be far away, the occasional *lavogne** testifying to their presence in warmer seasons. We came across one outside La Couvertoirade (so now I knew where the flock of sheep from last December got their water) and another one elsewhere. They looked out of the snow like gleaming mirrors, shifting from jade to sapphire according to the whereabouts and whims of the sun. Thanks to a recent Roquefort commercial on French television, I could picture them in summer, when white circles of sheep dance around them to the pastoral melody of their bells.

In winter the sheep are packed by the hundreds inside honey-coloured stone *bergeries* – also known as *jasses* – which are to the landscape of the Larzac what the *burons* are to the Aubrac. Lying low like rectangular igloos, they seem to merge with the soil, the better to shield themselves from the wrath of the wind and keep the herd snug and warm in winter. The larger *bergeries*, those with high vaulted ceilings and magnificent timber-work, did not escape the attention of the post- (occasionally pre-) 1968 *néo*-Aveyronnais, and many were converted into contemporary, spacious havens of tranquillity, the kind of place where a friend of José Bové's whom I visited that day now lives. Odette's son Philippe has a converted *bergerie* on the Causse Comtal which affords breathtaking views as far as the Aubrac. As recently as twenty years ago it was still the home of a flock of 700 ewes.

---

* Circular paved drinking-hole

193

Two days later we visited Jean-Pierre Romiguier at Layrolle, who explained to us the difference between the shepherd and the farmer and their different ways of life. Shepherds are poets, he claimed, who scan the skies as they move about on unconfined stretches of land and are guided by stars at night. The farmer is down-to-earth, sometimes to a fault, rarely pushing his horizons beyond his acreage of land. The shepherd has no land — here in southern France, it is either leased from the *commune* or rented from private owners. Unburdened by property, he roams about with his one piece of luggage, a substantial shoulder bag into which he packs his few belongings — basic clothing, food and medicines.

I thought of the stories of Abel and Cain and Jacob and Esau which I used to read as archetypal tales of sibling rivalry. In the Biblical stories, divine preference weighs in favour of the pastor (is it because he is the more spiritual of the two?), hence the shepherd and lamb imagery which runs like a leitmotiv through the Holy Scriptures, both literally and metaphorically. In the new light shed by Jean-Pierre the stories could also be interpreted as the dichotomy between man's choice of two ways of life at a given moment in his socio-economic evolution, some 5,000 to 6,000 years ago; precisely when, on this side of the Mediterranean, he was beginning to clear the forests and settle down. It was at that time too that he began to erect menhir statues, 120 of which have been recorded in the region, 60 in the Averyon, mostly in the southwestern part of the *département*, and 60 across the border, in the Tarn and the Hérault. Their concentration in this part of France is quite unique. For the first time he carved an image of himself (or his gods?) in human or larger dimensions, marking in the stone, perhaps, his own place in the universe.

Their faces have eyes and noses, but curiously no mouths in most cases, which intensifies the mystery, as if they were meant to withhold their secret. The expression is inscrutable, mirroring the enigma of our own existence. Some of the attributes of the male figures point to warring and hunting activities, but they certainly also raised sheep. In all likelihood, the first *lavognes* date from their time.

Jean-Pierre is no shepherd. His mother had hoped he would work for the SNCF (French Railway) and enjoy the secure life of a *fonctionnaire*, but he had different ideas and the pastoral world was one of them. Making a living out of a dream doesn't always work, but Jean-Pierre's materialised into a successful business. It started with an old shepherd's bag that Robert Aussibal, a historian friend, had come across. He believed it was made in the 17th century and thought Jean-Pierre might design an updated version of it and manufacture it out of leather. And so the company, Le Sac du Berger, was born. The bag is worn over the shoulder and combines rigid and soft hides in its different parts, so as to give it both a solid structure and a fluid feel. The central piece is made of cowhide, but the rest of the bag is sheepskin. It has various side pockets, which in the old days served as separate compartments for food, utensils, and medicines but can now be used for a mobile phone or a pair of glasses, for example. Jean-Pierre has infused life into an article that would have otherwise been forgotten or, at best, relegated to a museum. Moreover, he has managed to extend his clientele from shepherds to fashion-conscious city women. He employs seven or eight people and is planning on further growth. In an area where jobs are scarce, this achievement proves that dreamers can have their feet on the ground and be endowed with good business acumen.

It turned out that Jean-Pierre knew 'my' shepherd from La Couvertoirade, the one I saw on that moonlit December night emerging out of the white surge of bleating sheep and whom I had romanticised into a mysterious apparition from another age. No, he was a flesh-and-blood Frenchman, and he had not been on his way to milk his flock that evening, as I had assumed, because the *transhumant* shepherds breed their sheep for meat and do not work for Roquefort, I was informed by Jean-Pierre. There are only a handful of them down here, who own between them some 1,500 to 1,800 sheep. It was partly the Roquefort commercial that had misled me with its idyllic evocation of pastoral life around the *lavogne*. Jean-Pierre explained that most of Roquefort's milk is supplied by sheep farms which are much the same as cattle farms. As for my vision of La Couvertoirade's shepherd milking his hundreds of ewes by hand... in fact milking today is done mechanically, allowing productivity to rocket from 25 ewes per hour to 500/600. And in any case, the sheep that graze at La Couvertoirade are not milked.

I was beginning to suspect that the entire scenario of that magical night at La Couvertoirade had been a figment of my imagination created by the silver light of the moon, but was reassured that waves of sheep do roll down the slopes of the *causses* in the summer, although their numbers have been dwindling steadily. Most of them do live on farms and yield their milk to the Roquefort industry. The *transhumant* shepherd, on the other hand, continues the traditional pastoral ways, moving south to the Gard and the Hérault *départements* in winter, and back up north in the summer, to the *estives* either of southern Aveyron or of neighbouring Cévennes. The shepherd of La Couvertoirade would have gone down south for the winter by the end of December.

The words *transhumant* and *estives* rang the familiar bell of the Aubrac: to my surprise the sheep too are led annually to the mountain tops in pomp, treading the same *drailhes* (dirt track) year in year out, except that over here in the south this has been going on for thousands of years. Some of the roads built by the Romans started out as *drailhes*, and some of those you drive on today may have been Roman roads, *drailhes*, or both. Like the world of the *buronnier*, pastoral society had a hierarchy, from the *pastre* (shepherd), to the *traspastre* (his aid), then the *gojat* (the apprentice), and of course the indispensable shepherd's dog. Apparently the little mongrels are the best because they are devilishly smart and can keep an eye on as many as 1,000 sheep. Some shepherds also keep a few goats to lead the herds because, as one of them put it, they are more 'resourceful' than sheep, whose intelligence he described tactfully as 'collective'.

The sheep's *transhumance* is a less publicised and more intimate affair than the cows'. In some cases it is altogether a private event, the shepherds being reluctant to share it with outsiders. I was privileged to be allowed to take part in the event, and thanks are due to Jean-Pierre for having made it happen. My painter friend Christine came along too, and it was three o'clock in the morning in early June when we joined the group at Arboras, at the foot of the Larzac, still in the Hérault. It was a moonless night and at first I couldn't distinguish the sheep in the darkness, but the familiar chorus of bells reassured me of their presence. After brief introductions and handshakes we were offered a quick cup of coffee, but few words were exchanged. Jean-Pierre had warned me that the shepherds were not an extroverted bunch. Little by little my eyes got accustomed to the dark and I could make out the silhouette of the herd. However, it was only once the first rays of sun began to stream from beyond the Cévennes that the sheep fully emerged in their festive decorations, their fleece having been sheared and trimmed into elaborate patterns and painted into flamboyant bright pompon tufts. Their bells hung from hand-painted collars, a job that can take a shepherd several weeks to complete, and which he patiently repeats every year, just for his own pleasure.

René Serieys was accompanied by his son Bruno, a handful of friends, and his dogs Bill and Perlou. The women had remained in the rear, in charge of the all-important business of sustenance, and would join us in their van later on in the day. We had to make good mileage before we could stop for breakfast because the heat would increase as the day progressed. Climbing up north, we left the road and made our way up the steep stony hillside, overgrown with scrub oak and broom, ablaze with yellow blossoms at that time of year. The sheep were much more at ease on that terrain than I was, skipping uphill like goats. I, on the other hand, had to hold on to the bushes and stop to catch my breath every now and then, which provided me with an excuse to turn round and soak up the ravishing scenery of the Languedoc, marked with sun-washed squares of bright green vineyards. As soon as we reached the tarmac road at the top of the slope, the herd closed ranks and started trotting in step in an interminable surge to the continual ringing of a full-scale orchestra. Meanwhile Bill and Perlou were running all over the place, wagging their tails with extraordinary vitality, clearly enjoying policing the herd.

By midday we reached our lunch destination, a shady pine wood overhanging with the balm of resina, blessed with an underwood of broom and sweet fragrances, where the sheep continued to graze lazily while we enjoyed an exquisitely sunny *ratatouille* concocted by René's wife, Jacqueline, assisted by her friend Rose. With the flow of wine everyone's tongues loosened, finally, and Christine and I began to feel that we were being accepted. We would probably have been more wholeheartedly embraced by the community eventually, had we been able to stay on for several days. I realised that what is often perceived as insular distrust coming from rural natives is in fact no more than shyness. After all, from their perspective, we citizens of the big city can seem intimidating, even condescending. I am just as intimidated by their competence and resourcefulness regarding the essentials of life which are much more crucial to survival than my so called culture. By the time we were biting into the freshly-picked juicy peaches, a lively conversation was under way. I even ventured to ask a few questions while we had our coffee.

Then came holy nap time, when people and animals alike could do as they pleased: here a lone shepherd was fast asleep on his back under a tree, further away another shepherd was just dozing off leaning against a tree trunk; clusters of ewes cuddled together among the grasses, others were grazing sluggishly unable to resist the temptation of the scented herbs; some alternated between the two. Having come from the noise of the city, I let the rustle of the pines trickle down my ears. Occasionally an insect buzzed past through the silence, an idle bell accompanied the chewing of mouthfuls of broom; somebody was breathing peacefully in dreamland. Peeping through the boughs, the sun completed the pastoral nirvana with patterns of light which it cast on the grass. The march would resume at the end of the afternoon, once the weather cooled off. There is no need to rush when one is a sheep or a shepherd.

The *transhumant* shepherds are among Jean-Pierre's friends and clients, and several own his bags. What better guarantee of authenticity and quality? Undeterred by its weight, they appreciate the fact that the leather is alive and will eventually soften and gain patina. Add to it the pleasure of using an item that has been individually made, that is rooted in a geographical location and has a history, and that ultimately will see them through a lifetime.

Jean-Pierre's house nestles pleasantly in the lush green valley of the Sorgues, at the end of a country road that branches off the D7 at Latour-sur-Sorgues. The sound of streaming water greeted us as we got out of the car, indicating the presence of a lively river, the obvious location for a leather manufactory. Except that I was wrong once more: The leather market too has gone the global way and Jean-Pierre imports from Spain, Germany, Turkey, Morocco... He lives at Layrolle because he was lucky to find this large sheep farm which had been standing empty for ten years and was up for sale. He was also lucky to purchase it in a good state of repair, a magnificent example of a regional construction dating from 1860 which features impressive buttresses and timber-work under the massive vaulted ceiling. The sheepfold, traditionally situated downstairs, has been converted into a shop; the workshop is situated upstairs in what used to be the barn. Outside are two hectares of bucolic grounds, complete with a kitchen garden and fruit trees, surrounded by woods and watered by a stream that flows into the Sorgues. They call it Layrolle, like the place, because it's never been given a name.

Jean-Pierre's journey is edifying: by having left school and joined the job market early on, he had saved enough capital to buy the farm at an age when most people are barely on the first

Shepherd's shelter on the Larzac
©Patrice Geniez

▲ Friends ©Patrice Geniez

©Patrice Geniez ▼

The sheep transhumance – "holy nap time"
©Thirza Vallois

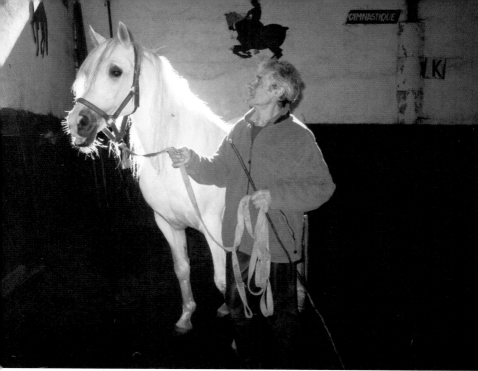

▲ Jean-Yves and Estoc ©Thirza Vallois

Le Rougier ©Patrice Geniez ▼

▲ Père André Gouzes with one of his flock, Sylvanès
©Thirza Vallois

Sylvanès, the cloister ©Thirza Vallois ▼

▲ The Russian Chapel above Sylvanès
©Thirza Vallois

The cycle of time ©Thirza Vallois ▼ ▶

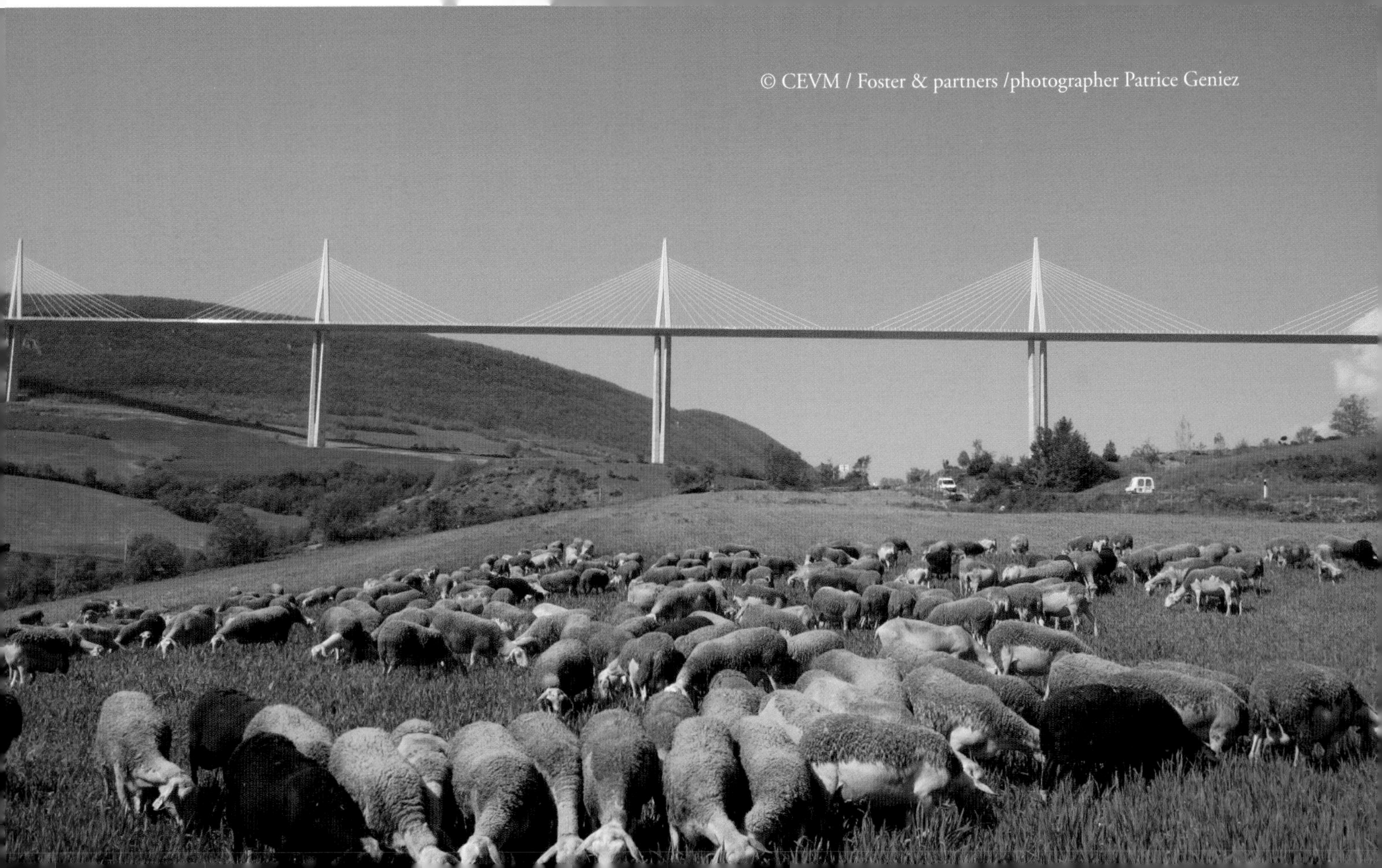
© CEVM / Foster & partners /photographer Patrice Geniez

rung of the property market. Talent, inspiration, vision and hard work, did the rest. Everything in the shop relates to pastoral life, from the little woollen sheep dangling from a key ring to wonderfully soft sheepskin slippers or vests, or huge umbrellas mounted astutely on wooden frames so as to act as a lightning conductor on the treeless *causses*. In the heat of summer, they also make excellent sunshades. Shepherds' crooks are another obvious accessory, made traditionally from the branches of chestnut or hazel trees.

Jean-Pierre has also redesigned the shepherd's full-length cape which protected him from inclement weather and marked his silhouette in the distance as he led his herds through the wilderness. By night it came in handy as a bedding. Jean-Pierre was inspired by an old model from neighbouring Cévennes but replaced the canvas with water-proof wool and also designed a coat version with sleeves to make it more suitable for modern living. Among the smaller items he carries I was amused by the traditional black leather wallet of the *maquignon*, the animal dealer. Since the transactions on the market place are done in cash, the wallet is fitted with two press studs, one for the beginning of the day when it is still empty, and another one for when it gets filled up with bank notes as the day draws on.

Roquefort cheese also took root in pastoral society, though no one knows how long back. All we know is that we owe this delicacy to a shepherd boy who lived in that hazy remote past we call "once upon a time" for lack of more specific information. Although we have no description of him, we may assume that he too carried his victuals in a bag, where the Roquefort cheese fermented into being, accidentally. The bag may have even been the kind of rudimentary arrangement Jean-Pierre described to me as the ancestor of the shepherd's bag, a crude sheepskin carried on the back and tied up in front by the animal's feet. Be that as it may, as usual it started with a love story.

It was hot on the Combalou plateau on that pre-destined day, and the young shepherd was sheltering from the sun at the mouth of one of its caves when, lo and behold, the beguiling silhouette of a fair maiden appeared in the distance, luring him on like an irresistible mirage. Smitten and oblivious of his sheep and his lunch—a loaf of bread and a morsel of cheese— he hastened out of the cave in her pursuit. The outcome of this amorous venture is unknown, gone the way of most tales, but it has been reported that when he eventually retraced his steps to the cave (some say it was four months later), he found his lunchpack where he had left it. When he opened it, however, the cheese was covered with greenish mould, into which he would never have dared sink his teeth, had he not been famished. And a good thing he did, for without realising it, he had bitten into the first Roquefort cheese, to which he succumbed with delight.

The oldest record of cheese-making in the area are the fragments of a cheese mould found on Mont Sargel. They date from the Neolithic age and are on display in Roquefort's archeological museum. This in itself does not prove that it was used to make Roquefort cheese, whose date of birth is likely to remain one of those unresolved mysteries that bury their secrets in the silence of times past. Yet Roquefort cheese does carry the mark of ancientness, as do its surroundings. Looking up to the cliffs of Combalou sets you pondering about durations and dimensions beyond your grasp.

It takes plenty of imagination to travel even further back, and picture southern Averyon submerged by two inland seas, to which bears witness the 180 million-year-old plesiosaurus discovered at Tournemire. When a new dawn emerged out of the chaos, two new mountain chains stood majestically to the east and west — respectively the Alps and the Pyrenees. Here, in the south of the Massif Central, the retreating waters left behind vast expanses of limestone, an extraordinary repository of fossils, a memorial to the defunct seas. The Tournemire plesiosaurus and samples of sea fossils are on display in the Museum of Millau. The newly-born *causses*, an aggregate of sand and shells, yielded a crumbly soil vulnerable to erosion by water and wind, which carved out of it a breathtaking array of cliffs, cirques, canyons and gorges.

These beautiful features can be seen at such spots as the Gorges du Tarn (in neighbouring Lozère) and those of the Jonte, the Cirque of Tournemire, not to mention the spectacular site of Montpellier-le-Vieux in the Causse Noir (so called after its black pine), where nature has twisted the grey rock into distorted shapes that look like the ancient ruins of a tortured, petrified city. Much of the Aveyron is covered with limestone plateaux, each with its distinct features, adding further diversity to the complexity of the Aveyronnais patchwork. Those of southern Aveyron — Causse de Sévérac, Causse Noir, Causse du Larzac come under the designation of Grands Causses, a vast territory of 315,640 hectares that enjoy the status of *parc régional*, which secures them environmental protection and the preservation of their architectural heritage. The Causse Comtal, north of Rodez, and the oak-covered *causse* dominating the Lot in the Quercy, in western Averyon, do not come under its jurisdiction.

The Alpine upheaval was followed by several lesser ones. Between three and seven million years ago, it was the turn of the Combalou plateau to be shattered out of its serenity by a landslide of layers of lime and marl, followed by two others, the last of which occurred only 15,000 to 20,000 years ago. When calm returned, a glowing saddle-shaped rampart stood facing the setting sun, hence the name Combalou from the Gallic '*combal*' for saddle. A multitude of cool, damp caves proliferated inside the rock, as well as endless fissures — *fleurines*, or *flarina* in Occitan, meaning 'blow', because they act as airducts and supply the caves with natural ventilation. The combined presence of the caves and the airducts create the unique conditions that allow the Roquefort cheese to ripen on this tiny strip of 2,000m long by 300m wide by 300m high, here and nowhere else in the world. A mysterious miracle for sure, and a good enough reason for the village of Roquefort-sur-Soulzon to have clung to the Combalou cliffside, its breadwinner and source of pride down the centuries.

For the reputation of the cheese goes way back to the times when the Larzac was the crossroads of several major routes linking Western Europe to the Mediterranean shores. In his Natural History (76 A.D.) Pliny the Elder refers to a cheese from Gévaudan (now Lozère) as "the most highly esteemed cheese in Rome", although it cannot be ascertained that he was referring specifically to Roquefort. With the fall of Rome in the 5th century, the road network fell into disuse and for hundreds of years the distribution of the cheese was restricted to the vicinity of its production. Banditry was rife, which accounts for the erection of a fortification — *rocca forti*. It is reported, though not established, that Charlemagne passed through here after his disastrous Spanish campaign in 788 A.D., and was offered a Roquefort cheese by the monks of St-Gall. When he began to cut out the revolting mouldy bits, the monks persuaded him to try what they considered the best part of the cheese. It seems that he was delighted and ordered two wheels of Roquefort to be delivered to him on a yearly basis. According to a different source, it was the abbey of Conques that supplied the Emperor with the cheese, two mule-loads which were dispatched to him every Christmas. Both reports are apocryphal and to be taken with a pinch of salt.

With the development of fairs circa 1000 A.D., the cheese travelled further afield and reached Creissels outside Millau where I had a taste of it in the company of Georges and Odette, and their friends, before my first visit to the Viaduct. However, the first clear reference to "a cheese made in cabins (*cabanes*) in the land of Larzac" dates only from 1070 A.D. The document specifies that the Lord of Cornus offered the abbey of Conques two wheels from each cabin. The reference to 'cabins' clarifies matters, since they were to the Roquefort cheese what the *burons* were to the Laguiole (and to the Cantal over the border) in a more recent past. Today, the women who work for Société, Roquefort's main producer, are still known as *cabanières*.

When the Knights Templar settled on the Larzac in the 13th century, sheep rearing was their main activity. It makes sense to assume they had a vested interest in Roquefort cheese, although there are no records to confirm this. Who cares! Roquefort Société has branded one of its three cheeses Cave des Templiers, capitalising on the fascination exerted by this medieval order. It is the strongest brand, meant to evoke the rugged life of the valiant soldier-farmers, and is appreciated by the savvy connoisseurs of the home market. The more balanced Cave Abeille 1863, on the other hand, is easier on the palate and has been selected for export, as I was satisfied to verify at my local Sainsbury's in London the week following my visit. At the same time, I was saddened to see 'The King of Cheeses' dethroned and subjected to an assembly-line treatment, stacked by indifferent hands among other blue cheeses, Danish, English, Italian, and French rivals — a far cry from the reverent care bestowed upon it back home. However, the *crème de la crème* of Société's cheeses is the divine Baragnaudes, which somehow manages an astonishing combination of softness and full-bodied sharpness, wrapped up in delicate aroma.

In the early 15th century, the royal house took direct measures to encourage the production of the Roquefort cheese and in 1411 Charles VI declared the Combalou a protected zone. This meant that no cheese could be seized from its cellars in case of bad debts. Charles VII, next in line, visited Roquefort, loved the cheese, and gave each inhabitant permission to keep one wheel of cheese for his own consumption, a privilege confirmed in a royal charter and renewed by future kings, from François I to Louis XIV.

Even more importantly, in 1666 the Parliament of Toulouse issued an edict which limited the Roquefort status to the location of its production. In effect this was the equivalent of the modern-day AOC, the much sought after Appellation d'Origine Controlée (Controlled Designation of Origin), which Roquefort was the first commodity in France to be granted again, in 1925, and on an international level in 1951. European recognition followed in 1996, with the establishment of the Appellation d'Origine Protégée (AOP) status (Protected Designation of Origin). The traceability of the cheese was made compulsory in 2001 to guarantee its authenticity, but at the same time the geographical zone of production has been allowed to expand way beyond the 1666 boundaries of the village of Roquefort.

Today not only can the entire *département* of the Aveyron sell its milk to the Roquefort industry, but also the neighbouring

Lozère, Gard, Hérault, Tarn and Aude, six *départements* in all, known as the Roquefort 'radius'. Contrary to the misleading television commercial with its circle of ewes drinking from a *lavogne*, most of the flocks that supply Roquefort have never set foot on the Larzac! Furthermore, only the last two phases of the production, the ripening of the cheese (14 days minimum) and its maturing (90 days minimum), take place in the cellars of Combalou. Before arriving here, the milk will have passed through one of eight cheese dairies, situated anywhere within the 'radius', where it will have been transformed into cheese, and that was big news to me too. This is where the cheese is salted and inseminated with *penicillium roqueforti*, the legendary and microscopic fungus at the origin of Roquefort's stardom, before being loaded onto the refrigerated trucks that deliver it to Roquefort, albino-like and insipid in taste.

Nevertheless, the act of sorcery that will turn it into the famous blue cheese does indeed take place in the caves of Combalou, and this is what entitles them to their prestigious pedigree. The magical metamorphosis extends over a period of four weeks in the silent sanctuary of the cellars, where no sunlight ever penetrates. This is where the *penicillium roqueforti* will gestate, ferment and develop inside the soft, fat, milky substance. In the old days one used to place rye and wheat bread in the cellars. Today the fungus is cultivated in laboratories and inserted into the cheese as powder, a gram of which contains between 20 and 30 million spores, enough to produce over 400 wheels of cheese.

The cheeses are pierced through and aligned vertically on the cellar's oak shelving for the duration of the ripening, so as to help them inhale the air let in by the *fleurines* and exhale the carbonic gas produced by the fermentation. Once all the shelves have been filled up, the cellar resembles a dim, oozing forest of cheeses, twice the area of the village itself. For the next several weeks it will be entrusted to the vigilant care of the *maître affineur* (cellar master), the alchemist in charge of the ripening and the only person allowed on the premises. His routine rounds are marked by the pounding of his steps, the one audible manifestation of life in this otherwise seemingly inanimate multi-layered underworld, lying eleven storeys underground. I say 'seemingly' because in actual fact a teeming, microscopic life is in progress, under cover, inside each wheel of cheese, without which the ripening couldn't occur.

It is the task of the *maître affineur* to supervise and stimulate the ripening by striking the right balance between the air coming in from the *fleurines*, and the heat let off by the cheese, so as to ensure the temperature in the cellar remains constant, at its natural 5º to 9º. Likewise the humidity in the cellars is kept at constant 95º to 98º. This is both a science and an art; it calls above all for flair, as exemplified by the highly celebrated and now retired *maître affineur* of Société, Maurice Astruc, whose face was as familiar to the French public as those of top celebrities. Endowed with the characteristic features of a native of the *terroir* — a corpulent morphology, a round, earthy, whiskered face, and an indispensable *casquette* (flat cap) — he used to pose for Société's commercials mothering a Roquefort in the process of ripening, the ultimate guarantee of affectionate care, and thereby of quality, in the face of all international bans and anti raw-milk hysteria.

This is all very well on the French home front, but today's global market requires more tangible safeguards, to which end the Red Ewe Label was established by the forward-looking Roquefort Confederation of Milk Producers and Cheesemakers, back in 1930 (which I also spotted on my visit to Sainsbury's).

Besides using the label to fight off forgery, the Confederation's main target is to maintain high standards by taking advantage of scientific progress whilst preserving old traditions. The quality of the Lacaune race, purveyor of the industry, has been improved through genetics resulting in a spectacular increase in its milk yield, 200 litres over the six months of its milking season. (For the sake of comparison, a cow will yield 6,000 litres in the same number of sessions). In parallel, special attention is given to the animal's food (fodder in winter, pastures the rest of the year), to maximise the quality of the milk and enhance it with the unmistakable flavour of southern France.

Never mind if the vast US market, or others, might be lost, as was the case in 1999 when the US retaliated against the European ban on hormone-fed beef by singling out Roquefort and slapping it with 100% duties. The dismantling of the Millau McDonald outlet was, in turn, largely in reaction to the US ban on Roquefort. When hit periodically by such punitive measures, the French will shrug them off with a haughty confidence in their own superiority and the assurance that the pleasures offered to and enjoyed by a savvy palate are of much greater value than those afforded by a fat bank account. And what better support than the enthusiastic testimonies of illustrious spokesmen from the Renaissance or the Age of Enlightenment, not least Rabelais, Voltaire and Diderot, who, in the famous *Encyclopédie* he co-authored with d'Alembert, defined Roquefort as "the king of cheeses, without doubt the finest cheese in Europe". And since Casanova recommended it as a stimulus for love, it is understandable that some amongst the French will view the US with a patronising mix of indulgence and disdain for its uncivilised nationals who are incapable of discerning between junk food and other such health hazards, and a full-bodied, unctuous, sensual Roquefort. Recent statistics may prove them right, since life expectancy in France now ranks among the highest in the world.

Roquefort Société, the result of a merger in 1842 of several small producers, is now a public company owned by the giant Lactalis, and holds a 61.17% market share. Its guided tours offer sound and light effects and finish, inevitably, at the boutique, where the three varieties of cheese are on sale. Papillon, the largest of the independent companies, organises visits too but they are less fancy. Despite Société's supremacy, Roquefort's six smaller privately owned companies— Papillon, Carles, Gabriel Coulet, Fromageries Occitanes, Vernières and le Vieux Berger — are standing their ground and doing well. Some have even carried off a share of Societé's custom in recent years. The smallest, le Vieux Berger, is highly praised and is served at Michel Bras'. This three-generation family business is run at present by Vincent Combes, who by keeping his business small (fewer than 10 employees) can enjoy *artisanal* status, a guarantee of individual attention and back-to-roots values in the mind of the French consumer.

All Roquefort's cheeses can be sampled at the restaurant of the Hôtel Moderne in nearby red-tiled St-Affrique, a pretty town by the river Sorgues. The intriguing name does not refer to the continent but to Affricanus, the Bishop of Comminges, who built the town's first church in the 6th century. The monument was replaced by several others over time, notably by a Gothic edifice in the 14th century which was destroyed by the Calvinists during the Wars of Religion. A plaque on a round tower by the Pont Vieux reminds the passerby that the Protestant women of St-Affrique put up a valiant resistance to the repeated assaults of the Prince de Condé in 1628. Although in this particular instance the Prince had to levy the siege, the Protestants were defeated in southern Aveyron, prompting many to emigrate, in particular the more entrepreneurial members of the community, and causing the area to decline economically. The present church dates from the 17th century, a pretty sight as its slender 78m-tall steeple rises above the Gothic Pont Vieux. Inside five stained-glass windows depict the life of St-Affrique.

We picked a Saturday for our lunch so as to take in the weekly morning market, which stretches along Avenue Victor Hugo and overflows with fresh organic produce from nearby farms. Endearingly, the Hôtel Moderne had stuck to its old name which, by dint of it being painfully unimaginative, has become pathetically poetic. It has also resisted a face-lift. Everything here exuded an air of times when modernity suggested the imminent advent of a glamorous golden age, be it in New York, Chicago or Paris, let alone small-town St-Affrique in a lost corner of France. The setting, the staff, even the clientele seemed to have remained unchanged since the days when the local bourgeoisie gathered here for celebratory family reunions. Consequently, we were served a wonderful meal in Gargantuan quantities, as promised in the expression *cuisine bourgeoise*. And since St-Affrique is not situated on the tourist highway, we also received our money's worth. The cheese tray extended beyond Roquefort to *pérail* which is made of ewe's milk, *bleu des Causses*, of cow's milk, and even *Laguiole* from up north. Obviously, the Roquefort selection stole the show, and included a delicious organic Papillon. Whilst delighting in them all, a necessary effort for the sake of comparison, I meditated on the famous *gastronome* Brillat-Savarin's statement: "a dinner without Roquefort is like a beautiful woman with only one eye."

Chapter 10

THE SALT ROAD

Salmiech is a sleepy little place, sitting prettily by the river Céor. Jean-Yves Bonnet will tell you that the name of the river derives from Ci-or, '*là où coulent les paillettes d'or*' (where specks of gold flow), which may or may not be true etymologically speaking, although the river did glitter like gold when I sat reading by the water and the sunrays filtered through the leafy tangles of trees along its banks. Besides, who cares so long as it is poetically pleasing, and Jean-Yves is a poet to the marrow of his bones who, no sooner had I crossed the threshold of his home, let an endless celebration of his homeland's radiant broom — *les genêts* — roll out of his throat. It sounded like a southern echo of William Wordsworth's "hosts of daffodils" and just as brilliantly golden:

> *Blossoms of gold, of light and of silk,*
> *Like butterflies laid on the tip of each twig,*
> *Heavy with scents that are hitherto bound*
> *From faraway shores where the sun has just drowned*

The nine stanzas in praise of local scenery and a pastoral lifestyle were recited with the rolling lilt that Jean-Yves had inherited from the Occitan language, the *langue d'oc* of the poet-musician Troubadours.

Today the *langue d'oc* has shrunk to a narrow province wedged between the Mediterranean and the Aveyron, but in

213

the Middle Ages it shone over a highly cultured civilisations that encompassed the whole of southern France. it was still the native language of Jean-Yves, who was born in the 1930s, early enough to escape the hegemony of French which was imposed a few years later. Now past 70, time has furrowed through his weather-beaten face, and has turned his once jet-black hair to silver, but his nimble slight body remains like that of an elf, and we all know that elves stay eternally youthful... They are also known to move about light-footed, although Jean-Yves prefers to do so on horseback.

When the recitation was finished he came up with a fairytale offer to take me riding across the broom-covered hills the following spring and experience the poem firsthand. The poem was written by the locally famous poet François Fabié, whose birthplace and home, le Moulin de Roupeyrac, at Durenque, on the Lagast plateau, is open to the public, offering an insight into a way of life now gone. Today it adjoins the village football pitch, and has recently been given rather too much of a facelift, but the serene tranquillity of the surroundings remains untouched, magically reflected in the deep blue water of the village pond. Situated between the Ségala and the southwest edge of the Lévézou, the plateau affords extended views of the *département.* By night, the skies display a galactic splendour that did not escape the notice of astronomers. When Jean-Baptiste Delambre and Pierre Méchain launched their seven-year expedition (1792–1799) to measure the meridian between Dunkirk and Barcelona, Lagast was picked out as one of the guide marks.

Jean-Yves's invitation sounded like a dream. Except that I hadn't sat on a horse for decades, and was no spring chicken. No matter how poetic, the idea was as over the top as Georges' having me write a book on the Aveyron. But then Georges too is a poet. And just as Georges had lured me into the project by giving me a foretaste of the Aveyron in October 2001, Jean-Yves suggested driving me down south right after lunch, in anticipation of our horse ride. It was early February, but owing to the proximity of the Mediterranean, the red hills of the Rougier reverberated with the intense brightness of summer which made it easy to shift the scene a few months forward and fancy the dark stringy broom alight with golden blossoms. By the time the jade ribbon of the Tarn was behind us, and the Dourdou had displayed its deep turquoise splendour on our left, Jean-Yves had completely won me over, just as Georges had.

In the end the spring horse ride didn't happen, due to lack of time on my part, but I did manage to join Jean-Yves on the Salt Route cavalcade in early July, a big event that enjoyed national media coverage and the object of my visit in the first place. Jean-Yves's aura in riding circles had a lot to do with its success. It reached well beyond the Aveyron, even beyond France. In the late 1980s, King Hassan II of Morroco flew out to Jean-Yves his personal hunting horse, also named Hassan, for special training. Jean-Yves travelled from Salmiech to Marseilles Airport and was given special permission to drive up to the plane to disembark the horse. The King even offered him the logistical assistance of the army to organise a Salt Route cavalcade down the ancient caravan routes of Morocco, but Saddam Hussein "started playing his tricks", as Jean-Yves put it, Desert Storm followed and the project fell through. So Jean-Yves stuck to the Aveyron, where he has been leading the cavalcade every July since 1984. The summer I joined them marked its 20th-anniversary jubilee.

It is believed that salt was first used during the Neolithic age, when man gave up hunting and started cooking the meat of his domesticated animals. In parallel, he also discovered the healing properties of salt, which are still celebrated in the village of Estaing on the first Sunday of July to commemorate St Fleuret, renowned for his healing powers. On that occasion the priest blesses the salt, whilst the farmers of the Aubrac present him with bread and *fouace*.

The Mediterranean coastline of southern France offered excellent conditions for the extraction of salt — shallow waters, few tidal changes, warm temperatures that stimulated the water's evaporation and helped early man notice the white residue. This was even truer in ancient times, when the coastline was hemmed by a string of lagoons, swamps and marshes. It is believed that Grecian traders were already extracting salt here in the 7th century B.C. When they founded Marseilles (Massalia) the following century, they turned the activity into a fully-fledged trade between the coast and the mountains. Rome followed suit, then the Christian monks, generating enough profit to attract the attention of the Royal House of France, which grabbed the lion's share of the trade by way of the notoriously hated salt tax, *la gabelle*.

Several salt routes — *cami salinié* or *cami de la sal* — furrowed through southern France, but Jean-Yves chose to follow the one that ran through his native Aveyron. Setting out from the Mediterranean saltworks of Aigues-Mortes, where they collected their salt, for ten days hundreds of participants followed him north, on horseback, by carriage or all-terrain bike, some even trailing along on foot. It was an awesome journey through a succession of breathtaking sceneries that you won't see from your car. We took in the vast deserted uplands

of the Larzac, the steep, stony woodlands of the Lévézou and
its moor-covered lakesides, fording occasionally a boisterous
stream, and finally past open fields of farmland on the
approach to Rodez, where the procession ended. At each
stopping-place Jean-Yves, dressed as a Knight Templar to suit
his penchant for the age of chivalry, presented the local mayor
with a pouch of salt and knighted him in a mock medieval
ceremony followed by a colourful equestrian show.

The fortified Templars' command post of La
Couvertoirade, our first stopping-place in the Aveyron coming
from the Hérault, provided an ideal setting for the ceremony
and a satisfying association with a military order whose initial
vocation was the protection of the pilgrim route in the Holy
Land. It is tempting to extrapolate that the Templars of the
Larzac engaged in similar military activities along the strategic
salt route, or in the actual trade of salt which would have
generated further income besides preserving their cheese,
except that, once more, there is no historical evidence that this
was the case.

On the other hand, it is an irrefutable fact that salt was a vital
commodity in pre-refrigeration days, a fact spelt out by such
expressions as 'white gold' or 'the salt of the earth', and a wide
range of vocabulary deriving from salt and relating to man's
livelihood, such as *solde* (pay), *salaire* (salary), even *soldat*
(soldier). According to Jean-Yves it is appreciated just as much
by animals which is why it is used as a bait to woo wayward
cattle back to the herd. The cause of many a war, *la gabelle*
enabled the taxman to become among the wealthiest men in the
kingdom, and by the same token among its most hated subjects.
Hence the palatial townhouse of the taxman Aubert de Fontenay
in the Marais area of Paris, sarcastically nicknamed the Hôtel

Salé (literally 'salty' but meaning costly in colloquial French), now home to the Picasso Museum. The fact that the salt tax was done away with during the French Revolution speaks for itself.

Regardless, Jean-Yves looked dashing in his costume as he gave the lead to the equestrian pageant against the lovely theatre set of La Couvertoirade, floodlit by the copper lustre of twilight. But the silvery mystery of that moonlit night of December was gone, and the magical silence encountered in the heart of winter had melted with the snow, like a dream lost on waking up to reality. Especially when I stumbled unexpectedly upon the familiar face of Jean-Pierre Romiguier outside his outlet of Le Sac du Berger. I had forgotten he had a shop there. Reality extended further to dinner, served at long rows of tables, as at all Aveyronnais gatherings. The formidable din, a combination of lively conversation and bad acoustics, drowned all hope of interviewing fellow guests. Even the accordion was at pains when it tried to hold forth, except for the odd occasion when a cluster of male voices joined in on a whim, infallibly unmelodious and hopelessly out of tune. Not that it bothered anyone. It was not about music but about having a good time.

I was seated opposite the likeable Mayor of Millau, Jacques Godefrain, whom I had first met at the inauguration of the piers of the Millau Viaduct. On my right was the engaging Marie-Jo Laborie, Madame le Maire of La Couvertoirade. So La Couvertoirade even had a modern mayor, just like any regular French town and village! And a woman mayor, at that! Forget about sheep-rearing Patriarchs or cross-bearing knights dotting a carbon-copy landscape of the Holy Land! Besides, although Marie-Jo's family tree in La Couvertoirade can be traced back to the 17th century — not quite the times of the

Templars, but still— her daughter is enjoying a scientific career in Seattle. I was equally surprised to find out that the very Robert Aussibal who had introduced Jean-Pierre Romiguier to the old shepherd's bag was Marie-Jo's brother-in-law. And likewise that Jean-Pierre and Jean-Yves Bonnet were friends! Small world. But then everyone seems to be connected or even related here, even across social and professional boundaries and the unmarked boundary between northern Aveyron and the south.

During the dinner it came up that Jean-Pierre was making a shepherd's cape for Jean-Yves who would be riding to Compostela the following September, fulfilling at last a lifelong dream. As a child he used to play at the foot of the *château* of Béranger de Landorre, the lord of Salmiech who was appointed Archbishop of Compostela in 1322 and held the position until his death in 1330. His remains were taken to the Dominican Chapel in Rodez, but the chapel was destroyed during the French Revolution and I haven't been able to elucidate what has happened to them since. Endowed with an exceptional sense of diplomacy, Béranger was a major player on the European chessboard, promoting spectacular reconciliations between such bitter enemies as Philip the Fair of France and Pope Clement V. Jean-Yves recalls the hopeful gold diggers who, like himself, hung around the *château* during his childhood, but for a different reason. The Céor yielded to them no gold, only trout. Jean-Yves had little use for gold. It was the *château*'s landlord of yore that captured his imagination, the incarnation of the chivalrous ideal. Riding his horse to Compostela at the age of 70 was a tribute to his revered predecessor. And the choice of September for his pilgrimage was not fortuitous, Béranger having made his official entrance into Compostela as its new Archbishop on the 26th of that month.

Like so many Aveyronnais Jean-Yves is a profound observer of nature, and has taught me some precious lessons about the beauty of chivalrous love through his relationship with his horses. *Chevalier* (knight), he pointed out, derives from *cheval* (horse), and each of his horses gets his individual attention, education and parenting, and in return is eager to please. In other words, their relationship is based on complementary reciprocity. Gentle talking, patting and a handful of carrots make the horses willing, while going through the movements and paces with them, as he would with an equal partner, gives them real pleasure. Jean-Yves will tell you about the alchemy of miming and likes to call himself the Marcel Marceau* of horses. Miming, he claims, is the common ancestral language of all living creatures and how humans acquire their mother tongue. It is transmitted through the eyes, the facial muscles, vocal cords, and every part of the body. It will get you much further than preaching or coercing. So when Estoc refused to go down on one knee during a demonstration, rather than raise his voice, Jean-Yves knelt down by his side and in no time they were both on the ground interlocked in the joy of communion. Jean-Yves claims Estoc is the world's cleverest horse, who can execute 60 different movements. He claims this is the world record and would like to see him entered into the Guinness Book of Records. He can pull out his tongue, place a hat on Jean-Yves' head, and mimic his grimaces. Jean-Yves never raises a whip at a horse and never spurs it on with his stirrups. When I enquired about the stick he was holding, he replied that it was just his conductor's baton.

---

* A famous French mime

Way before Robert Redford in Montana, or real-life Monty Roberts in Santa Barbara in California, Jean-Yves had been whispering to horses in the Aveyron, and to all nature's creatures, emulating one of his fellow countrymen from way back, Victor of Aveyron. He is also known as Victor of St-Sernin, after the village where he was caught the third and final time, in 1800. (This is also the home village of the Aveyron's most famous menhir statue, la Dame de St-Sernin, now on display at the Musée Fenaille in Rodez). To the general public the boy is better known as l'Enfant Sauvage (the Wild Boy), owing to François Truffaut's famous movie.

It is believed that the boy was raised by a wolf, or pack of wolves, in the woods of Lacaune (after which the area's breed of sheep is named), where he had twice been captured by hunters but managed each time to escape. The third time he was locked up as a freak and became a national curiosity. The Home Minister, Lucien Bonaparte, took a personal interest in his case and had him moved to Paris for clinical observation, while his life story was played out to packed houses at three of the capital's theatres. Rumour even had it that he was the mysteriously lost Louis XVII, the dauphin of the guillotined king. This would contradict another hypothesis as to the fate of the young king, according to which he escaped to the Château de St-Amans by Villefranche-de-Panat in the Lévézou. There he met a native maiden whom he made pregnant. Apparently, one of the restaurant owners from nearby Salles Curans, which we passed on our way along the Salt Route, believed he was one of their descendants.

In 1811 Victor was moved to the Impasse des Feuillantines in the Latin Quarter, home to the famous Feuillantines Convent before the Revolution, and still surrounded by bucolic grounds at the time. Today rue des Feuillantines is a regular street off rue Gay-Lussac, and a bus stop announced electronically by a female voice on the 21 and 27 lines. Those among the passengers who have seen Truffaut's movie are probably unaware that this was the Paris home of the Wild Boy of Aveyron until his passing in 1828, and also the home of his more illustrious and somewhat younger neighbour who went by the same name, one Victor Hugo.

Jean-Yves believes the boy died because he had been forced into the prison of civilisation. He drove me to St-Sernin-sur-Rance to see the bronze statue of the *sauvageon*, as he referred to him sympathetically. He too was a sauvageon and withered away within the prison walls of his school. At night he used to run off to sleep with the horses in the stables. Later he fixed up an '*hermitage*' in the wilderness of the Lévézou, where he lived alone with some animals, including a few wolves. He still keeps a pair, Charlemagne and Chipie, and responds to their howls in their own language. Miming, he says, is a two-way traffic, denoting respect for nature's variety (rather than hierarchy). It was his grandfather, Philippe, who instilled in him the connection to nature, a role model who had fired his imagination with his wonderful stories, told in Occitan by the fire. Jean-Yves scoured the countryside with Grandfather in a horse-drawn cart and recalls the special day when they rode to Rodez for the first time, to see the early silent version of Jungle Book. It goes without saying that Mowgli left a deep impression on the six-year-old.

His first memories of horses, however, go back to when he was three. This was in the village of Carcenac where they visited relatives who had several draught horses, perhaps ten. An ancient sarcophagus, unearthed somewhere in the vicinity, was converted into the village trough — there were so many of them in the countryside that no one thought twice about recycling them. Jean-Yves remembers being seated by his cousin on one of the horses so that he might get a better view of the 'trough'. By the age of 14 or 15, he had started buying his own horses, and was the first to introduce riding horses into the Aveyron. He also became the Averyon's first riding instructor, an eccentricity that was frowned upon by the villagers. Mamie Bonnet, Jean-Yves's mother and everybody's Mother Earth, confirmed that her son's testimony was true to life.

At the youthful age of 94, she still reigns single-handed over the kitchen, where her tiny person busies herself for hours on end and has a presence audible enough to fill up not only the kitchen but also all the space of the adjoining dining-cum-living room, for most of the day; the shuffling sound of her feet, the intermittent running of water, the opening and shutting of drawers, the tinkling of cutlery, the knocking, scraping and scrubbing of pots and pans, the occasional beating of an egg (needless to say there are no electric utensils around)... You can follow every one of her movements without having to enter the kitchen. Soon the exciting splutter of sizzling and frying will signal the beginning of the cooking process, which will evolve eventually into the comforting smells of simmering and baking. In between she keeps shuffling to the omnipresent telephone that emits the same old-fashioned ring of pre-mobile phone days, just like in the film *Biquefarre*. Only once she had finished feeding us at the huge dining table with its oilcloth from days gone by, did she allow herself, finally, to flop into the armchair for a pause. "How will Jean-Yves cope once I am gone?" she asked me anxiously.

On my first visit, Mamie was *désolée* because she had burnt the apple tart, of which I wasn't aware. I actually found it deliciously crunchy. Four months later, when I tried to reach Jean-Yves on the phone, it was Mamie who answered, acting as secretary. As she'd only met me once, and that was several months before, I was sure she wouldn't remember me and launched into a long-winded introduction to help her along. To my surprise, the nearly century-old lady cut me short before I could finish my first sentence, reiterating once more that she was sorry that she had burnt the tart when I visited. When I met her again at the end of the Salt Route cavalcade and told her I would be coming back in September because I wanted her to fill me in about Jean-Yves's childhood and see him set off for Compostela, her eyes brightened like a child's: '*Oh, je vous ferai à manger!*' (Note the gastronomic and psychological distinction between *faire la cuisine*, which suggests the ambitious attempt at the art of cooking, and *faire à manger*, which implies the casual throwing together of ingredients, *en toute simplicité*. I found out early on that although *faire à manger* involves no gastronomic claims, like *un petit repas de rien du tout*, the result often lingers longer in one's memory. Odette's *farçous** have the same effect on my palate, and are the best I've ever had.

Throwing ingredients together had been Mamie's lifelong occupation. As the former innkeeper's wife she had fed generations of stagecoach passengers, all of whom alighted at the Auberge Bonnet when travelling through Salmiech. When the Germans turned up during the Occupation, it was quite a tricky business because one had to warn the Jewish families and the *maquisards*** whom she was hiding in the inn to make

---

* Aveyronnais pancake usually mixed with herbs and parsley
** Members of the Resistance during the German Occupation

a dash for the nearby woods. She remembered one Jewish family of furriers from Paris and even some English Jews (what on earth were they doing in France?). She also remembered the chills that ran down her spine one morning when she saw a pistol lying on the kitchen table, which one of the *maquisards* had left there with the typical carelessness of youth, she said. She managed to dispose of it just before the arrival of the Germans. Stating half proudly, half critically that her son was the very devil, I felt like answering her "like mother like son".

Jean-Yves may not be an organic farmer, but his philosophy and concerns are much the same as those of Sébastien Persec from Laguiole and Henri Dardé from Najac, both of whom are members of the Confédération Paysanne. Lamenting the state of desolation in the countryside, he pointed to the tall arching boughs along the road, hanging heavy with wild peaches, plums and pears, most of which were rotting away for lack of hands to pick them, even free of charge! Grapes and figs were beginning to turn purple and would suffer the same fate in a couple of weeks, by which time I would be gone, and charged through the nose at my local supermarket for an insipid variety in plastic packaging. Jean-Yves's laments intensified as we sniffed the nasty smell of chemical fertilisers coming from the newly cultivated fields. In the old days, manure was provided the natural way, by the droppings of animals, horses being the best, he explained, then sheep, and lastly cows. Today we grow worms and stick them in the earth! We have lost our ancestral memory that enabled us to forecast the weather. We have lost the connection with the wind and the light and the smell of the air that guide the birds and the beasts. Grandfather Philippe still had it, he who could divine a hidden spring underground and the radiation emitted by different bodies, which enabled him to also act as a healer. Like Gérard Fabri, a healer from le Bousquet, by Pont-de-Salars in the Lévézou who, on several occasions relieved me and several friends of undefined ailments. I recalled Capou's injunction — "Just listen to the river" — and his surprise that I had confused it with the wind and got lost in the woods...

Jean-Yves has no use for the weather reports on television. Instead, he sniffs the air and observes a toad or a snail. If there is earth on the tail of a slug, then he knows it's going to rain... As if in support of Jean-Yves's point, nature offered me a glimpse of what she does best and laid at the far end of a field a cow with her newborn calf crouching by her side, still covered with the goo of its afterbirth. Jean-Yves's eagle eyes noticed the pair even though he was doing the driving and was focused on the road. Without him I would have missed the unique sight of the mother licking her newborn to its feet. Shortly afterwards it was standing on its wobbly legs, goaded by mama to take its first steps into life. When we drove back past that field in the evening, the calf was already part of the herd.

Red and golden hills alternated past us, a pocket-size square cemetery planted with a handful of dark cypress trees in the middle of nowhere, old stone houses here and there. Jean-Yves's lament became a diatribe. It was due to our greed for oil that things have gone wrong, the poison we pump out of the bowels of Inferno with the Devil's benediction, the fatal curse that will be the death of us. As will the EU, who have dispossessed us of our *terroir*. What happened to the Rouergue's twelve varieties of apples? Gone the way of their English counterparts to make room for global, tasteless novelties. Go on the last Sunday of October to the chestnut festival in the magnificent *bastide* town of Sauveterre-de-

Rouergue and drink the tasty apple juice made from those old varieties, the like of which I've never had. It is served on the perfectly preserved medieval square, together with roasted chestnuts and folk music and dances. Jean-Yves acknowledges that in olden times you had to put up with a king, but nowadays there are hundreds of them, he says, swarming out of Brussels. At least in the old days the lords abided by the code of chivalry. Today it's all about money.

The evening meal at La Couvertoirade finished with song and music, but the real Salt Route adventure began for me the next morning, when I was seated on a horse-drawn carriage. I had expected a touristy jaunt, like the memorable ride along the Amalfi Coast in Italy when I was in my youth. I was entrusted to the good care of Raymond Ginestet whose weatherbeaten face and Rouergat lilt seemed to guarantee a safe crossing. His mares went by the names of Fanny, which sounded perfectly friendly, and Karma, which could only be of good omen. Besides, it turned out he was a neighbour of Raymondou from Farrebique and had made an appearance in the 1983 sequel of *Biquefarre*. He even remembered Baba vaguely. It felt cosy that everyone should know everyone, and Karma and Fanny's steps were even keeled as they trotted rhythmically up the tarmac road through the outskirts of Millau. So far so good.

Raymond had been horse-driving champion of France and that too was reassuring. Unfortunately, he let slip that this was a more dangerous sport than horse riding, causing my muscles to contract instantaneously. Indeed, once we turned into the stony dirt paths, jolting and rattling up the steep hill, then bouncing chaotically headlong down vertical slopes, even a name like Karma seemed to offer no protection in the face of certain death. The only way to survive was by standing up at the back of the vehicle with both hands clinging desperately to the bar and one's knees slightly spread and bent in a monkey position, '*faire le singe*' as the expression goes. After several hours in that position my hands were numb and I was incapable of walking straight, but at least I hadn't been thrown off the vehicle!

André Veyrac offered to take care of me for the next stage of the Salt Route. He too was a pure Aveyronnais, although his broad-brimmed hat and large build gave him the look of a Robert Mitchum in cowboy gear. His carriage was lighter and more graceful than Raymond's, and since his lovely wife Viviane seemed calm and confident, I assumed nothing could go wrong. The last of our foursome turned out to be Jacques whom I had met several times at Georges and Odette's. He was just as surprised to see me on the Salt Route as I was to see him. Meanwhile Viviane threw out casually that although her husband was an expert Aubrac breeder, in terms of horse-driving he was a semi-beginner, and that their pair of mares were a Polish import with no traceability and no information as to how they had been trained. They went by the names of Vodka and Whisky, suggesting anything but a smooth ride. As though sensing my apprehension, Vodka, who was every bit my equal in terms of cowardice, got edgy right away and altogether frantic at the sight of cattle grids, which set her jerking and swerving, and finally rearing up with a long whinny.

Memories came to my mind of poor Ferdinand, the heir to Louis-Philippe's throne, who was killed in 1842 on the Avenue des Ternes off what is now Place Charles de Gaulle-Etoile in Paris, when his horse bolted and tipped over the carriage. In keeping with the usual French lackadaisical recklessness, no one wore riding helmets which made me feel vulnerable each time we were thrown off balance by an oversized stone. There was no need to worry, everyone reassured me, because Whisky's even temperament counterbalanced Vodka's frenzy and regulated her pace with the detachment of a pendulum. Taking several deep breaths, I did my best to focus on Whisky and let my pulse adjust to the rhythm of her trot, until little by little the improbable happened and I felt one with nature, literally, first with the warm sun beams, then the breeze, finally the blend of exhilarating fragrances. Jean-Yves had said that no mode of journeying could allow us to be at one with nature to the same degree as horse riding. His theory is that the blood circulation between rider and horse stimulates the pores to open up and sharpens the senses. Viviane kindly offered me the seat by her broad-shouldered, Robert Mitchum of a husband. Perched above Vodka and Whisky, I trotted along the Wild West stony trails of the Lévézou, fearless and daredevil, for the first time feeling truly in osmosis with rugged Aveyron.

Chapter 11

OPENING UP TO THE WORLD

On the morning of 14 December 2004, Millau was shaken out of its hibernation for the celebratory opening of its Viaduct. For a brief moment, the little town became the centre of attention, playing host to French President Jacques Chirac who flew down from Paris for the occasion, and to the international media who flew down from all over the world to break the good news. Giant screens had been set up in the centre of town to allow the Millavois (the residents of Millau) to be part of the celebrations, vicariously, although many of the high school pupils used the opportunity to organise protest demonstrations, Latin Quarter style, complete with confrontations with the riot police. It felt surreal to see side by side *La France d'en haut*, imaginative and creative, about to dazzle the world with her cutting-edge technology, and *la France d'en bas*, mummified into inertia, unable to work her way out of obsolete institutions, in this case that of education. The pupils' complaints were too parochial for a media scoop and went unnoticed, but to me, having been through it all in Paris two generations earlier, it felt strange to hear the slogans of my youth repeated on the streets of Millau, especially on the symbolic day that marked its opening up to the future.

Unlike the angry youths, Alain Montrozier marked the occasion by bringing out a new vintage, les Versants du Viaduc, which can be bought directly at the winery in Aguessac, a few minutes' drive north of Millau along the lovely Tarn Valley. I had a first taste of his excellent wine at the Château de Creissel restaurant, but when I visited him at Aguessac, Alain also gave me a tour of the magnificent stone village of Compeyre above his winery, home to century-old cellars where the vinification of Alain's special vintage, Maître des Sampettes, still takes place.

Meanwhile *La France d'en haut* gathered around her president west of Millau, to admire the new record-breaking megastructure soar like a bird above the clouds. The bridge's architect Norman Foster likened it to a delicate butterfly. To me it looked like a majestic regatta of ethereal sailboats, eerily suspended between heaven and earth, a vision of unspeakable beauty, the stuff that dreams are made of. Foster's major challenge was to work out a design at once sturdy enough to resist the forces of nature, yet slim enough not to obstruct the landscape. What he achieved is an alchemist's *tour de force*, allowing 290,000 tonnes of concrete to dissolve into featherweight transparency. Paradoxically, the bridge actually enhances the landscape, and vice versa. The beholder is astounded.

But the overriding challenge of the project was the coupling of the bridge itself with the site chosen for its construction. This was sheer madness. Geologists had warned against building on the brittle limestone soil prone to landslides (one of which nearly happened in August 2003). Its endless cavities may well be favourable to the miraculous ripening of neighbouring Roquefort cheese, but it hardly seemed likely to provide safe anchorage to a 290,000-tonne megastructure. This is also a valley subject to nightmare scenarios of gale force winds. Obviously, technology has made giant strides since November 1940, when 'Galloping Gertie', the Tacoma Narrows suspension bridge in Washington state, came galloping down, but still, the slender 2.460km steel deck of the Millau Viaduct had to be launched over a 270m chasm with turbulences that can peak at 130 kmph (that's hurricane force). Was Michel Virlogeux, the dreamer behind the project, out of his mind? With all due respect to the 100 bridges to his credit, not least the magnificent cable-stayed Normandy Bridge, this time he was planning to throw a multi-spanned roadway over one of the deepest and windiest valleys in France, at Eiffel Tower heights.

The construction of bridges is among the most daredevil of architectural challenges, which is why the Devil's collaboration was sometimes called upon to see them completed. In return for this service he demanded the soul of a living creature or else he threatened to destroy the bridge. Many of Europe's medieval bridges bear his stamp in various languages — Devil's Bridge, Teufelsbrücke, Ponto di Diabolo and Pont au Diable. At times even monks resigned themselves to negotiating with him, notably the Benedicts of St-Guilhem-le-Désert, in the neighbouring Hérault *département*, when they built the spectacular Pont du Diable over the chasm of the Hérault river, in 1030. Admittedly, it was named after the Devil only in the 14th century. The medieval bridge builders often managed to outwit the Devil and did not pay their due. Was Michel Virlogeux hoping to do the same and carry the age-old legend into the 21st century, as suggested in a fun thriller written by Jacques Godfrain, the Mayor of Millau? If so, he would be pushing the Devil (and civil engineering) further than ever before.

Did a 5-hour bottleneck of summer holidaymakers justify throwing a multi-spanned roadway over heights comparable to an 80-storey skyscraper? Jacques Godfrain argued that this new axis would be shorter, more economical to use and more scenic than the two existing north-south routes along the Rhone Valley and the Atlantic. But this could be lethal ! The unnumbered lives lost during the construction of New York's Brooklyn Bridge came to mind. Fortunately, Eiffage, the company in charge of the project, prioritised the safety of its workers and was proud to come out with only one fractured foot and broken rib. The Eiffel Company commissioned to build the steel deck, and part of the Eiffage conglomerate, also took a big risk, putting at stake the illustrious name behind their long-standing reputation. Although today Eiffel's name is associated foremost with his celebrated tower, it was his railroad bridges opening up the rugged Massif Central that made Gustave Eiffel an engineering legend. The Garabit Viaduct, which he built over the Cantal side of the Truyère river, was the world's tallest bridge when it opened in 1885 and, not unlike the Millau Viaduct, was challenged by a deep, windy valley. He was assisted by Maurice Koechlin, who also collaborated in designing the Eiffel Tower and the iron framework of the Statue of Liberty.

In order to beat the wind, Eiffel and Koechlin introduced the then revolutionary truss concept into the structure. In the case of the Millau Viaduct, it was the entire launching technique that Marc Buonomo and Jean-Pierre Gerner revolutionised by inventing a sophisticated system which combined mechanical, hydraulic and computer technologies. The actual launch was carried out by 64 transfer jacks secured on top of the piers and the temporary support towers, and on the abutments. They were made up of a frame equipped with two chocks that were barely visible from ground level. Six hydraulic jacks installed under each frame and connected to a central hydraulic station drove the lower chock to lift the deck and the top chock to push it forward, at the speed of 7 to 9 metres per hour. The operation was monitored by a central computer in the launching control centre, which sent instructions to the relay microcomputers installed on each of the piers and the support towers. Needless to say, everything had to work in perfect synchronisation.

On 28 May 2004, everyone held their breath as they watched the two halves of the deck make the final leap towards each other. For eighteen months they had been sliding forward convulsively across the piers and the support towers, 6cm at a time, a process all the more challenging because they had been launched on either side of the valley from slightly different heights. This gave the roadway a subtle incline which improved the visibility for drivers, but complicated the maneuvre. Furthermore, to prevent a floating feeling, the deck was given a slight curve and 3-metre screens to reduce the effect of the wind by 50%. These also proved effective against the fear of heights, although they were made transparent so as not to obstruct the view. It took the ingenuity of satellite-guided hydraulic rams to monitor the launch, and the virtuosity of GPS to get the two halves of the deck aligned within one centimeter. In other words, it required the most advanced technology to keep the Devil out of the way. This technology was not yet available in 1989, when the project was first submitted to the French government. The miracle of the Millau Viaduct was also in its timing.

And, paradoxically, too, in its timelessness. For it stands on a vast empty land where little seems to have altered since dawns unknown. The few roads that cross it often follow the route of ancient flocks of sheep, as do many of the trails now used by ramblers. We followed some of them on a precocious spring day in early February, aiming for the best view over the Viaduct, according to Guilhem, a mountain guide who has walked every bit of the Larzac. We hiked for several hours, during which time we met not one living creature other than the odd bird. The warm sun, the balm of resin, the honey-coloured rocks, the early blossoms, (echoing the Aubrac, the Larzac boasts a spectacular profusion of floral species, not least sixty different varieties of orchid), the solo chirping here and there, all combined to make it one of those blessed moments when nature gets the mix just right, and you forget yourself and become part of it. The Viaduct had gone quite out of my mind until Guilhem suddenly stretched out his arm and pointed to it in the distance, a faint silver filament running across the horizon.

I had seen the Viaduct scores of times by then, at different stages of its construction and on many occasions since its completion. I had seen it shine transparently white against a bright blue sky and wrapped mysteriously in veils of mist. I had seen its masts rise out of billows of fleece, and subtly lit by night. I had seen it from every possible angle, from a distance and up close, in every kind of weather and in all seasons. I had penetrated the tallest pier, I had climbed one of the support towers, and I had seen the sails come into view one by one, way above the clouds, as we drove up the curve of the deck. But I had never yet witnessed it in such absolute symbiosis and harmony with its environment as now, disproving the notion that concrete is inevitably divorced from nature and offensive to the eye. Despite the magnitude of the bridge, from where I stood with Guilhem at that moment it seemed to fade into infinite, hazy, purplish skies, like some disembodied, time-transcending apparition. Perhaps it is because the Larzac was passed over by the industrial age that ancientness could flow so smoothly into the 21st century. This is also probably why the sight of age-old sheep grazing at the foot of the science fiction-esque Viaduct is taken as a matter of course.

When it came to erecting the 700-tonne pylons over the Viaduct's piers, the engineers of the year 2004 employed the very same old technique used by the ancient Egyptians when they raised their obelisks. The 87-metre pylons were pivoted little by little to a vertical position, just like 5000 years ago, then lowered to their anchorage point, except that at these mind-boggling heights, the help of hydraulic systems was required. This pivoting method had already been put into practice on French soil on 25 October 1836, when Rameses II's obelisk was erected at Place de la Concorde. Philippe Lebas, the engineer in charge of the operation, was no less apprehensive than the men of Eiffage:

> "*For a misunderstood order, a badly secured cable, a bent bolt... would have caused a dreadful catastrophe: the shattered obelisk, the loss of millions, the hundred or so workmen crushed inevitably by the collapse of the rig. I confess I could not think, without some sort of anxiety, of the deep responsibility that weighed upon me,*" he reported.

Eiffage also had to reckon with huge costs — €394 million — incurred entirely by the company, the French government having washed its hands off the project after twelve years of shilly-shallying. In return Eiffage was granted a 75-year concession to recoup its investment and draw whatever profit they might from the toll charge. It was a race against time to complete the bridge and start cashing in as fast as possible, and it was a triumph to be opening it to traffic one month ahead of schedule. On the afternoon of the official opening, the residents of Millau were granted one free ride, at a reduced speed, so as to marvel at and photograph the monument, but from 16 December on, Eiffage meant business. I was told that one driver who had travelled a long way and slept by the bridge the night before in order to be among the first to cross, was fined when he slowed down to take pictures.

A 24-hour video surveillance system picks up the slightest abnormal traffic pattern or incident from the control station, although on rare occasions this Big Brother does get outwitted. Thus, the body of the Viaduct's first suicide victim was found at the foot of pier no. 5 on the morning of 14 January 2005. Six months later, José Bové and his friends also successfully dodged the surveillance computers and managed to block traffic for three hours by letting loose a 150-strong flock on the Viaduct's deck. They were drawing attention to their claim for compensation for the previous summer's drought, perceived as an inalienable right in the all-providing welfare state of France. However, such incidents have been rare, and so far the Viaduct's financial performance has been excellent. 4.430,000 vehicles crossed the Viaduct between December 2004 and December 2005. The figures dipped slightly the second year, probably because the novelty effect had somewhat worn off, although the blame was also laid on the football (soccer) World Cup, an event that keeps millions glued to the television screen. Regardless, the overall profits have so far exceeded the estimates by nearly 20%.

I was surprised to hear that the awesome Millau Viaduct was guaranteed to last 120 years. I had assumed that bridges were built with the expectation they would last indefinitely. True, the first bridge thrown over the Tarn two thousands years ago no longer exists. It was built of stone, leading to the scenic road to Lodève, now in the Hérault. But the various Devil's

Bridges across the steep ravines of medieval Europe have been standing for at least 600 years and show no sign of giving way. The aforementioned Pont du Diable at St-Guilhem-le-Désert, for instance, has heroically resisted the spectacular floodings of the Hérault for nearly a thousand years. Are today's computer-generated bridges programmed for a brief life span like the rest of the disposable commodities produced by our consumer society? If the gorgeous Millau Viaduct does not survive beyond December 2124, or thereabouts, the Devil will have had the final laugh after all.

In the meantime, however, the Viaduct is likely to be a godsend for Millau and may well revitalise its declining economy, once world-renowned for its glove industry, earning it the name of la *cité gantière* (*gant* meaning glove). After all, it is largely because bridges were vital to economic development that the Devil enjoyed obstructing their construction. It is too early to predict how much new business the Millau Viaduct might attract, but it could certainly be a long-term asset to the tourist industry and existing businesses. The catchphrase of the Viaduct's inaugural billboards — MILLAU S'OUVRE AU MONDE (Millau opens up to the world) — conveys this hope. There is no way of counting the millions who come to admire it, but those among them who went to the visitors' centre in 2006 totalled 390,000. Most are French and European neighbours, but they have come from all corners of the world, including official delegations. On 22 and 23 September 2006 the Mayor of Millau played host to three successive delegations, from Quebec, China and California. Well, I thought at the time, if China was coming to the Aveyron, then Millau must definitely be opening up to the world, and it was a historical occasion I had no intention of missing.

Unfortunately, although the delegation was made up of high ranking officials of China's Popular Assembly, none of them could speak French or English and all conversations had to be conducted via their interpreter, which inevitably created a barrier. I assumed that behind their inscrutable smiles they were at least as astonished by the bridge as we were. The French official who was liaising with them lost no time in setting me straight by whispering in my ear, "sssshhhh....don't tell anyone but they have at least thirty like this one ..." And no, he continued, the opening of the Millau Viaduct was not making the headlines in China, and the delegation did not come all the way to visit it, only from nearby Toulouse where they had been attending a seminar about pollution issues and social welfare in rural areas (and meanwhile signing some business contracts). The visit to the Viaduct and to the Roquefort cheese caves was thrown in on their way to the south of France for a bit of fun before flying home.

Still, Mr Fu Zhihuang, who led the delegation, did express genuine interest in the bridge. He was introduced to me as the head of the Financial and Economic Commission, but later I found out that he had trained to be an engineer and had served as China's railway minister a while back (China has three separate transport cabinets in its government, for rail, roads and air). He was in fact the man behind the record-breaking, pan-Himalayan Lhasa railway line, climbing 5,072m (16,640ft) above ground level. The 1,142km (710mile) of its final section alone cost $3bn. Ironically, it was at the Millau Viaduct in remote Aveyron that my introduction to modern-day China began. No, she isn't only flooding the west with cheap toys, textile, shoes, and now four wheelers. She is also engaged in building a stupendous transportation infrastructure for the future and that includes an overwhelming number of colossal bridges.

One of the early engineering achievements of Communist China was the building of the 1100m-long Wuhang bridge over the Yangtze, back in 1957. The 1.5km Yangtze River Bridge, a double-decker bridge for trains and cars, was another source of national pride when it opened, in 1968, because it was designed and built entirely by the Chinese after their falling out with the Soviet Union. Sixty additional bridges were planned to be built over the Yangtze River between 2004 and 2020, bringing the total number to 100. In Shanghai, the new 3.900m-long Lupu Bridge, which opened in 2003 over the Huangpu River, has the world's longest arch (550m), whilst the 36km-long Hangzhou Bay Bridge, now under construction south of Shanghai, will be the world's longest ocean-crossing bridge. There are also the tunnels dug beneath China's territorial waters. At the moment of writing, China has started pushing beyond her borders, into Indonesia, and as far as the Danube river in Romania, that is, into European Union territory....

As my brain struggled to register this staggering information, the Chinese expedition to the Millau Viaduct took on the aspect of Gulliver's landing among the Lilliputians. Yet, despite the humbling data and figures, Mr Fu Zhihuang expressed an admiration for France, for her culture and traditions, quality of production, elegance and style. In the Aveyron, although he had barely spent half a morning breezing in and out of Roquefort Société and the Millau Viaduct Visitors' centre, he was struck by the cohabitation of ancientness and modernity. It was comforting to have one of China's pivotal figureheads back my own perception of the area as I had tried to convey it in this book.

The visit continued with a buffet lunch at the Mairie of Millau, where the Chinese and French flags floated side by side.

I wondered what Gulliver might be thinking of the toy-like, honey-coloured Mairie, where the lives of 20,000 inhabitants were administered, as against, for example, the 30 million residents of Chongqing, a sister city of Toulouse and the fastest-growing urban centre in the world, with half a million new arrivals every year. Undaunted, the Lilliputian Jacques Godfrain threw the gauntlet down and proclaimed humourously that Millau has recently begun to export its gloves to China.

When 24 hours later we returned to the Mairie with the delegation of Californian senators, I was amused to see the stars-and-spangles hoisted at the very spot where the red flag of the People's Republic of China had preceded it the day before. The buffet menu was identical, but the American delegation mostly numbered women, including its head, and most were casually dressed and informal in manner, in sharp contrast with the Chinese. This time around, Monsieur le Maire got much more pro-actively involved in promoting the town's glove industry, taking the guests to one of the manufacturers and leaving them ample time to shop and support the local economy. The world's most famous pair of gloves, however, the ones donned by Rita Hayworth alias Gilda, was not manufactured in Millau, but he would have very much liked to see them housed there. During our visit to the glove section of the Millau Museum, he launched an appeal in the direction of Hollywood to that effect, hoping it would be relayed by the delegation.

Glove-making developed in Millau because of its geographical position in the heart of a sheep-breeding region. Like in all thrifty rural societies, every bit of the animal was either consumed as food — milk, cheese and meat, or recycled for other usages, predominantly its wool and skin, but also its dung which the winegrowers of the Tarn Valley and the Languedoc used as fertiliser. It was the Roquefort cheese that was at the origin of the sheepskin industry in medieval times, since in order to increase the ewes' supply of milk, their lambs were slain when they were one or two months old (still the case today) making their skins available to the tanners of the Tarn river and the Dourbie. Pierre Raymond was the first tanner to be mentioned by name, in 1193. However, the industry only really picked up in the 18th century, and glove-making specifically, in the 19th, when the number of Millavois tripled from 6,000 to 18,000. Almost everyone was employed by the industry, the men preparing the skins in the tanneries, amidst a sickening stench and in sweltering temperatures, the women often working from home, doing the sewing, which enabled them to tend to their domestic duties simultaneously. They could be seen all over town, seated at their front door sewing gloves, enjoying the sun and a much healthier air than their husbands.

Because the skin of the Lacaune breed is of exceptional quality, and was further improved by the ecological conditions of its breeding, Millau could target the luxury market and became the purveyor to the most renowned *haute couture* houses both in Paris and overseas. By 1931, it had superseded Grenoble as the 'glove capital' of France, although the Depression raised a premonitory red flag, pointing to the vulnerability of an industry largely dependent on the whims of fashion. Yet despite the market's highs and lows, prosperity continued until the early 1960s, peaking in 1963 when 1,100 jobs were provided by 17 tanneries and 6,000 by 82 glove manufacturers. A record 4.7 million pairs were produced that year.

Sales began to dip after 1963 and decline inevitably followed in a fast-changing market, taken over by synthetic materials, mass production and cheap labour in southeast Asia. It is too early to predict what the economic impact of the Viaduct might be, but with the world's economies moving fast towards globalisation, the odds would not seem in favour of Millau. Yet providence may have descended to the town from the heights of the Aubrac in the person of Gérard Boissins, one of the founders and ex-CEO of the celebrated Forges de Laguiole knife manufactury, who has recently taken over Millau's oldest glove manufacturer, Causse, a family business going back to 1892. He has been joined by the entrepreneurial Parisian Aveyronnais Jean-Louis Costes, his partner in Laguiole, and a very talented young couple, Manuel and Nadine Rubio, who are the artists of the company and design not only the gloves, but also the brochures, packaging and advertising material. For several years now they have been designing gloves for the most prestigious *haute couture* houses — Hermès, Chanel, Vuitton and Christian Lacroix, to mention but a few — and have twice been awarded prestigious prizes, notably the Talent du Luxe award in 2004, alongside Michel Bras. Indeed, the new Causse Gant works for the luxury industry only. There is no point in competing with China on cheap goods, especially since the strength of the French lies in quality and tradition, as Mr Fu Zhihuang pointed out to me at the foot of the Viaduct. Gant Causse's own label is of no lesser quality, but not nearly as dear, and can be bought on site; or in their Paris boutique on the upscale rue de Castiglione, off Place Vendôme.

Olivier Causse has also joined the team, bringing a *savoir faire* and experience acquired over more than a century. The location of the new company has been shifted to the former premises of Guibert Frères, once Millau's prominent glove manufacturer and tanner, providing 1,000 jobs. They were handed over to the care of a leading architect and friend of

Jean-Louis and Gérard's, Jean-Michel Wilmotte, whose credentials include the redesigning of several of the Louvre's wings and galleries. Here he has created a beautiful minimalist haven of spacious serenity light years away from the inferno of the tanneries, a glimpse of which can be caught at the Museum of Millau. Guibert Frères' old steam boiler stands outside the main building as a nod of respect for the past. This is important to Gérard, as was the choice of premises that had once been a landmark of the industry. Like many people here, he believes in the importance of preserving traditions and historical continuity. The glove industry has personal meaning for him because his family was from Millau and his mother, like so many thousands of women in the town, used to make gloves. Today, however, only 60% of the gloves are made of local lambskin. The rest is imported from all corners of the world — pigskin, deer, crocodile, whatever the whims of fashion dictate. The Causse brand can be bought on the premises, and visits are organised by appointment.

Meanwhile, the one-time Templars' home at La Cavalerie, better known in recent times for the fight against the extension of its military camp, is also courting the fashion industry, hoping to cash in on the Viaduct with a discount-shopping village of 30 designer shops. It is due to open in 2008 on an area of $15,000m^2$ between the A75 interchange and the old posthouse. Although the idea of a shopper's haven on the empty and ideologically-charged Larzac may at first glance seem surreal, the position of La Cavalerie, close to the exit of the motorway, will create jobs and may well make this a profitable venture. After all, it was owing to its position on the route between north and south that La Cavalerie developed in the first place, and that was at least two thousand years ago, perhaps much more. Besides, the Templars and Hospitallers' presence here was motivated solely by economic reasons, which is why the Larzac has been standing empty since the dissolution of the Hospitaller Order during the French Revolution. In the face of the myth created in the 1970s against the extension of the military camp, the only economic activity on the Larzac, other than the Roquefort industry situated on its fringe, was generated by the presence of the military at La Cavalerie. So, should the discount-village project take off, I shall see no wrong in detouring to La Cavalerie on the off chance of unearthing a Giorgio Armani or some other designer bargain.

That said, there were no such temptations when I returned to the Larzac in July 2006. Instead I headed for the fortified village of Ste-Eulalie-de-Cernon, across the A75 motorway from La Cavalerie, to see an open-air performance of Les Frères du Silence, an *opéra populaire*, composed, written, choreographed, staged and produced by Yvan-Marie Ruffié, another fervent Aveyronnais who has the stony Larzac in his blood but is actually from Marcillac. He is also passionate about local history and wove a tale of passion into the background of the Cathari and Templars' persecutions. Playing it out under the crystal clear Larzac night, with with the old walls of Ste-Eulalie as a backdrop, seemed the obvious thing.

We drove there along a winding country road, past clumps of box and leafy woods, early enough to have dinner with the troupe — 200 amateurs supported by a handful of professionals, among them Michel Wolkowitzky from Sylvanès Abbey, of whom more later. Most came from the local area, but some from as far north as the Auvergne. They were of all age groups and all willing to give up their spare time throughout the year for rehearsals. Seated next to me over dinner was Thierry Martin from l'Hospitalet-du-Larzac, who played the priest in the opera. He enjoyed the role all the more, he told me humourously, because he came from a Protestant family. His mischievous smile persisted as he told me that on the night of the annual village fête, in July, an outlandish farandole is danced in front of the church — la Buffatière. Before he could go any further, I broke in to surprise him with my knowledge. He was even more surprised that I had found out about it thanks to the carvings on the miséricordes in the cathedral of Rodez. On the other hand, I did not know that Millau had an aerodrome, where Thierry works in 'real' life. Situated between l'Hospitalet and La Cavalerie, a 5-minute drive from Thierry's home, it is used for smaller, private (up to 80-seat) planes, and may come in handy for the hurried pilots among you.

Ste-Eulalie is no less lovely than La Couvertoirade and has more of an authentic, year-round village life. This was the seat of the commandery going back to the Templars whose first acquisition on the Larzac was the early church of Ste-Eulalie, for which they paid partly in coins and partly in cheese. After dinner we had time to enjoy a relaxed drink on the village café terrace, overlooking the old cobbled square and its 17th-century fountain prettily framed by three plane trees and one lime. Everything was bathed in the roseate glow of a long-drawn summer evening, including the 17th-century marble Virgin atop the church door. It looked pretty much the same when the famous revolutionary orator Mirabeau came here to visit his uncle, Admiral Riquet-Mirabeau, the last commander of the Hospitaller Order before its dissolution. Only the four original elm trees are gone, having been replaced in 1880 by the present trees because they threatened to collapse on the animals that came to drink from the fountain. Now hailing from Malta, and from Clerkenwell in London, the Order of St John of Jerusalem, as the Hospitallers are commonly known in Britain (l'Ordre de Malte, in France) continues its charitable work, the only Christian Order to have sustained its vocation for 800 years.

The Conservatoire Larzac Templier et Hospitalier, based in Millau, who promote the heritage of the two Orders and their contemporaries on the various sites on the Larzac, provide excellent audioguides (also in English and other European languages). These are for hire at the visitors' centres of the respective sites and are highly recommended.

Yvan-Marie, of the *opéra populaire* talked at length about how important it was to preserve one's roots and heritage, but also to follow one's imagination and ideas, where real truth lies. He also believes that life could only be authentic in rural society, flowing with the rhythm of nature. And then there are all those stones and rocks of the Aveyron that he feels so anchored to. "You know," he said, "it takes time to bring a stone to life." He sounded like St Exupéry's Little Prince.

Two hours later, I was seated in the dark among the audience, watching the young children of southern France lament the destruction of their ancestors' Occitan culture against the medieval rampart and spectacular light effects. There was nothing out of the ordinary about children enjoying performing in a rock opera very much of their time, but you wouldn't have expected them to be so involved in a historical episode 800 years removed from their own lives. The local community got involved in the project too. A good number had volunteered to lend their hand – the electrician, locksmith, cooks, dressmakers, the ushers, those who were selling the programmes, and many others. It was a team project, like the ones orchestrated by Nadine up north in the Carladez and the Viadène and it created a communal sense of belonging. I recalled a comment made by the Dominican Father André Gouzes about contemporary urban society which, he says, is the sum of multitudes of solitudes, because today's city dwellers have lost their roots. In the close-knit community of his native Brusque, at the southern edge of the *département*, heritage was transmitted from grandparents to grandchildren through legends narrated by the logfire. André likened his grandfather to "an old oak tree" with roots that struck into "the utmost depths of the memory of our ancient soil", going back to prehistoric times. Alas, there aren't many roots left in present-day Brusque. Perched prettily above the Dourdou at the foot of the ruins of its 11th-century castle, most of the houses have been converted into holiday homes.

André too is another one of those free-spirited poets of the Aveyron whom folly prompts to engage in wild, Quixotic, yet ultimately successful projects. In André's case it was the resurrection of the former Cistercian abbey of Sylvanès, which was a derelict ruin when he stopped there occasionally as a child while heading north from Brusque with his father. The abbey church had survived because it was restored in 1909-1910 to serve the parish; the chapter was converted into a barn; the fabulous vaulted scriptorium, where the monks had once copied out manuscripts, was taken over by a flock of sheep. By a miracle, the eastern side of the cloister had also survived. The rest was gone.

I first visited Sylvanès in early February 2004, after my brief introductory drive through the Rougier de Camarès with Jean-Yves Bonnet. We had had several early spring-like days, during which I had also detoured to the wonderfully preserved *bastide* town of Sauveterre-de-Rouergue and the nearby Château du Bosc, the summer home of Toulouse-Lautrec during his childhood, which he would have inherited had he not died prematurely. At present, this is the home of Nicole Bérangère Tapie de Celeyran, the painter's great niece, now in her 80s, but still an extraordinarily vibrant guide who brings the beautiful and moving place alive. The sun got even brighter the following day, as Jean-Yves's car rushed and rumbled towards the south, past stretches of empty red hills, meeting every now and then the deep turquoise Dourdou. We parted ways at the road fork, where Jean-Yves turned west, headed for the stables of Belmont, while I continued towards red-stone Camarès, a thriving *bourg* before the wars of religion drove its entrepreneurial Protestant families away, notably to Switzerland.

Climbing up the hillside above the Dourdou, together with its tall church spire, Camarès is further graced by the lovely Pont Vieux. Although the church dates only from the 19th century, the bridge goes back to 1133 and is still rock solid. It is closed to vehicles only because it is narrow and reckless driving may make it unsafe for pedestrians. Today the Dourdou is crossed by the 19th-century Pont Neuf, beyond which lies the D10, running past green fields and another cluster of red and pink houses as it makes its way through Andabre. A few minutes later I arrived in Sylvanès.

I had been warned not to expect the spectacular setting of Conques, but the name did suggest a certain sylvan serenity. And it had to be close to water, otherwise the monks would not have chosen to settle there. I was hoping it would be a lively spring, preferably the source of a river that I could then follow and play out the scenario denied me in the Aubrac at the outset of my journey, when everything was saturated with the water from the mountain snows. Later, I was unsuccessful again when I hoped to follow the Aveyron from its spring by Sévérac-le-Château and make an emblematic pilgrimage through the *département* that bears its name. It was mid summer and there was barely any water at all! Just a pathetic trickle, and two young sweethearts idling their time away in the shaded seclusion. Picnic tables and benches, and a bit of waste and litter lying on the ground suggested you might prefer to try a different spot at weekends or holidays.

I did find Sylvanès by a little river, tucked away at the bottom of a narrow, wooded valley, the Cabot. A green meadow spread in front of the long red-tiled red-stone buildings, evoking a clearing in a forest. Another stream bounced down the slope and joined the river further down. On the way to the abbey, I had noticed a group of derelict, abandoned houses among big old trees. There was a shabby, locked gate in front of the drive, topped by a big inscription — LES BAINS DE SYLVANES — a vestige of better times. It turned out that Sylvanès has a hot spring (as do Andabre, Cayla and Prugnes) and already had a spa in Roman times. Two of its pillars have made their way to the living room at the Mas de Salel lodge, by Montagnol, the former living quarters of a flock of sheep that used to work for Roquefort, I was told by Françoise, the proprietress. The bright blue, two-wheeled cart with the flower boxes, next to the car park, once served to carry the cheese to the Roquefort cellars. I thought Françoise had the cart painted blue to make it pretty, but she told me this was always done, to keep the flies off. Apparently they don't like blue.

Another spa was opened here by the monks in the 17th century, La Source des Moines, a commercial venture with an adjoining hostelry that allowed the abbey to supplement its revenue and live comfortably after a long period of decline. It was a short-lived prosperity though: on the eve of the French Revolution there were only four monks left. Even without a revolution the abbey would have probably closed down, since an edict dating from 1768 ordered the gradual closure of all monastic establishments with fewer than 15 inmates.

When watering places became popular in the 19th century, the village of Sylvanès hoped in turn to cash in on its hot spring and opened a new spa. Dreams of glory climaxed when Empress Eugénie expressed an interest in taking the waters here, but, to everyone's disappointment, the remoteness of the place made her change her mind and opt instead for Vichy. The spa was still functioning when André Gouzes was a boy, but eventually it went the way of the abbey. In all likelihood everything would have disintegrated into the valley over time, perhaps into oblivion, had André not gathered his energy, vision and faith to have the monastic buildings first restored, then turned into an original spiritual centre where Christian worship and cultural events of any or no religious affiliation cohabit.

André (or Père, or Frère – he is a bit of each) Gouzes was away on my first visit and I was met by Michel Wolkowitsky, a professionally trained and excellent singer, who both performs and runs the abbey. I knew little about the history and workings of Sylvanès at the time, and since Michel is not a churchman I wasn't quite sure how he and André Gouzes shared their respective roles within the framework of the establishment. Eventually I understood that Michel was in charge of cultural activities, notably the International Summer Music Festival of Sacred Music which has by now gained national and international recognition. Only later I found out he was the Abbey's director (André says he is the 'boss'), and that André Gouzes too was a musician. As a matter of fact, it was music that had brought the two men together, in Toulouse. André composes and conducts church music and his *Liturgie chorale du peuple de Dieu* has been translated into a dozen of languages, reaching out as far as the US and Japan. I was intrigued by the title, taking it to extend to all faiths, as I grasped the spirit of Sylvanès from leafing through programmes of previous festivals. These embraced all corners and cultures of the world, from Tibet, and India to African America, Britain, Spain, Russia or Latin America — you name it — side by side with Mozart's quartets, for example. Followed a quick tour of the church, chapter and Scriptorium, too brief and speedy to allow me to pause, behold, absorb, or be inspired, because I had to leave for Rodez and catch the plane back to Paris. It felt like a recce before the actual shooting of a film. I sensed that this was an unusual place that required more time before I could grasp it.

It was unusual from the outset, since its founder, Pons de Léras (or l'Héras), had been a lord turned highwayman, operating with his band of brigands on the strategic Pas de l'Escalette, the hilly pass connecting the Mediterranean and the north via the Larzac, mentioned earlier. His life story, an edifying pilgrim's progress leading to repentance, followed by pilgrimages — to St-Guilhem-le-Désert, Compostela and Mont St-Michel — and finally to retreat, is reported by Hugues Francigena, a monk of Sylvanès, whose testimony was written between 1161 and 1171. On their return, Pons and his party stopped at Rodez where they received the support of the Bishop Adhémar who suggested they stayed there, but Pons preferred to settle in the Camarès. The name referred to the area at the time (to which bears witness the name of the village biscuit manufacturer, Biscuiterie *du* Camarès, rather than *de* Camarès, a family business run by husband, wife and daughter — worth dropping by).

Hugues described the Camarès as "covered with forests, steep uplands, sheer hillsides, watered by rivers and streams". The landlord, Arnaud, Pons de Léras's close friend, was happy to offer him land for the establishment of a hermitage. Silvanium, as it was then called, seemed just the right spot. It also had a predestined name, because by swapping the first 'i' for an 'a', it became Salvanium, meaning salvation. Hugues reports that the hermitage was raised to the status of abbey in 1336 and attached to the Order of Citeaux (the Cistercian Order). This was barely three years after the completion of the magnificent Pont Vieux (the 'Vieux' is a much more recent addition) in Camarès, which Pons and his party would have crossed. It must have been a source of pride to its contemporaries to no lesser a degree than the Millau Viaduct is today. So much so that whereas the Viaduct bears the name of its town, Camarès the place was named Lo Poun after its bridge. In the same spirit, His Lordship was known as Arnaud du Pont and incorporated the bridge into his coat of arms.

A poet like André was bound to be fascinated by the romantic ruins of Sylvanès, especially on that night when, as an adolescent, he had run away from home barefooted, in tattered coat and hat, and they were revealed to him shrouded in mist. But he was also taken by the spiritual journey of Pons de Léras, for whom he felt the kind of empathy Jean-Yves shared with Victor, the *sauvageon* from St-Sernan. André too had the temperament of a *sauvageon*, running wild, climbing up trees, or going hunting or ferreting with Grandfather, "the Lord of the Mountains" from whom he may well have inherited his spirit of independence. When the ferret disappeared in the burrow, André glued his ear to the earth and listened to the mysterious drama taking place underground, but when the ferret reappeared with the blood-covered body of a rabbit, André was frightened. Yet at other moments the same ferret would be all gentleness and slip under André's shirt for a cuddle. The dichotomy between violence and gentleness is a potent presence in the rugged, elemental Rouergue, the pendulum that sways between light and darkness, be it sunshine versus snowstorms, the little ferret, or the opposing forces of darkness and light that had marked the life journey of Pons de Léras. André, too, was initiated to the night during his adolescence. His two 'dark angels' then were Baudelaire and Rimbaud, but they also opened up to him the infinite potential of creative liberty.

As for the light, it was largely from the church that it emanated, still the spiritual spine of rural society during André's childhood, despite the breakthrough of the Republic's secular forces. André remembers the annual pilgrimage to the chapel of St Thomas de Cantorbury in the forest of Brusque, whom I had earlier come across in Mur-le-Barrez. Unlike Empress Eugénie, it would seem that the churchman was not put off by the remoteness of the Rouergue, if he really stopped here as legend has it. Legend also has it that his relics are sheltered in the church of Brusque, having been offered to the parish by Raymond VII of Toulouse, who had received them from King Louis VII.

Above all, André was impressed by the liturgies and rituals that punctuated the cycle of the seasons, 'spiritual illuminations' supported by the deep voices of the men of the congregation. Once more, like in the Aubrac, I was struck by how closely religion is intertwined with the soil in these parts, like in Biblical times, when agricultural activities were tied to worship. André spoke of 'enchantment', of the joy of letting oneself be penetrated by what he calls the Mystery of God. Add to this the music played on the piano by his mother, who died prematurely when he was only a child, the intellectual excellence later absorbed from the Dominicans, and the no less excellent musical training he was granted owing to his talent. Add too his boundless curiosity, hypersensitivity, humility, enthusiasm, and generosity. And finally add the unflinching support of Michel. The sum total is the resurrection of Sylvanès.

I have been back to Sylvanès several times since. I attended several concerts in the church, surrounded by the magnificent simplicity of the architecture and the purity of the acoustics. But I wanted to go beyond this and share some of André's Mystery of God. I would not have cared to do so, if I hadn't sensed that, like Jean-Yves Bonnet, André could not be fitted into a straitjacket. I also liked the fact that, not unlike Jean-Yves, his education was acquired through 'gleaning' along the way, although André likes to describe it as 'poaching'. *'Je suis le braconnier de Dieu'*, he says.

Easter, the new beginning of the seasons' cycle, seemed the obvious time for my visit, bringing to a close the journey that had started in early spring up in the Aubrac. Of course it depends on the angle you choose to look at it from, since the inception and early gestation of life takes place in the dark, before spring as did Creation according to the book of Genesis. André was on a different plane. He relates the passing of the seasons to their passage into another dimension of time, to transcendence. Did I have to travel all the way to a lost little valley on the southern confines of the Aveyron to realise that the celestial kingdom might not be a place but an a-temporal realm?

It is irrelevant to André whether or not the venture of Sylvanès outlives him, because all human ventures now and here are transient. The ruins of the medieval castle of Brusque, and the bell tower that has survived the old church, must have been a daily reminder of that. André has composed thousands of pages of liturgy, and, significantly, has not completed his work. For him, liturgy marks the mystery of time, and is a human replica of the cosmic dance of the celestial spheres. It also marks the alternation between the shadows of night and light, a concept also contained in Cistercian architecture which, more than an art, is the expression of the monastic way of life and ideal. Stripped of ornamentation, its beauty lies in the purity of a mathematical order, echoing the order of the universe. Jacques Godfrin tells me that the pine cones sculpted on the chapters of two of the church's pillars are emblematic of regeneration, since they close and open by turns, respectively at sunset and sunrise. Who were the brilliant minds who designed these masterpieces for the glory of God and Christ, in total humility, without leaving behind their names? This was nearly 900 years ago. The astonishing acoustics of Cistercian architecture, which make the faithful's 'Halleluias' resound through every corner of the church, surely were worked out by a brilliant physicist, whose name has gone the way of the architect's. They accompany the silence of prayer and meditation and sustain vocal celebration with equal perfection, perhaps nowhere more so than in Sylvanès, whose unusually wide nave, the widest in France, envelopes those present like a maternal vessel.

For forty years, André has been sweeping choirs off their feet, all over France and beyond as far as Quebec and Japan,

connecting them to the cosmos. His own compositions take
Gregorian chanting and Bach as their inspiration, kindred souls
from the past —as are the members of the Order of Jerusalem
from the Paris St-Gervais, whose presence in the Aubrac
surprised me at first. Now that I have pieced together a fair
amount of the Aveyron the tie between the Order of Jerusalem
and Sylvanès becomes self-evident. André also feels strongly the
appeal of the Orthodox church, stemming perhaps from the
'spiritual illuminations' of his childhood in Brusque, and the
deep male voices that accompanied them and moved him so
much. This led to another folly, in 1994: the building of a
traditional Russian wooden chapel 800km away from Moscow,
which was then dismantled and shipped aboard a 15-wagon
convoy across Europe to Sylvanès. Here it was put together again
and perched on top of a hill among the woods, where André has
taken up residence, befittingly closer to the heavens.

And finally the organ. My longstanding friend Odile has
never been to Sylvanès, but she mentioned to me that she had
once responded to a nationwide fundraising campaign for the
building of a new organ for an abbey she believed was situated
in the Aveyron. I guessed at once it was Sylvanès. Who but
André and Michel would have managed to raise money for
such a cause and on such a scale? And it is an astounding
organ, commissioned from Daniel Birouste one of the
country's leading organ builders, who hails from Plaisance in
the Gers, better known for its *foie gras*, It took 10 tonnes of
steel, 55m² of sheep and lamb skin, 3,500 screws, 3,900 kilos
of lead and pewter, 5,000 pipes, and 30,000 working hours to
put together this fabulous instrument. It was placed on the
western wall of the church, looking out to the altar from
within a splendid chestnut case, unornamented and dignified,

in harmony with the surrounding architecture. The subtleties of shadow and light are its only decoration, in the same minimalist spirit as the stained glass of Conques that could also be considered 'Cistercian'.

Some may object that the Cistercians had no organs, but that's precisely the point. The Sylvanès venture moves on with the times. Its new organ does not shy away from the advantages of modern technology and is computer compatible, an instrument of the 21st century with a rich palette of sounds that allows it to play the register of most schools, from the Renaissance to today. Others worried that the organ's volume of sound might interfere with the unique quality of vocal expression achieved in the church. Even Michel had had his doubts at the beginning, but he was won over by the miraculous timber, the bright new sounds and intensity of tone.

Without the contribution of thousands of regular citizens like Odile this would never have happened. Each had their own motivation, like the pilgrims to Compostela, be it an act of faith, a fondness for Sylvanès or a simple love of music. To some the donations were memorials to lost loved ones, including children. There was a Jewish woman who had been hidden with her family from the Nazis by total strangers in a nearby village, and who contributed to the organ as a way of saying thank you to their community. The names of all those thousands are engraved in the pipes of the organ.

Sylvanès is prospering. As the Millau Viaduct opens up the Aveyron to the world, Sylvanès builds bridges to the world's multitude of cultures. And whereas Millau welcomed the political representatives of China to its Viaduct last September, Sylvanès will host a Chinese shadow theatre in July 2007. Meanwhile, on the far side of the meadow, another kind of resurrection is planned by way of a modern spa. I am not quite sure how I feel about the three dozen bungalows that will mushroom there, although they won't be built right next to the abbey. It is important to remember that, just like the Source des Moines in the 17th century, the spa will bolster the local economy. I hope Sylvanès will get the balance right, which, so far, has been the secret of its success, even though the poet in André likes to attribute the success to a spark of folly. There is certainly an element of that, yet Michel is unafraid to state that Sylvanès is also a business.

The Easter weekend was drawing to a close. We gathered at the Mas de Salel for our final dinner and were barely seated when the young student opposite me asked what I thought of the 35-hour working week. Before I knew it, a heated discussion had sprung up about the upcoming presidential elections, whilst Christ stepped back discreetly, leaving the floor to the terrestrial agitation of an impassioned political debate, left, right and centre.

BY THE SAME AUTHOR

Around and About Paris – From the Dawn of Times to the Eiffel Tower
Thirza Vallois writes about her city with passion and, more importantly, the unmistakable authority of first-hand knowledge... These superb guides should soon achieve legendary status. – William Boyd in the *Spectator*

Around and About Paris – From the Guillotine to the Bastille Opera
* With its wit, erudition and lively writing, it knocks most books on the City of Light for six. – Geoff Andrew in *Time Out*
* Vallois captures – and opens up for all to taste – the incomparable sense of the past one experiences walking the streets of Paris. This is a book for those who think of Paris as an urban paradise – the curious gazer, the laid-back ambler, the wanderer, the seeker of this city's wonders.
Here's to *Around and About Paris*. On your next flight to Paris, don't leave home without it. – Patty Baudouin in the *Boston Book Review*.

Around and About Paris – New Horizons: Haussmann's Annexation
* An astonishingly informative companion – *Times Literary Supplement*
* For in-depth coverage of the sights, sounds and smells of Paris, nothing tops Thirza Vallois' *Around and About Paris* books.
– Janet Delong in the *Paris Free Voice*

261

There are guides to every aspect of Paris... and then there are Thirza Vallois's extraordinary *Around and About Paris*... Packed with history, anecdotes and curiosity, they bring the city alive. – Anthony Sattin in the *Sunday Times*

Treat yourself to this treasure
Booklist, The American Library Journal

Romantic Paris
This is the best book yet from the author of the highly-acclaimed series *Around and About Paris*. Vallois has a stunning command of this town's history and culture... And her new guide is an unabashed celebration of the capital of romance. – Bob Roberts in the *Paris Free Voice*